MUSIC MIND GAMES

REVISED EDITION

MICHIKO YURKO

© 1992 MUSIC 19

WARNER BROS. PUBLICATIONS INC.
15800 N.W. 48th Avenue • Miami, Florida 33014
A Warner Music Group Company

Music Mind Games is dedicated to my beloved
children, Meredith, David and Andrew.

Published by Warner Bros. Publishing Inc.
15800 N.W. 48th Avenue, Miami FL 33014

Copyright © 1992 Music 19
a Division of CPP/Belwin, Inc.

Printed in the United States of America

Editor: Sandy Feldstein, Mary Fujii Henshall
Production Coordinator: Sandy Sneed
Designer: Michiko Yurko
Photographer: Earl Goldstein, Maryland
Mike Uno, Hawaii
Judy Todd, Virginia
Graphics: Mike Blowers
Art: Kathy Purser

ISBN 0-89898-561-7

INTRODUCTION

I had the pleasure of meeting Michiko Yurko in the 1970's and was immediately taken by her approach to music education.

The concept of teaching music through enjoyable games in a totally noncompetitive environment is evident throughout her work. This approach is so enticing that students of all ages seem to immediately smile and quickly become engrossed in the learning process. Michiko's materials are so well thought out that teachers and parents instantly understand the sequence of learning and the interactive, flexible nature of the music games.

Michiko Yurko's sensitivity to children, her understanding of pedagogical goals and sequence and her superior musicianship are all evident in **Music Mind Games** . . . materials that musically educate the total child.

We, as publishers, are proud to be a part of the future of music education.

Dr. Sandy Feldstein
COO and President of Warner Bros. Publications Inc

ACKNOWLEDGEMENTS

I want to thank the thousands of students, parents and teachers who have participated in my classes since 1974. Because of you, I have created these games and streamlined my ideas. I was greatly encouraged whenever you laughed during one of my games or happily understood another little piece of the puzzle of music theory. Your energy fueled my desire to write this incredible book. Your enthusiasm gave me strength.

I want to thank the many dedicated people who have helped *Music Mind Games* to be published. Sandy Feldstein and Sandy Sneed at Warner Bros. have been unswerving in their belief in my work and their patience in letting me have the time to create. Their dedication to producing the finest product at a reasonable price has continued to impress me. Thanks to Sandy Feldstein for his invaluable editing.

Mike Blowers, *Music Mind Games'* graphic artist and typesetter has spent countless hours on this project. Through his work, my ideas have become beautiful realities. And a special thank you to Connie and Bill for all their advice and support and to Kathy Purser for her charming drawings.

The work of three photographers are contained in *Music Mind Games*. Judy Todd took photos while I taught classes at the Central Virginia Suzuki Institute. Mike Uno snapped hundreds of photos at the Hawaii Suzuki Institute. Earl Goldstein of Glogau Photography Studio spent several afternoons at my former studio shooting photos of me and my private students, simulating what we normally do in class over many months.

Many hugs and kisses go to my mother, Mary Henshall for her extraordinary efforts in editing and proofing this book. What I thought might be a three week read-through stretched to nearly five months of reading and rereading. Her efforts were herculean.

To all of you who want to make music theory and learning enjoyable, I salute you. Your dedication to the students you teach can only have a positive effect on all of us.

TABLE OF CONTENTS

CORNERSTONES

by Michiko Yurko

1. Assume that students know nothing but are brilliant and can learn anything.

2. Given the right environment for learning, students will demonstrate great ability and intelligence.

3. Learning that is joyous and intensely satisfying should be a natural part of life. Students hardly realize they are learning because they are having so much fun.

4. Students remember what they do themselves.

5. Students who meet with success each step along the way will enjoy learning and want to discover more.

6. If students are confused, it's not because they are slow, it's because the teacher is presenting the materials incorrectly.

7. A great teacher doesn't teach, but allows students to learn by providing them with enough to challenge but not overwhelm them.

8. A teacher must have endless capacity to improvise and create situations so students can succeed.

9. A teacher is someone who is cheerful, a bit of an entertainer and especially someone who feels empathy for students.

10. A teacher must never embarrass students in front of others or in private. If mistakes occur, the teacher's role is to help students learn how to correct them.

11. Successful learning occurs in many small steps rather than one big step.

12. See that the students learn the concepts first then commit them to memory through repetition.

13. The true objective of teaching is the permanent retention of information.

PHILOSOPHY OF LEARNING

language of the earth

Learning to read music is like learning to read a language of the earth, a language loved and enjoyed by peoples of all lands. Music is constantly being created, takes many forms and can be molded to take on its own unique appeal to various cultures. Some of the world's music expresses the feelings of individual ethnic groups such as a simple, lilting melody of an African tribesman's flute as he plays for his family at sunset, the chanting sounds of a Tibetan monk, the rhythmic melody of a group of Polynesian singers or the ancient songs of American Indian tribes.

In western cultures music is created and enjoyed by people in many ways. It may be a rock group made up of fun loving, idealistic high school friends, a Beethoven symphony being performed in a great performance hall by a world renowned orchestra or a song sung by schoolchildren to their parents at a school play.

Behind these glorious sounds of music is a magnificent system of written music. With western music, this system enables the reader to interpret the exact pitch, rhythmic duration, tempo, emotion and loudness or softness of a series of notes. All of this comes to life via the composer's use of a highly systemized series of dots, lines, symbols and words. It is a language which has evolved over countless centuries and is delicately expressive yet as sturdy as any mathematical equation.

Is it enjoyable to learn to read?

Learn to read music and you understand a language of the world. Learn to read, that is, if you like page after page of theory workbooks. Or can manage to stay alert during lessons of memorizing notes on lines and spaces. Or remember how many of this note equal how many of that note. Or understand the circle of fifths chart.

Ask musicians which music class was their least favorite and you will probably hear, "Music theory".

At an Arizona music camp in high school I remember sitting in a classroom copying scales into my staff notebook as the instructor wrote them on the board. Not only was I confused about what it all meant, the subject was presented in such a dry manner, I was not at all interested in what we were doing. The instructor wrote while he talked, and we sat and copied. There was no action, no sound, no involvement. Nothing reached me, nor anyone of us. There was often a shower in Flagstaff, so we spent most of our time wondering if it would rain while we were in class or soak us as we dashed back to the cafeteria for lunch.

Many years later as an adult I was the instructor for a group of teachers in Tulsa, Oklahoma, gathered for a three-day workshop on my ideas for teaching music theory. Before getting started, I asked them to tell their names, hometowns, teaching situations and reasons for coming to the workshop. Some were teachers and a few were dedicated parents who wanted to teach their children. I had to smile at one teacher's reason for coming.

"I'm not sure why I'm here. I really hate music theory!"

I laughed understandingly. "I love your honesty. And I'd love to hear your thoughts after the workshop." Teachers who had already been using my materials were smiling at each other.

Within minutes of playing the first games, I felt her attitude changing. During the next two days with the students, she was beaming. Before I left to catch my flight home she said, "Now I love music theory! What a difference. The students were eager to come to class and learned so much from you. It's great. My daughter was in your class and didn't even know she wasn't supposed to like it!"

Does it take talent to learn music?

Many people who cannot read music think that reading music is difficult. I suspect they also believe that it takes special talent to learn how to read music since they feel playing a musical instrument or singing well is something that requires talent. And everyone knows that you inherit talent, that you have to be born with talent . . . or do you?

Let's talk about this subject of talent. I can think of no better spokesman on the subject than Dr. Shinichi Suzuki. He is the creator of the Talent Education Method that has brought the joy of wonderful music into the lives of hundreds of thousands of students and their families, worldwide, as they study the violin, piano, viola, cello, bass viol, flute, voice, guitar and harp. Dr. Suzuki teaches that:

> *Talent is no accident of birth.*
> *In today's society a good many people seem to have the idea that if one is born without talent, there is nothing one can do about it, and they simply resign themselves to what they consider to be their "fate." Consequently they go through life without living it to the full or ever knowing life's true joy. That is man's greatest tragedy.*
> *Man is born with natural ability. A newborn child adjusts to his environment in order to live, and various abilities are acquired in the process. My thirty [now sixty] years' experience has proved over and over again that this is true. Many children grow up in an environment that stunts and damages them, and it is assumed that they are born that way, and they themselves believe it, too. But they are all wrong.*
> *An undesirable, disagreeable adult is one who was brought up wrong. A person unable to do good work is one brought up in that way. I believe that most readers will agree with what I have said. So-called fate, of course, one cannot deny. We can do nothing about our being born into this world nor about our having to die sooner or later.*
> *Good or bad, however, once born we have to live with ourselves until the day we die. There arises then the inevitable question of how to live. If our ability was not developed for us, we have to develop it ourselves. Instead of being defeated by misfortune, we have to make something good of our lives. There is no need to give up in discouragement; it is possible for every person to improve himself.* [1]

This philosophy is basic and revolutionary at the same time. It simply means that every student can succeed.

---

[1] Shinichi Suzuki, NURTURED BY LOVE, (Exposition Press), c.1969 p.7

There is no result without cause. Wrong education and upbringing produces ugly personalities, whereas a fine upbringing and good education will bring forth superior sense and feeling, as well as nobility and purity of mind.[2]

Every student has the ability to learn

I want to teach in such a way that every student learns and learns well. If a student isn't understanding or remembering the lesson, then I must change my approach. Rather than thinking that the student is slow or unable to learn, I try another idea.

I strive to find the key to unlock a student's ability.

This is the art of pedagogy. This is where a teacher must have endless capacity to improvise and create situations where the student can succeed. And it's a wonderfully rewarding outlook to have. And it's really quite easy.

Any teacher is tremendously fulfilled when a student learns something, learns it well and finds joy in the process. After experiencing that positive feedback from students, a teacher wants it again and again.

Here's what happens. These successful students greatly encourage the teacher. Then the happy teacher finds it easy to enlighten even more students. Simply put . . . it becomes a cycle of successful learning and gained self-esteem for all involved.

The great natural ability of all students

When I look out at a group of students I feel I am looking into the faces of bright persons. I want them to learn all I know and more. I want them to stand on my shoulders, to be better than I am. Then, humankind advances and improves.

Young people whose curiosity has not been stifled are amazing creatures. They are like scientists exploring their surroundings. They should be given the opportunity to wonder and to be curious. With only a little help from a teacher, they will feel a marvelous combination of pride, fulfillment and growth when they investigate their questions and find their own answers.

There's much to be explored and learned. If given the right environment for learning, students will demonstrate great ability and intelligence. The materials I've designed support these beliefs.

Dependable, well thought-out, versatile materials

You'll find the materials I've created easy to work with. They can be used in your special way to create the learning situation that your students need from you. They are versatile as well as interchangeable. It is remarkably easy to use them and in the process, master the fundamentals of music theory.

The materials are large enough so a student can easily absorb the information. They are colorful since everyone naturally prefers color to black and white. The colors are soothing to help keep the class in order.

---

[2] Shinichi Suzuki, NURTURED BY LOVE, (Exposition Press), c.1969 p.24

They are designed not to be noisy or feel uncomfortable in your hand. This helps learning <u>feel</u> pleasant and also assists the class in maintaining its discipline.

To give the lessons variety and also provide a cross check of understanding, students will work together with one set of materials for certain games; then in later games, they will have their own materials and work side by side.

Cooperative learning, not competitive learning

It's important that the students treat each other with respect and kindness. Since the nature of the games is to provide them with the opportunity to win while they are learning, I want them to be supportive of each other rather than competitive.

All the games are uniquely designed so students work together for a common goal rather than trying to beat each other by finishing first. Contrary to most game playing, everyone wins. And it works amazingly well when everyone wins.

I want learning to be a joyous experience that students enjoy together under the guidance of a teacher who is enthusiastic and supportive.

We have fun in class! When we have fun it conveys a nonverbal message that the subject of music theory is a manageable subject to master. Students don't worry or become stressed since the information is well within their reach. They have time to learn.

However, class dynamics requires that we move along at a very fast clip. Young minds are quick. And lucky that they are, for they help keep our adult minds agile.

Learning is naturally easy

Learning is a natural part of life and something that can be done without effort. Step outside in the morning and learn what the temperature is so you know what to wear. Look in the mirror after a haircut and know if the reflection is flattering and likable. Spend enough time around another person and, without effort, you will learn many things about that person. In fact, you learn a lot about a new person in just a few moments, if instincts are trusted.

Learning does not have to be a trial, a test or a disappointment. Learning does not have to be a situation where one feels small minded or unable to understand or to feel unlikable.

Learning can be easy. It can be joyous and intensely satisfying. It can be encouraging and fulfilling and leave us hungry for more. Learning must be all of these things.

How to entice students to want to learn

So, what is the matter with the traditional concept of formal learning?

Perhaps teachers haven't thought about using basic philosophies to trigger a student's interest. Without interest, nothing can grow.

First it is necessary for teachers to understand that their purpose is not so much to teach, but to simply allow students to learn. It is also their most important responsibility to make lessons so enticing that students are anxious to learn. This enticement can take many forms, and all of them must be genuine. Teachers must feel a freedom to be themselves, to teach in a style that best suits their own personalities.

I like to combine a feeling of friendship, relaxation, excitement, sensitivity, vigor, calmness and fascination with learning. I project the feeling that time is standing still and there is no hurry to learn anything. I will stay with a subject, stopping only when the students have learned all that they can. When the interest level slips ever so slightly, I move on to something else. I like to cover an appealing variety of subjects.

When I teach with a feeling of friendship, the students know they can trust me. I maintain a slight distance so that it is clear to everyone who is in charge. I never relinquish this role and maintain it, not through discipline, but by gaining the respect of my students. First, I achieve this by sincerely admiring them as remarkable, special, uniquely created individuals. I constantly strive to recognize each person as an individual, to be sensitive to his or her needs and try to never make anyone feel uncomfortable. I'm open, friendly and sensitive to the special humor that each age group so instinctively craves.

Using the floor

In a traditional teaching situation, the teacher stands at the front of the class and the students sit and watch. This is a situation for teaching, but not necessarily one for learning.

The games in *Music Mind Games* are played on the floor to create a more intimate environment. This enables the students to direct their attention more easily, and more importantly it focuses the attention on the group.

With students and the teacher sitting on the floor, the focus is more on the materials and the students and less on the teacher. Thus the materials teach, and the students take charge of their learning.

This creates a subtle yet vital difference in what happens to the learning process.

Relaxed, focused students learn more easily

I'm never more frustrated as a teacher than when the class is quiet and well-behaved. This may sound strange, but I prefer students who are alive. Quiet, well-behaved students are not free since they are concentrating too much on how they've been told to act.

I want students to smile, to laugh and maybe even get a little silly. Then they are in a state that allows them to learn in the most natural way. Since they are joyful and interested, they are also creatively focused on what I want them to learn. And in this state, the information they absorb will have an excellent chance of being retained.

However, I do not want my students to loose control of themselves and begin acting as if they're on the playground, running freely. If I sense that happening I try a creative way to pull everyone back in. Once on the third day of a workshop in Hawaii a group of 8 - 13 year olds were beginning to spiral out of control.

As I passed out *Dictation Slates* I told them, "We need quiet during this game. That means no one except me is allowed to talk. There will be no warnings . . . AND, whoever talks will have to bring me something to eat tomorrow."

I greeted their surprised faces with a finger across my lips and continued, "Let me tell you some of my favorite foods

. . . just in case one of you talks. I like fruit, crunchy things and although I try not to eat too many sweets, I like chocolate." The parents were chuckling since they too had noticed their children getting too rowdy. After each dictation pattern, I smiled and named off a few more favorite foods. The class regained it's control and were very successful with their dictation patterns.

Out of seventeen students, three did talk and sweetly brought me little treats the next day.

Learning can be quick

All the games in **Music Mind Games** have been taught over and over again to work out the kinks and streamline the process so one game flows into the other. When I teach, I am constantly assessing the ability of the students to absorb the information taught by the game in a smooth, unstressed manner. Over the nineteen years that I have been teaching these games, I have improved many ideas so students can learn with a minimum of effort and a maximum of confidence building. Although each teacher using the materials affects the process in personal ways, the games are presented in a manner to achieve the utmost success.

For example, the system for melodic dictation allows students to be taking dictation within minutes. Younger students will take more time to integrate the process, but older, school aged students can move faster. At a workshop in Hawaii a mother/teacher told me how amazed she was that her son Noah, age 10, was able to take dictation so quickly. The class had quickly assimilated the games in Chapter 5 in a few minutes and were easily into Chapter 9 games. For all 14 of the students who had been studying piano, violin or cello for several years, this was their very first experience with dictation. Absolutely everyone was successful.

In another class at this workshop I was preparing a group of students of various instruments and abilities to play *Musopoly* on the fourth and final day of the workshop (I saw each class for one 50 minute session each day). They played the first three games for learning tempos and mastered them in a few minutes, but there was less time to memorize all the notes on the grand staff. All we did learn was where the five C's are found and located the G in the treble clef and F in the bass clef. On the day we played *Musopoly*, 8-year-old Michael, a violinist, had the chance to name all the bass clef notes, something he'd never practiced. While the class cheered him on, he named every note correctly and won lots of the game's *Rhythm Money*.

Let's remember what we learn

There is no value in teaching something if it will just be forgotten. Reading music is a skill that a musician will use for life. It must be retained permanently.

I constantly strive to present the information in its truest form so that students' minds can absorb a logical sequence of facts. That is why my book is called **Music Mind Games**. I want to help students not only learn about music, but to think better and remember more.

I want to help train the intellect but disguise the process with entertaining games. The musical concepts are important, but the mind's development is also essential. Teaching like Socrates, by asking questions rather than giving answers, opens the mind to exploration and discovery. The result is joyful confidence and the desire to learn more.

I've created many overlapping mind games which approach a particular subject from different angles. This helps the students achieve the internalization that is so necessary for long term retention. Knowing the facts of music theory must be deeply remembered so that students have the confidence to read music and play securely. When one bit of learning leads to a little more understanding, then the subject becomes focused and stable.

Teaching not testing

When my first child was ten months old, I attended Glenn Doman's BETTER BABY INSTITUTE in Philadelphia, PA. We met all day for six and one-half days, mostly listening to lectures and watching a few fascinating demonstrations. Part of his program is showing young children large printed cards of words, math equations and other "bits of intelligence".

Dr. Doman taught us that information is like a gift to be given and one should not ask for it back. In other words, allow students to learn what you seek to teach them, but don't be so quick to test them to see if they remember it. If you teach it thoroughly with much repetition and in an interesting manner, they will learn it.

As you play the variety of games I've developed you will be able to see if the concepts are taking hold. There are many games that teach a similar idea except the materials are just a little different, or they are used in a new way. This repetition helps the information take hold in the students' minds.

Being positive and speaking positively

*I remember a fairy tale I read as a child. It was from a large book with delicate illustrations where my imagination and I often got lost. My sister Linda gave it to me on my ninth birthday and it's simply called **The Fairy Tale Book**.[3] The last story is called, "Fairies" and is a short tale about a widow with two daughters. I have paraphrased it slightly.*

The oldest was just like her mother, who was spiteful and mean. The younger girl was generous and gentle, as her father had been, and she was perfectly beautiful as well.

Like likes like they say, and the mother loved the older girl dearly. She hated the younger, who did the housework and cooking for the three of them.

One day the younger daughter met a poor old woman at the well. True to her gentle kindness, she gave the old woman a drink from her pitcher.

The woman thanked her. She said, "Because you're helpful and gentle, I will give you a gift. Every time you speak, a precious jewel or a beautiful flower will spring from your lips." Then she vanished. She was a fairy who had come to test the girl's good heart.

With her pitcher full, the girl went home. Her mother scolded her for being so long at the fountain. "I'm sorry, Mother," said the girl. As she spoke, two roses, two pearls, and two diamonds fell from her lips.

"What's that?" screeched the mother. "Where do they come from?"

The girl was both obedient and truthful. She explained what had happened. In the telling, she spread a carpet of diamonds and flowers about her.

The mother was angry that the fairy had made a mistake and should have given such a gift to the older sister. That afternoon she forced the lazy, unwilling girl to fetch the water.

At the well was a lady in beautiful clothes. The lady asked for a drink.

"I'm no servant," said the rude girl. "This is my pitcher, not yours. Get your own drink, if you're thirsty."

---

[3] *THE FAIRY TALE BOOK, (Golden Press, Inc.), c.1958, p.155*

"Very well," said the lady, who was the fairy in a new disguise. "I'll give you a gift to suit your manners. Every time you speak, a toad or a snake will slither from your mouth."

And that's exactly what happened. Since even her mother could not tolerate having her house filled with slippy, sloppy, slithering things whenever she spoke, the older sister was thrown out and wandered the world, alone.

The younger sister was chased into the woods by the furious mother only to be discovered by a prince who fell in love with her beauty and good heart. He led her home to his palace. They were married, and reigned happily for years and years and years.

Besides using this story to guide my choice of words in my everyday life, I use it to try to help my own children speak kindly to each other. Although we have our share of toads and snakes to toss out the back door on any given day, I do have quite a collection of jewels and flowers that I treasure.

A collection of thoughts

Discard everything that is unnecessary.

Aim to be simple.

Relax, abandon yourself. Fear nothing.

Compress time. Aim at succeeding, don't waste an instant.

Don't take yourself seriously.

Don't hurry, don't rest.

Use self-humor.

Don't be afraid to be a little foolish.

Have endless patience.

If faced with overwhelming odds, occupy time with something else.

Have endless capacity to improvise.

Bring abstract ideas into concrete form.

Assume that students enjoy learning.

The teacher's attitudes influence everything.

Believe that children are perfect, and we're just building upon their strengths.

Support everything with a visual aid.

Insure no possible way to fail.

A teacher must be upbeat and positive.

If the goal is only to learn facts, then we lose the chance to know that learning is exciting.

IDEAS FOR TEACHING

hat makes a successful teacher?

A great teacher is cheerful, a bit of an entertainer and especially someone who relates to students. S/he must have high ideals and be able to feel the human side of how it feels to learn.

If you can remember how it felt to be young and to be a student, you will know how to teach. Think back into earlier years and remember your teachers. Who comes to mind first?

I remember a violin teacher who was a college student when I studied with him. He was very good at the violin but not at teaching. He went through exercises with me and assigned pieces, but his suggestions never impacted nor changed my playing. Although he told me what was wrong with my playing, he didn't teach me how to practice. Even though I knew his suggestions were valuable, I didn't improve. Not relating to me as a person, he sought only to improve my violin playing. He was boring and I was too bored to concentrate. After not too many lessons, my mom let me quit.

I remember a piano teacher who had a fine reputation. It's just that she was good at something I wasn't interested in. I liked playing piano, but at the first lesson she assigned several dozen chords and their inversions. I felt overwhelmed and understimulated at the same time. Anyway, I wanted to learn repertoire rather than reading from FAKE books. So, Mom agreed to let me stop after a few lessons.

When I was in high school I auditioned and was accepted to study private piano at Arizona State University. I can remember Dr. Arnold Bullock very well. I would sit at one of his grand pianos in the middle of a large Oriental rug that had two holes worn clear through to the wooden floor beneath, right where our heels rested when we played the pedals. His space on the rug also had two holes in the same spots. Dr. Bullock had become a white haired professor teaching many lessons at these pianos.

He was an accomplished pianist, but I didn't quite connect with him. I remember trying not to fall asleep . . . during my lesson.

Dr. Bullock was certainly a nice teacher. He loaned me recordings (I still feel badly about the one I accidentally melted in my car in the hot Arizona sun) and entered me in competitions, which despite warnings that I wouldn't win because I hadn't practiced enough, I did win. Somehow he kept me involved playing classical piano though high school and for that I am most appreciative.

Then came George Katz, graduate of Julliard (first in his class the same year that Van Cliburn graduated second) and an amazingly gifted, disciplined and well-educated musician. He was strict, encouraging and his ideas for musical interpretation were endless. Why did I relate to him so well?

He taught me. He didn't only teach me piano. He taught me.

He took the time to get to know me so he knew what my abilities were and never gave up until he guided me to reach the goals he'd set. He expected only the best and convinced me that I was capable of the best.

Since his directions were clear, I knew what was expected of me. I knew what I was to practice and how. I knew what was supposed to be done. He was in charge.

And he was kind. I don't ever recall feeling badly about something I had or hadn't done. If I didn't do something right, I simply needed to do it again.

I worked hard. I practiced and practiced and practiced. I wish I had some of those lessons times back again because I enjoyed the growth I felt while I was with him.

Students want to grow. It's a wonderfully enriching feeling to have someone take enough interest in you to care about how you are developing.

Finding the balance between too easy and too hard

A great teacher develops the sensitivity to provide students with enough to challenge but not to overwhelm them. How much is enough? Watch their eyes. Watch their body language. Listen to their comments. Stop before they want to stop.

Be spontaneous and joyful as you teach. That doesn't mean you need to laugh and smile all the time. That wouldn't be natural. But do have fun and relax with your students.

I don't make strict lesson plans for my classes. I have a few ideas about what games we could play, but I always wait until I see the students to know what to teach them. Some days the weather influences their moods, or maybe they will become so interested in a new game that we'll spend the whole class on it.

Become a student

Nothing will help you develop ideas on how to teach better than becoming a student again. Maybe it will be helpful to take a class in something unrelated to music. Try something you're interested in but maybe something you're not terrific at.

I tried ice skating one winter. I liked the growth. The teacher was kind but kept me on a direct path. I enjoyed practicing, but I especially liked how I could skate a little better each week. I was fearful of falling, so I tried things at my own pace. After so many years of focused attention on my fingers, it was refreshing to try to bring my entire body into action.

I liked being in a class with other people so I could watch them when they did something better than I. I also felt good when I could do something more easily than they could. There was a good balance.

I tried aerobics another winter. That was physically demanding, but I appreciated the kindness of the teachers. They rotated schedules so I had a chance to do the same routines with different teachers. "Work at your own pace," they would yell to us over the loud, driving music. I developed the most when the teacher was positive, encouraging and talkative. If a teacher wasn't upbeat, I felt overwhelmed. If the teacher had charisma, looked happy throughout the class and seemed to reach out to us, I felt strong.

Sometimes great, but not always

It's not always possible to be a great teacher. Even great teachers have off days. There are days when the students seem a little bored, too wiggly or have forgotten everything from the previous lesson. And there are days when a teacher may feel out of focus, unprepared, too demanding, unable to get a hold on the class, tired or ready for two weeks on a tropical island with a fully equipped beach house and a cook.

Ahhh, that does sound inviting, doesn't it?

But, getting back to reality.

I'd like to share some ideas that I've discovered over the years about the art of teaching. These are important little details that can affect your disposition and that of your students as you enjoy learning together.

A minimum of talking

Too much explanation can be confusing. Use a minimum of words to pleasantly explain a game. I've included conversation I actually use in teaching my own students.

I'll use *Musopoly* and myself as an example. Years ago when a class played *Musopoly* for the first time I used to set up the game and tell the students how to play it, rule after rule, requesting that they ask no questions until I was completely finished. Then they would begin to play.

Now I toss the game board in the middle of the room, hand them the cards to set out and the dice begin to roll. The game is quite logical and the students enjoy discovering about it as they go along, asking questions as necessary. It's more fun for them and there's more time for play.

Keeping the class under control

I enjoy when my students feel relaxed, free to make mistakes and be themselves during class. It's also important that all of us exercise self-control and be respectful of each other.

During the actual class it's the students, rather than I, who should keep themselves under control. This is the most positive way to conduct class, and it allows me to use my voice for teaching and praises rather than orders, reprimands or threats.

Most students welcome this atmosphere and rise to my expectations. Occasionally though, there's someone who needs a little guidance. When this student acts up, seeking more attention, I deal with it right away.

At a one-week workshop in Alaska, a bright girl named Susan simply talked too much. She had a comment for everything we did and didn't do. She was deliberately refocusing the class towards her. I whispered to her as I was passing out cards, "Susan, I want you to please stop talking so much." I didn't want to embarrass her nor give her extra attention for undesirable behavior.

She didn't change. A few moments later I whispered to her again, "Susan, I want you to stop talking so much, and this is the last time I'm going to ask you." It worked. In the next few moments I watched to find something she did well, then I smiled and spoke to her in a positive way. She still talked more than anyone else, but it fit within the boundaries of our class.

One time a young boy in a workshop class in Oregon didn't respond to my second request to stop talking. "John, I want you to please go sit on that chair for a few moments." He watched his classmates play a round of 2-3: FINE. While the students were busy, I handed John a set of *Alphabet Cards* and said, "Would you like to join the class again?" He was fine, and I was able to find lots of times to praise him for good behavior.

Sometimes separating two good friends before we bow helps. "Kathleen, you stand here. And Joan, you stand over here, please."

I want to preserve the misbehaving students' dignity whenever I have to help them get their act together. If I embarrass them even once in front of their peers I know that I will loose my chance to gain their respect and thus their cooperation.

Deliberate mischief

What about a student who misbehaves and tries to take over the class to gain attention? Is there a gentle yet effective way of dealing with this situation?

There's a game in Chapter 3 where students throw the *Toss Note* on the *Grand Staff Board* and call out if it's on a line or space. Occasionally someone tosses too hard and hits me with the *Toss Note* (that's one reason why it's soft!). I join the laughter and hand the note back to the student. "Do I look like a line or a space? A bit gentler this time, okay, Brian?"

Now and then someone will deliberately toss the note off the staff to get attention. I give her another chance with the exact instructions as before. If this continues, I hand the note back, look directly into her eyes and say, "One more chance, Lisa." If she persists, I hand the *Toss Note* to the next player. "Please have a seat, Lisa."

Taking turns

When games involve turns, you can either go around the circle or select students randomly. Another idea is to let the student who just had the turn choose the next person. As s/he glances around at classmates I suggest choosing the person who's being the quietest. This simple idea keeps everyone's attention on the game and everyone settles down rather than calling out, "Me! Please, me next!"

Subtle corrections

If students make an error, it's best to help by correcting the materials and saying just a few words. Remember that if you draw too much attention to them it may be embarrassing. They may not be able to concentrate on your suggestions. Help them later, individually.

Not success for just some students

In school there are students who do well, those who do fairly well and some who don't always catch on to what is being taught. I don't think those students are unintelligent, I think the curriculum is not at their level and that they need more time. If learning is based on a time schedule, then those who need more time will fall behind.

Soon their self-image tells them they aren't so bright. They get used to not catching on. It's unfair that some students do not succeed.

It's not only school that affect the student's ability to learn. Learning patterns are established before formal learning begins. Ibuka's **Kindergarten is Too Late** discusses the importance that preschool life has on children. If the home life of children is nurturing, encouraging and properly paced for success, children's self-esteem will grow. They will feel capable and able to learn.

If teachers and school life can foster these positive attitudes, students will feel successful and they will prosper. All students deserve this opportunity.

Teaching or correcting?

There's a valuable concept that lies in the heart of Maria Montessori's philosophies of educating children.

Teach teaching, not correcting. If a student makes an error, it's because s/he doesn't understand. Rather than correcting, ("that's wrong, it's this way,") the teacher should reteach the information ("C is found two ledger lines above and below the staff."). Students want to do something correctly and when they understand it, they will do it correctly. They want to be right.

They may need to be retaught several times before the information takes hold. That's totally all right.

Pace of the games

There are many differences between professionally made television and home movies, but one important one is how quick the action is. Watch cartoons, children's toy commercials or Sesame Street, and you'll see how fast the pace is. The human mind has the capacity to learn very quickly if the information is presented clearly.

Students will retain better focus and concentration if games move along at a steady pace. Watch so that no one is getting bored.

Whenever I pass out cards, observers jokingly ask if I ever worked in Las Vegas. Cards are flying and the students love it. I don't lose control of the class but refresh the students and give them a second wind to carry on with the next game.

Mix it up while their eyes are closed

After they have been introduced to a concept, give them a chance to try it on their own. Many games use this idea. Here's how it works. Snap your fingers, the signal for them to close their eyes. It's best not to say "don't peek". Usually they won't think of it unless you suggest it. Instead say, "It's more fun if you keep your eyes closed really tight." Clap your hands twice so they will open their eyes. "Raise your hand and I will call on you. Did I tell you I always call on whoever is being the quietest?" Otherwise everyone will dog pile on the cards!

Students take real delight playing this way. There's something so fun about having a trick appear while one's eyes are closed. It's even more fun if the trick can be solved, and a compliment is given. Even shy children will relax and want to play. Remember that this is for learning, not for testing. Help them to be right each time.

What should you do if a child is not able to fix it?
   1) Smile and fix it yourself. Offer a short explanation. "The C card is after B.'
   2) Let another child fix it and then praise both students for their efforts. "Good, both of you!"

Please, create your own games, but . . .

Enjoy the materials and enjoy the games. If you feel as if you'd like to improvise and make up games, please do. I have just one request.

Please remain faithful to the philosophies I've outlined for these materials. To illustrate:

One day I was at the printers putting some final touches on the art work for the *Blue Jello Cards*. One card had two whole rests and another one was full of eighth rests and sixteenth note triplets.

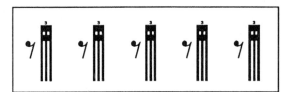 

Mike, our graphic artist for the **Music Mind Games** materials, laughed and said, "Boy, if I was a kid I surely would be bummed out if I got this card," and pointed to the one with the triplets.

"Oh, but I never put the kids on the spot like that. I don't use these cards as flash cards," I quickly explained.

"No?" Mike couldn't seem to imagine any other way to use them.

"It's too much like testing, and kids don't like to be tested."

"I certainly agree with that," nodded Mike.

So, please keep in mind the philosophies behind these materials as you improvise ways to use them.

A reason for learning from Beethoven

Beethoven believed music students should be well versed in music theory by age thirteen. Then their expressive abilities can be captured in original, correctly written compositions.

Being fluent in dictation and rhythm is a valuable asset in composition. That is why so much of this book is devoted to those areas.

It also helps students to read and perform better if they understand music theory. And if they have been taught with joy, they will look favorably upon the whole arena of musical life.

A moment to shine

Everyday, every student should have a chance to shine, to glow for a moment in the sunlight of success. Teachers who help create those special times are truly enriching the lives of young persons they've been fortunate enough to teach. The sunlight that's created will continue to spread in countless ways, reaching many for a long time.

IDEAS FOR GETTING
ORGANIZED

ow many times to play a game

You may want to play some games over and over, week after week. Others you may just play once. Another game may be played for a few weeks, then not again for several months. One might be played, then forgotten for a year or so. Brought out again with a new twist to make it trickier will be fun.

I don't mean to be vague, but that's how this method works. Some students will catch on quickly and be anxious to move on to more challenges. You may cover highlights of *Alphabet Cards* games in Chapters 1 & 2 in a session or two and be ready to move on to thirds and other intervals.

Or, your students may be younger and need time to acquire the concepts, so you play games in those chapters for a few years.

During this time you'll also do rhythm games, dictation games, learn some of the orange symbol cards, play games with the staff and other musical activities.

I promise you will have lots to choose from, and the games will be always be successful for you. Promise.

PART
ONE

3

How to organize a class

It is important to try to cover several main areas in each class:

Rhythm   Dictation   Alphabet or staff

Depending on the level, I add musical symbols and tempos. With advanced students we play games with scales, triads and chords.

Here are ideas of games that are appropriate at different levels. These are merely suggestions. There are over 200 games in **Music Mind Games**, so these are just a brief sampling.

Please take into account how long your students have been studying and what their backgrounds are. Depending on the situation, these games could be played during one or more class sessions.

Also, I've played the games listed for "five-year-olds" with students who are twelve-years-old on many occasions. Students are introduced to music at many different ages. It's never to late to begin. So, don't take the ages I've listed too seriously. However, if you do have the chance to begin students at a young age and keep them, they can easily accomplish this list. I'm fortunate to have several excellent high school age students who began piano lessons with me when they were in preschool.

4 year olds:	1-3:	FAT SNAKE	10 year olds	13-7:	*REAL RHYTHM* SNAKES
	3-3:	LINES & SPACES WITH FACES		17-10:	SUSPENSE - NOTES
	4-1:	*BLUE JELLO CARDS*		18-6:	RHYTHM SOLITAIRE
	5-3:	REPEATED NOTES AND INTERVALS		19-9:	SHARP SCALE FINE
				24-1:	SONG PUZZLE DRAW
5 year olds:	2-2:	SNAKE VARIATIONS	11 year olds	15-4:	COUNTERPOINT SNAKES
	4-8:	*BLUE JELLO CARDS* BINGO		16-4:	INTERVAL CIRCLE DICTATION
	5-4:	*MELODIC BINGO* COPY GAME		18-9:	MEREDITH'S TOWER
	6-1:	THESE FIVE C'S		20-2:	WRITE A SCALE - FLATS
	7-2:	NOTE OR REST?		21-1:	FOUR KINDS OF TRIADS
6 year olds:	6-4:	*GRAND STAFF CARDS* C'S	12 year olds	16-1:	THE LAST NOTE IS FIRST
	7-4:	CARD CHART		18-11:	SPEED
	8-3:	FIX THE ORDER - THIRDS		20-7:	CAN YOU TELL ME - FLATS?
	9-4:	TAKE AWAY		21-2:	MAJOR SCALE TRIADS
				22-1:	SCALES AND CHORDS
7 year olds	7-7:	WAR WITH *NOTES & RESTS CARDS*	13 year olds	15-6:	RHYTHM MATH CHART
	8-4:	WIN A TRIAD		16-7:	INTRODUCING HARMONIC DICTATION
	9-5:	HEAR ANY THIRDS		21-7:	SECRET SCALE
	10-5:	I'D LIKE TO SELL A . . .		21-13:	INVERSION DROP
	11-1:	DYNAMICS		23-3:	INTRODUCING RELATIVE MINOR SCALES
		Begin reading music			
	14-1:	*MUSOPOLY*			
8 year olds		Practice sight-reading in class	14 year olds	16-9:	DICTATION ROW
	8-6:	INTERVAL CIRCLE		21-14:	ONE NOTE - MANY CHORDS
	9-6:	WRITE MINE		22-7:	SEVENTH CHORD INVERSIONS
	11-7:	LEARNING THE OTHERS		23-6:	MINOR SCALE DICTATION
	12-3:	TEMPO MIX-UP			
	13-3:	BECOME A BEAT	older:	repetition of games to maintain memory expansion to more advanced concepts	
9 year olds	13-5:	WHAT SONG IS THIS?			
	15-2:	MAKING MEASURES			
	16-5:	*SONG PUZZLE* SNAKES			
	17-4:	*BINGO* BOTH CLEFS			
	19-1:	SHARP MAJOR SCALES			

Beginning and ending class

I like to begin and end each class with a bow. This Oriental custom has become common in karate, judo and other classes. The bow is a greeting between students and teacher. It says that the class is beginning and it's time to put other thoughts aside until after the final bow. It's a reminder to become focused and ready for learning.

I teach a "dinosaur bow".

A what?

Before bowing I wait for each student to assume the correct position for bowing: Relaxed, yet tall, focused body. Hands at sides. Eyes up. Feet less than an inch apart for balance. And most important, a smile. ("Dinosaurs had big teeth.") If anyone needs fixing, I offer pointers until everyone is ready.

I wait until I hold everyone's eyes in mine. My eyes indicate when to bow, thus helping to create control before the class even begins. Then heads and eyes are gently lowered a little, supported by straight backs. The hands should stay in place, elbows bending slightly. The hands should not slide down the sides of the legs during the bow.

So that the bow isn't too fast, everyone whispers the long name of a dinosaur before coming up. ("Stegosaurs, triceratops, or tyrannosaurs rex".) Little kids will giggle and older students will say the dinosaur name silently.

Raised eyes meet again and then everyone sits down for the first game.

Before the closing bow I might remind students of any assignment or announcements and thank them for their good manners during class. "Thanks for coming today. I really enjoyed seeing you. Have a nice week."

Names of students

This is an essential point for relating to your students and gaining their cooperation and awakening their spirit for learning.

I assisted at my son's preschool one year. During music class I noticed that the music teacher rarely used the students' names. Even though she had worked with some students for two years, she would say, "You, go over and play now," instead of a much more personal, "Kathryn, it's your turn to play the bass tone blocks." Everyone in the class was just "You," as if all the students were just variations on the same thing. In defense of her, she did come in contact with hundreds of little students each week. However, even when she knew their names, she did not use them. The class lacked warmth and no one seemed to develop a personal relationship with her.

Many people feel they aren't good at remembering names, as if a short memory is as permanent as the size of your foot. Well, it is definitely possible to practice remembering names so you will become better at it. Clever people have devised tricks to help us remember names, and sometimes they work. I think the most direct way is to use someone's name over and over, each time looking at each one's face to help associate the face with the name.

When I watch a television broadcast of the President's press conference I always notice how more personal it seems when the President calls a reporter by name. "Yes, Diane?" or "That is a good question, Sam . . ." It seems as if one person is truly talking to another. Can you imagine the different impression if the President said, "You. What do You want to ask me?" or pointed his finger at someone and said, "You?"

Students are especially touched if you call them by name. It means they really exist for you and are special human beings. It means you're interested in hearing their answers and their ideas.

Notice how you feel when someone you care about uses your name. Try it in your own family.

Names at workshops

At most week workshops I am assigned to teach five classes of about 12 students each day. Since that's about 60 new names to learn, I get a chance to keep my memory in shape. Looking at class lists ahead of time doesn't really help. Taking some time on the first day to get acquainted does.

To begin with, I introduce myself to the class and tell the students a little about myself, such as what I teach at home and what some of my interests are. I tell them a bit about my family and what my favorite foods and colors are and what I like besides music. I tell the adults a bit about where I teach, how long I've been doing it and maybe a comment or two about my students.

"And what was my name?" I ask after all that talking.

"Ummmmm. Mrs. Yurko?" someone will volunteer.

"Right! Now I'd like to learn each of your names." By now we are all sitting in a circle on the floor. Turning to the student sitting next to me, I ask her name.

"Amanda."

"Hi, Amanda," I smile at her. Then turning to the class, I ask, "Can everyone say Amanda?"

"Amanda," says everyone together. Next I'll look at the person sitting next to Amanda. "What is your name?"

"Bradley," he says smiling broadly.

"Hello, Bradley. Can you all say his name?" I ask.

Everyone looks at Bradley and says his name. Then we all look at Amanda and say her name.

Next, we learn the name of the person next to Bradley.

"Hello, Susan. And who's sitting next to Susan?"

"Bradley."

"And next to Bradley?"

"Amanda."

And so we continue around the circle, learning one new name and then repeating all the other names. If the class is large and the students are smart, we may learn two names at once. We may practice everyone's names by going around the circle in thirds. That means we say every other name, then back around the circle, still in thirds, saying everyone else's name. The students begin to relax and enjoy themselves. They are learning the names of new friends and beginning to feel a part of the class.

After the students have introduced themselves I ask, "Do you think I can say everyone's name? Okay, cover your name tags before I try."

There's the sound of hands slapping tight over name tags and giggles as I get ready to take on the challenge. Around the circle I go, looking at each student before I say his or her name. If I miss, I make it a point to say that name over and over to help remember it and also to reassure the student.

Then I ask, "Do you think I can remember your names if you're all mixed up? While I close my eyes, you move to a new spot and sit next to two new people. Ready? Go!"

While I cover my eyes I can hear the sound of muffled laughter as scurrying students change places.

"It's getting dark in here. Are you ready yet?" I ask with a smile.

"Ready! Open your eyes!" they call out.

"Cover your name tags before I open my eyes." Then I open my eyes.

"Wow. This is going to be a challenge," I joke with them. Around the circle I go trying to remember names, but thanks to all the repetitions, it's easy now. What before were shy, maybe frightened children are now smiling, giggling, eager students.

The mix-up also has a hidden purpose. Sometimes students may come to class with a friend or two. Or all the boys sit on one side and the girls on the other. This mix-up helps to spread everyone around.

Learning names has several purposes: 1) to let me learn names and let them learn each other's names to help make new friends 2) to help students relax 3) to let each student feel special 4) to mix up students who, because they knew each other before class, might have been tempted to talk 5) to let the students know that this class will be enjoyable as well as challenging and 6) let them get used to me before I began to help them learn more about reading music. It's worth every minute.

After learning names, we all feel more comfortable working together, and the students are eager to begin playing with the materials they've seen on the tables.

Temperature of the teaching room

I learned something else of importance at Doman's six day Better Baby Institute. We were warned to dress warmly.

Seems Dr. Doman learned that NASA had done experiments to determine the perfect temperature of the oxygen astronauts should breathe while in their space suits. We were told that it was 65 degrees.

Great — the brain likes 65 degrees and the body likes 72 degrees. Guess who won?

You guessed it . . . I wore several warm sweaters on the first day and by the second day, I wish I'd brought along the blanket from my hotel bed.

Yet, hour after hour, we all stayed alert, fresh and able to focus on the information given us.

Since then I've kept my teaching rooms cool - - although not as cool as 65 degrees! I find it keeps all of us from getting sleepy and we work more efficiently.

Furnishings of the teaching room

Depending on where you are teaching, at a school, studio or home, some of these things will be at your choosing and some will not. As with any situation, do your best and be happy with it.

Cleanliness: This is simple. The room must be clean.

Clutter: This is also simple. There shouldn't be any . . . well, not too much. A few stacks of papers is one thing but boxes of music, Christmas decorations, yesterday's pizza box and your children's shoes are distracting.

Colors: Simple, pleasant, soothing colors are best. Friendly colors can be calming and interesting at the same time.

The rug: Since nearly all of these games are played on the floor, this is the most important consideration. Choose your carpeting or rug carefully. A neutral color is relaxing. And invest in an industrial type padding. It will give extra cushioning so everyone can feel comfortable for a long time.

The Japanese have a saying: "Buy the best, cry once."

Windows: These are wonderful. Keep the shades open, let in the sunlight, and refresh yourself now and then by looking outside.

Closets: I once designed a studio and borrowed some floor space along one wall and had the carpenter build closets behind two double doors. They contained wall to wall shelves and had some vertical partitions so the *Bingo Cards* could rest upright. There was lots of shelf space so cards, notes and *Alphabet Kids* sat ready to be grabbed up for a game.

Trash can: An important addition.

Bathroom: If you're teaching in a public building, this will be provided. If you're in your own private studio, try to arrange so the bathroom is used only by your students. Everyone will feel more comfortable with this. A wall container of small cups is a nice gesture, and a box of tissues is a must.

Lighting: Teaching rooms should be well lit, comfortable and not too bright. Florescent ceiling lights are efficient and can provide a full expanse of soft light. Long armed, movable halogen lights make terrific piano lights.

Furniture: Comfortable seating for parents and observers is necessary. A table for homework helps older students make use of their observation time. If the rug is soft, visitors will often choose to sit there.

Entry room: The outside door to that former studio of mine originally opened up directly to the outside cold or heat so an entry room (6' x 9') was added. The room had it's own heating source under a bench that ran along one wall. Along the opposite wall and half of another were double rows of coat hooks, one low for young people and another high for adults. The door had full length windows plus a window above the bench. The inside door to the entry room was half windows so from where I sat at the second piano I could see people enter and leave. The carpeting was big brown squares that could be easily cleaned or replaced.

The telephone and doorbell: If you are teaching in your own studio you may wonder what others do about the telephone. An answering machine is one solution, but I don't use one. If a student will be late or must cancel, I want to know it when they call. Since I have parents present in my studio, I ask them to please answer the phone and take messages for me.

If you must be interrupted by either phone or door, leave your students with a short assignment to do over and over until you return. If you have parents present, one of them may enjoy taking over the class for a moment.

Your furnishings and teaching room will be individualized and there are many designs that will work well. Just keep in mind that the physical surroundings not only affect the students who spend a few hours there each week but especially you who may be there for thousands of hours as the years roll by.

What to wear

This is a most important consideration for any teacher. Can you remember scrutinizing the clothes your teachers wore each day? In the 1970's one of my professors wore suits he had worn in the 1940's — but it was rather appropriate since we all felt he didn't really relate to our generation anyway.

Another teacher wore comfortable, up to date clothes. We felt we could relate to this teacher and relaxed in his presence. He was also humorous and encouraging.

At one workshop I taught with a teacher who wore cut off shorts and T-shirts each day. Although I enjoy casual clothes, I felt this sent an inappropriate message for a learning situation.

Another teacher wore the same clothes three days in a row. Packing light is a virtue, but this was carrying it a bit too far! Students like to feel that a new day brings new chances for success. To see a teacher wearing fresh, interesting clothes affirms that.

Since the games in this book are played on the floor, it is fine to wear casual clothes that adapt to floor play.

Your clothes do reflect your attitude about how you want to relate to your students, and **what you** wear will send an important nonverbal message.

Shoes: During the two months I lived in Japan I got used to taking my shoes off anytime I went into a private home, temple or school. The entrance to all homes has a street level area where outside shoes are slipped off and left. One then steps up and into a soft inside shoe which is worn only in the house. Once back home, I felt more comfortable without my outside shoes and noticed how much cleaner my floors and rugs stayed. Thinking of all the places my shoes traveled in a day, I decided I didn't want that in my home.

In my teaching studio everyone has gotten used to wearing socks (although on hot days we see toes). This makes it more comfortable and safer to sit on the floor and play the games.

Assignments for home

Usually I don't give homework from theory class since my students are practicing their piano lesson each day. However, sometimes there's a little fact that I want them to think about for a few moments each day to keep their memories fresh. I try to make the assignments creative.

"Whenever you brush your teeth this week, please say your thirds backwards three times."

"Whenever you and your mom or dad are stopped at a traffic light, I want you to say "treble clef - G clef" and "bass clef - F clef".

"Can you teach your dad how to do "F C G D A?"

"As you fall asleep this week I want you to think of the grand staff and put each of the five C's in the right place. Let's try it once right now. Close your eyes."

"Everyday at the very beginning of your home lesson, spell three dominant seventh chords using different roots."

During a class in San Juan, Puerto Rico I taught a group of students "ritardando" and "a tempo". As an analogy I compared the terms to what a car does as it stops for a red traffic light and then resumes its speed when the light turns green. "On the way home from class today, please count the number of times your car or bus or whatever "makes a ritardando and an a tempo". It was funny hearing their stories the next day!

Groups

Many games are described for play with twelve or fewer students. If your class is larger, divide the students into pairs or small groups and ask them to take turns. They will certainly enjoy the company and learn by watching and helping each other.

Cleanup

After each game is finished, all the materials should be organized and put away. The students will get used to this and joyfully participate. If we have a lot of materials, like for *Musopoly*, we will form a "fire line" to get everything back to the closet in a cooperative manner. This is always fun for everyone.

There are more hints for cleanup in the games.

IDEAS FOR PRIVATE TEACHERS

I teach private piano students in my home studio and over the years have developed a schedule that allows for good teaching time as well as quality time for my own children. Here are some ideas I've used at different times over the years.

Observation first

When parents call about lessons I answer their questions briefly and invite them to observe lessons. There is no charge for observing. This gives them a chance to know first hand what my program is like. If they like what they see, they may come back as often as possible.

I do not keep a waiting list but tell observing parents that whoever observes the most gets the first available time. Most observe for several weeks or months. The longest a student and parent observed was for nearly a year. When she and her mother began lessons, it was smooth sailing and still is.

One boy and his mother came for nearly five months. Although the mother was interested, the boy never looked up from the books he brought with him. I doubted <u>his</u> interest in piano and the mother figured this out, too, and stopped coming.

I find this observation period very valuable, and it helps my students stay with lessons once they begin.

PART ONE

4

Parents' classes before lessons

I meet with the parents who will join the program. We meet for several sessions and discuss four topics: 1) Philosophy of learning 2) The importance of listening to fine music and how to fit it into your day 3) How to have an effective home lesson 4) How to behave at the studio lesson.

The parents take a short lesson each time and set an example for daily practice at home.

Begin in small groups

I like to begin groups of four students ages 2 - 5. When I've tried two students to a group, there may be competition and three students may become unbalanced. The groups meet once or twice weekly for one hour. We begin with a bow, then each child has an individual lesson while the others listen and play with quiet toys out of the line of vision of the student.

The students enjoy being with others, they are inspired to do their best, they don't develop a fear of playing for one another and everyone learns from each other.

Each child progresses independently of the others. There is not a hint of competition <u>ever</u>.

After several months, I take one class every fourth lesson or so and do theory games with them. We always save time for performance.

A weekly theory class

When the students need more time than 10-15 minutes per session, I expand the class and allow a half hour for each lesson. I schedule these students into a theory class each week. Parents tell me these classes are a favorite of their children. Students are expected to continue to observe one or more lessons besides attending their own. To encourage this, the parents and I organize a rotating schedule so they can observe different students. This is ideal but not always possible.

week 1	week 2	week 3	week 4
Henrietta	Gus	Ann	Roxanne
Ann	Henrietta	Roxanne	Gus
theory class	theory class	theory class	theory class
Roxanne	Ann	Gus	Henrietta
Gus	Roxanne	Henrietta	Ann

With a theory class in the middle of lessons, the student stays for an hour or so but comes only once a week. Older students bring homework. Occasionally a student will come on different days for lessons and theory class. This schedule can be expanded to include more students.

Time for my own children

Since my children are now in school, I save the half hour after they get home for them, instead of teaching. We talk about our days, and they get started on snacks and homework. This time is vital to our relationship.

Setting up classes: age or playing level?

Actually both are important. However, if I begin a student at a later age, say 9 or 10, I will put him with students his age even if they've been studying awhile. It doesn't work to put an older beginner in with younger students. The humor is different with various age groups. My students know that I value fine playing at all levels so the beginner feels comfortable and is inspired to advance more quickly.

Performance

As part of my group class each week, we include a short recital, usually at the end of the hour. We do a variety of things, but usually everyone plays a solo that he or she has been preparing all week.

This gives students the chance to become comfortable in front of an audience made up of a small group of friends.

Occasionally students try out a new piece, but usually they perform a polished one that has been studied for months.

Students smile at the audience, announce title and composer then take a bow. I teach them to look at the audience again and smile.

After they seat themselves comfortably and properly at the piano they are to sit in rest position until everyone in the room is quiet. I suggest they hear the first part of their piece in their heads, look at the notes they are to begin on and then put their hands on the keyboard.

After the piece is finished, hands return to rest position before they leave the piano and take a final bow. Week after week, the students enjoy the chance to play for each other and to polish their performance skills.

We have some fun ways of deciding who is to play first.

1. *Alphabet Cards* I hold out one set. Whoever draws A plays first and so on in order. If the students are learning the backwards alphabet, then whoever draws the G goes first and so on in order, backwards.

2. **Clues and clothes** This one isn't related to music reading, but it is very popular. I describe something about what a student is wearing and everyone tries to guess who it is. Whether they guess or not, that student is next.

It's fun since my clues are tricky. I pick out some tiny detail, like a label on the bottom of a shoe. If a boy is wearing socks with a few stripes the clue might be "This road goes round and round". If a girl is wearing a dress with lots of flowers I might say, "More fragrant than perfume."

I'm careful not to let my eyes give away the student. Also, rather than letting the last student play by default, I give clues for the last two performers so everyone can guess who's who. This way everyone enjoys special recognition.

3. *Real Rhythm Cards* I select the same number of cards as there are performers, each one a different value. I arrange the cards upside down so that just a bit of one end is peeking out from underneath a board.

As you may have guessed, this is a variation on "drawing straws". Whoever has the shortest rhythm value waits the shortest time and thus plays first. The longest value will wait the longest and plays last.

4. *Rhythm Cards* Each student draws one or more cards. They lay their cards on the floor and compare to see whose cards add up to the most number of beats.

5. **Alphabetical order - with a twist** "In alphabetical order by the third letter in your first name" or "In backwards alphabetical order by the first letter in your last name" or "In alphabetical order by the last letter of your middle name" or . . .

Who's prepared to play One month I noticed that my students weren't playing as well as I might have liked. Although I'd asked them to choose their piece a week in advance and prepare it each day, when it came time to play, many of them only then began to decide. One day I said, "Whoever chose a piece a week ago and is prepared to play it, may perform today." Only one student played that day. But at the next class, everyone was ready.

Most favorite and least favorite Here's an idea that will inspire your students to practice two pieces of their choosing. This works well with a sight-reading piece or repertoire pieces.

"Next week I would like each of you to prepare two pieces to play for everyone. I want one to be your favorite piece and the other your least favorite piece."

"Wow!" The students looked at each other, rolling their eyes.

"Now the fun part of the recital will be to see if you can fool us with your performance by making both pieces sound so good that we can't tell which is which. If you play one piece well and the other one badly, it will be easy to guess. But if both are great, we might be fooled. However, don't plan on playing two unprepared pieces, either!"

What a benefit to have them practicing a piece they were otherwise unmotivated to polish!

Involving parents

In many of my teaching situations the parents are present. Usually it's the mom, but often dads come. Whenever possible, I invite them to come down and play the games with us. Their children love it, too.

Often, I ask the parents to play a role unusual in normal parenthood . . . to be the one without the answer. My directions are simple and whispered to the parents, "Make mistakes and have fun."

This gives the parents an easy out if they truly don't quite understand what's going on. They relax in their role of being free to make mistakes.

The reason I use the parents in this role is simple. Imagine these two situations.

Situation one: Some students have mixed up a Card Chart for their parents to fix. They are sure they've made it so difficult that no one will ever straighten it out. Their parents smile and begin to work. The students see that they're doing all right, so they sit down and begin to play and act silly, no longer paying attention to the game.

"Come on down and see how we did," call out the parents.

"Looks okay from here," someone calls back.

Situation two: A group of students have mixed up a Card Chart for their parents to fix. They are sure they've made it so difficult that no one will ever straighten it out again. Their parents smile and begin to work on it. It soon becomes evident that they are making mistakes, and lots of them.

"Oh, no! That doesn't go there, Mom," calls out Jane.

"Shhh, Jane. Don't help them," says Sherri.

Soon the students are laughing behind each other's backs as they try to contain themselves from giving away the answers. The parents chat away in mock seriousness, making deliberate yet in their own way, logical mistakes, asking each other's advice along the way. The students can't take their eyes off the cards as they watch their parents struggling.

"Okay, we're done. This looks great," exclaim the parents.

"Oh, you think so?" The students are full of laughter, eager to show how well they know their stuff and happily amused at their parents' mistakes.

"Can we fix it now, please?" the students beg me.

"Is it too hard for you?" I ask.

"Are you kidding? This is easy," says Stanley. Smiling parents back up to give the students room as they dive for the cards, quickly arranging them correctly. If a mistake is made, someone easily catches it. The game concludes with a roomful of smiles.

SUMMARY OF MUSIC MIND GAMES METHOD

When we read music, a multitude of important concepts are massed together on one page. Present at any moment are endless combinations of precise pitches, diverse rhythmic patterns, intertwining chordal structures, changing dynamic levels, multiple variations of tiny dots, slashes and lines with distinct meanings, subtly different tempos and an assortment of foreign language terms. Add the composer's stylistic characteristics and it's a lot of information to process simultaneously. Besides understanding all this information, the music must be immediately reproduced on an instrument that requires a high level of expertise.

Whew!

Let's take this one step at a time.

I have divided music theory/reading into six categories and developed games to allow each area to be thoroughly explored.

1. **Musical Alphabet and Intervals**
2. **The Grand Staff**
3. **Rhythm**
4. **Melodic and Harmonic Dictation**
5. **Signs, Symbols and Tempos**
6. **Scales, Key Signatures, Triads, Seventh Chords**

As basic ideas are understood, students can begin reading. The concepts in the games and the reading pieces will compliment each other. Please read **Chapter 24: Let's Read Music** for guidelines on when and how to introduce music reading. Concrete ideas presented in a logical sequence will eliminate uncertainties and gaps in understanding.

To help you locate the various chapters within these groupings in **Music Mind Games**, they are identified by various printed screens. If you need to look up particular games you want to use, these screens should expedite your search.

There are 575 photographs and hundreds of illustrations in **Music Mind Games** to help you understand how to play the games. The photographs give you impressions, feelings and ideas as to how the students I've taught reacted to the various games.

The materials used during the photo sessions are handmade prototypes of the **Music Mind Games** materials that are available. You may notice some variations in the art work, colors, paper and construction.

PART ONE

5

1. MUSICAL ALPHABET AND INTERVALS

Materials used in games:
1) *Alphabet Cards*
2) *Musopoly*

Chapters: 1:   JUST THE ABC'S
            2:   SNAKES!
            8:   THIRDS ARE ONE MORE THAN SECONDS
           14:   *MUSOPOLY*

I remember sitting in freshman theory class listening to my classmates pause as they attempted to answer questions concerning harmonic dictation or harmonic analysis. "Let's see, a tonic to a mediant in the key of F. That would be a major FAC triad descending to a . . . a . . . d . . minor dfa triad." It was apparent that they were hesitant in their answers because they were not comfortable with an alphabet that was backwards or mixed up.

"Ummm, the sixth below G is . . . ummm . . . ah . . . C, no B."

I decided we all needed practice in scrambling up our musical alphabet so we could focus on the real issue of tonalities and chordal progressions.

When I began teaching, the first materials I made were *Alphabet Cards*. First the students learned the order of the letters, then laid them out in long SNAKES to learn that the letters A - G are repeated over and over again to become the musical alphabet.

These games proved to be such a success that I named my first book, **No H in Snake: Music Theory for Children** (Alfred Publishing Company - 1979).

Now there are many games using letters. Students have a fun way to become fluent with the musical alphabet and all sizes of intervals. Dealing with just the letters, not the pitches or their relationship on the staff or the instrument, allows students' minds to become flexible and secure, one successful step at a time.

2. THE GRAND STAFF

Materials used in games:
1) *One Staff Board*
2) *Grand Staff Board*
3) *Clefs Puzzle*
4) *Ledger Line Sheets*
5) *Bingo Cards* and *Bingo Dots*
6) *Notes with Letters*
7) *Grand Staff Cards*
8) *Musopoly*
9) *Dictation Slates*
10) *Magic Notes* and *Magic Wands*
11) *Cardboard Keyboards*
12) *Mini Notes*
13) *Large Dice*

The games in this area are not simply quick tricks to help the students remember the names of the lines and spaces. They are carefully ordered games to enable students to understand the logic behind the staff.

The clefs are not printed on the large staff boards so that through manipulation the students learn about their shapes and their placement on the staff. Once they begin sight-reading, they are more aware of the clefs and the other important information found at the beginning of each piece.

Before trying to learn the names on the staff, students learn line from space and high from middle or low using a fun bingo game.

When it's time to learn the grand staff, all the notes of one letter are learned at the same time. Notes are learned with interval relationship, and students practice placing them on the staff (without the unnecessary bother of silly jingles). Then they are memorized with intriguing games so that they can be named quickly.

Grand Staff Cards are unique in the music world since students learn to identify single notes in relationship to the entire grand staff. Not ever used as "flash cards", they are used in many games to help with instant recognition.

3. RHYTHM

Materials used in games:
1) *Blue Jello Cards*
2) *Blue Jello Rhythm Puzzle*
3) *Real Rhythm Cards*
4) *Notes and Rests Game*
5) *Rhythm Money/Rhythm Playing Cards*
6) *Rhythm Bingo Cards*
7) *Gold Coins*
8) *Magic Notes* and *Magic Wands*
9) *Large Dice*

From the beginning of their study, students feel that rhythm is easy and manageable since it is introduced with sound rather than by explaining mathematical note and rest values, time signatures or measures. *Blue Jello Cards* and the *Blue Jello Rhythm Puzzle* are used during the same period of instruction.

Blue Jello Cards - students see simplified (no note heads except for half, dotted half and whole notes) notes and rests of all combinations of rhythms. Without a bit of instruction by the teacher, students learn by imitation and soon join in saying and clapping the rhythms.

The *Blue Jello Rhythm Puzzle* allows students and teachers to create rhythm patterns and play games that include rhythmic dictation.

The *Real Rhythm Cards* are revolutionary to the music education world and become an invaluable tool for understanding rhythmic relationships. Each card contains one note or rest and is made in a proportional length for the value of the note or rest as it appears in sound. This teaches note and rest relationships and allows for many games with rhythms. The cards allow students to clearly visualize the sound value of each note or rest. Students also use these cards to write out songs or rhythms.

The *Notes and Notes Game* begins as a simple matching game and progresses to many intriguing games where notes, rests and time signatures mathematically relate to each other. Single notes and rests and common combinations of notes are on individual cards without being sized to their note value. *Gold Coins* and *Magic Notes* help students relate values of cards.

Rhythm Money and *Rhythm Playing Cards* are the same materials. They come 52 cards to a deck and are used for many terrifically fun card games. There are four each of the thirteen basic notes and rests.

Rhythm Bingo Cards are in two levels and used for individual and group games of dictation as well as clapping.

4. MELODIC AND HARMONIC DICTATION

Materials used with games:
1) *Number Slates*
2) *Dictation Slates*
3) *Magic Notes* and *Magic Wands*
4) *One Staff Board*
5) *Notes With Letters* (blank side)
6) *Melodic Bingo Cards*
7) *Song Puzzle Cards*

Chapters: 5: I CAN HEAR IT - DICTATION PART 1
          9: NOTES ON THE STAFF - DICTATION PART 2
         16: EXPANDING EARS - DICTATION PART 3

Dictation is the single most useful musical concept in helping students to understand how to read music. Although so necessary, it is often overlooked by music teachers. The steps are simple and the games are enjoyed by students. Parents are amazed at their abilities.

Students are told that sequential numbers match sequential pitches. Simple stepwise patterns are played for them to write in numerals using the *Number Slates*. Mistakes are easily corrected.

Students can soon write and correct patterns played for them using *Dictation Slates* and *Magic Notes*. The colored, movable notes make it easy to take simple or complex melodic and harmonic dictation. Besides being pretty, the notes have a thin rim of metal so cleanup with the magnetic *Magic Wands* is delightful fun. Clever games help students master writing what they hear.

Dictation games can also be played as a group using the *One Staff Board* and blank side of the *Notes With Letters*. The *Song Puzzle Cards* are common songs with one measure per card. Players reassemble the songs and play games to reinforce their skills. These cards combine rhythmic and melodic dictation. The *Melodic Bingo Cards* help students see that groups of notes form "melodic words".

5. SIGNS, SYMBOLS and TEMPOS

Materials used with games:
1) *Orange Symbol Cards*
2) *Yellow Tempo Cards*
3) *Large Dice*

Chapters: 11: SIGNS AND SYMBOLS
12: TEMPOS
14: *MUSOPOLY*

With so many interesting musical symbols to learn, over 160 *Orange Symbol Cards*, each containing one musical symbol have been created. Students are able to learn what they mean through musical example as well as musical definition. A logical progression allows students to learn all the cards with a fun variety of games.

13 *Yellow Tempo Cards* contain the major tempos words. Cards are arranged in order using sound and definition.

6. SCALES, KEY SIGNATURES, TRIADS, SEVENTH CHORDS

Materials used with games:
1) *Alphabet Cards*
2) *Blank Cards*
3) *Pink Sharp/Flat Cards*
4) *Mini Sharps and Flats*
5) *Staff Sharps and Flats*
6) *Bingo Cards* and *Bingo Dots*
7) *One/Grand Staff Boards*
8) *Clefs Puzzle*
9) *Dictation Slates*
10) *Magic Notes* and *Magic Wands*
11) *Scale Triad Cards*
12) *Seventh Chord Cards*
13) *Scales and Chords Game*
14) *Cardboard Keyboards*
15) *Large Dice*

Chapters: 19: SHARP SCALES AND KEYS - EASY!
20: FLAT SCALES AND KEYS - EASY!
21: MASTERING TRIADS
22: *SCALES AND CHORDS* - SEVENTH CHORDS
23: EXPANDING TO MINOR KEYS

Using *Alphabet Cards* and one *Blank Card* for the 8th tone, students create scales by hearing a scale played and identifying the pitch that needs altering. Some information is given and much is discovered by the students. Games using a variety of materials enable students to understand and remember the tonality of all major and minor scales and the identity of key signatures. They will be able to write key signatures and all the primary chord structures.

In studying triads and seventh chords, major is purple, minor is blue, diminished is green and augmented is pink. The ear learns to identify these sounds and the fingers quickly learn how to spell the chords. Clever games challenge even teachers.

What can I say to you? I am perhaps the oldest musician in the world. I am an old man, but in many senses a very young man. And this is what I want you to be, young, young all your life, and to say things to the world that are true.

Pablo Casals

IMPRESSIONS FROM OBSERVERS

Over the years I have welcomed having other teachers observe me. I like hearing their remarks and appreciate their willingness to share their impressions and thoughts. I have decided to include a sampling of their comments in **Music Mind Games** because they can be helpful to other teachers.

I am very close to my teaching. What I mean is that I do it as easily as I breathe. I have come to realize that I am most relaxed when I am teaching. It is a part of me and I have become it and it has become me.

In writing this book, I have tried to tell not only what I teach, but what I do when I teach. From the time I began writing **Music Mind Games**, it was eight months before I could manage even one word of Part I. I had a splendid time detailing each of the games contained in Part II, but in order to write about how I teach and what I believe, I needed to step outside of myself and recognize what my teaching is all about. I'm thankful to many friends and family for the inspiration I needed to do just that.

I've tried to be thorough and insightful. However, after reading what others write about my teaching, I recognize that it was a wise decision to include their viewpoints for you.

ONE

For several years I had heard enthusiastic reports of the teaching of Michiko Yurko but had not had the opportunity of meeting her or observing her teaching. In February of 1990 she taught at the workshop sponsored by the Suzuki Association of the Greater Tulsa Area and I was privileged to watch her teach theory to a class of students who were perhaps five and six years old. I was impressed in many ways:

1. She immediately made the students, mostly strangers to each other and to her, feel comfortable.

2. The teaching definitely was on the level of the students — not above nor below them. She quickly found out "where they were", reviewed a bit and moved on from that point.

3. The teaching was imaginative, including each child (sometimes together, sometimes in turn) in the many activities.

**PART
ONE**

6

33

4. Though a variety of activities proceeded through the hour, they all seemed pointed to the goal of relating notation to sound.

5. In some situations like this one, the impression is sometimes given that, though much teaching is being done, not much learning is taking place. In Michiko Yurko's class it was apparent that <u>both</u> teaching and learning were active and exciting.

I would welcome other opportunities to watch Michiko Yurko teach — there is much to learn from her.

RALPH HARREL
Dean Emeritus
Fine Arts and Communication
Southwest Texas State University

TWO

I have observed Michiko Yurko's teaching of her music theory method since 1977. From the beginning and through the years, I have been impressed and challenged by her excellent teaching in so many areas.

To be specific:

Creativity: The theory games are loved by students of all ages. Michiko designed the games and materials in such a way to give limitless variety and expansion to the basic fundamentals of music. I have used this method with my own piano students since 1977. The longer I use it, the more impressed I am with all aspects of its design. My students always love coming to theory class and never hesitate to tell me that theory class is their favorite thing about taking piano lessons!

Michiko continues to incorporate new ideas which expand and improve the games. She is certainly a master at class structure, pacing, relating to the students, challenging them, reaching them at their level and helping them to discover on their own.

Ability to nurture others: Michiko has trained many teachers in this method — motivating each of us to discover our own ways and create new ideas.

I have used the materials to construct the circle of fifths on the floor, a circle of tetrachords, all chords and triads; minor scales; intervals and inversions; as well as teaching the form of pieces. Michiko has always encouraged me and even used some of my ideas in her own teaching.

Organization and distribution: The distribution of patterns and basic materials has enabled hundreds of teachers and thousands of students to benefit from the method — all of whom, by the way, believe that "theory is fun"!

What a wonderful accomplishment!

Rita Hauck, Suzuki piano Teacher Trainer from Cincinnati, Ohio

THREE

When I first saw Michiko teaching in Stevens Point, Wisconsin in the mid 1970's, I was most impressed with how she related to the students through the materials. I am a psychologist, and I found her manipulation of these materials to be similar to the way psychologists are trained to manipulate the materials used in psychological evaluations. To the students they look like "games," but to the trained psychologist, they are tools of evaluation.

These colorful and clever materials do not bespeak their consequences when manipulated skillfully by teachers. It is only when an observer watches them with the students that their full potential can be realized. To be sure, they are extremely well thought out, well designed and imaginative, but it is teachers and students who give them life!

From my experience, I have found that some teachers who watch me using her materials think that "anybody could do this." I feel it takes masterful skill; it takes understanding of learning principles; it takes the ability to do task analysis on the spot and back up or move forward at a moment's notice. In short, I am glad I have been able to watch Michiko to help me learn how to effectively manipulate these materials.

I sat watching Michiko day after day when I first discovered what she was doing. I knew this was a delicate and complex operation when done as effectively as she does it. That is why I traveled to her home when she published *No H In Snake: Music Theory For Children* to attend one of her workshops. I admit, I copied technique at first. As in all things, the details — the seemingly small things are very, very important. I knew even the littlest detail mattered a lot.

Dr. Jeanne Brazier, Glen Ellyn, Illinois

FOUR

In October 1983 I was in a class Michiko taught at Central Washington University in Ellensburg, WA. I have been using her ideas and I would like to tell you that my students thoroughly enjoy the activities. They have such fun and so do I! Her book has been more than a resource for activities, though. Her spirit emanates from its pages. On those days when I'm weary of teaching I need only to open to any of the games, and I'm faced with her high level of professionalism in developing all these activities and the intense sensibilities that she has for students. I have always left her book with a renewed enthusiasm for teaching and working with young people towards a high degree of music.

Laura Robinson
Washington

FIVE

When Michiko gives the students tasks to do and problems to solve, she does this in such a way that the students are eager to get started. It is exciting to observe the students working together and communicating ideas amongst themselves with Michiko standing aside, thus allowing them to be independent yet still learning. Michiko's ideas are imaginative and creative and can only add a great deal to the student's understanding of musical concepts.

Nehama Patkin, pianist, lecturer, movement teacher
Victoria, Australia

SIX

Even as a child my daughter Michiko was creative and innovative, and she had an instinct for involving others. Here are two examples:

When only 9 years old, her 4th grade class was planning a unit on Hawaii. Her wise teacher stepped back and let Michiko take charge. Among her ideas, she brought in a young man who was from Hawaii. She taught a group of girls to perform the hula; they made "grass" skirts and leis. There was background music, the room was transformed into a mini Hawaii, complete with a bubbling volcano (later entered in a science fair). Not only did parents and other classes come to the program, Michiko invited the press. A reporter came and did a news story with a picture. These students didn't just read about Hawaii, they <u>were</u> Hawaii and would remember it the rest of their lives.

In the spring my spirited daughter produced and directed a play based on the book ***The Box Car Children*** by Gertrude Chandler Warner. There was a talent show preceding the production and tickets were even printed up. One afternoon when the janitor came to sweep my room he leaned on his big pushbroom and chuckled as he told me about my petite girl.

"You should see her at the rehearsal. One boy wouldn't do it right so she sat on him!"

Again, parents and other classes came when it was staged in the auditorium complete with lighting, scenery, props and music. Not just reading or hearing about it, those performers became the characters in ***The Box Car Children***.

And that, 30 years later, is the magic of ***Music Mind Games***. Students don't just listen to or read about music theory, they are totally involved in it. Her games are fun! I've watched Michiko in action. She sparkles with enthusiasm, and the students catch that spark. (Don't worry, you'll never catch her having to sit on anyone now.)

I am writing this almost 3000 miles away from where Michiko is finishing her book. As I proofread, I marvel how now as then, she dreamed of doing something never before attempted and made that dream come true. She will be surprised at what I've written and especially so with what I'm going to say now.

Michiko, I'm so glad I got all involved in your book and am forever marvelling how you did it. Yesterday I talked with someone very musical who gave up being a music major because she couldn't take all the theory.

The measure of one's life isn't just the happiness you find — it is what you do to make the world a better place. Children, teachers, everyone will be better musicians because of your book. It is a great contribution. You have not been on this earth in vain, but have brought joy and fun to music! Take a bow!

There's an ancient Chinese proverb:

> *Tell me . . . I forget.*
> Show me . . . I remember.
> *Involve me . . . I understand!*

That ancient philosopher and my beautiful Michiko are kindred spirits.

Mary Fujii Henshall
Nampa, Idaho

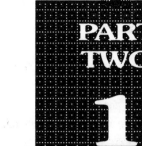

JUST THE ABC'S

Since the first seven letters of the alphabet are used to identify notes in western music, it's logical to begin our study of music reading with them.

Most youngsters can easily rattle off their ABC's but really knowing them may be another story. The games in this chapter will help their minds take over the rote memory and turn it into clear understanding.

These *Alphabet Cards* games give students a visual reference for what they've heard and seen for years. And at the same time, they have fun moving the letters around.

No matter what the age, I usually begin a class with GAME 1-A: WHAT LETTER IS THIS? Any age group will feel safe and eager for more when you begin with a game they can easily understand. Then we move on to an *Alphabet Cards* game at their level.

The games in this chapter are for younger students (ages 2 - 6) who may be able to say and recognize their letters, but who need games to help comprehend them more completely. If there is any doubt about the ability of your students, play these games. Since they are such fun, an older sister or brother observing a class might just ask for a set of *Alphabet Cards* so s/he can play, too.

When these games seem easy, quickly shift to a game in the next chapter.

GAMES
IN THIS
CHAPTER

GAME 1-1: WHAT LETTER IS THIS?

OBJECTIVE:
To determine if the students can identify the letters:
A B C D E F and G

IN BRIEF:
Teacher tosses a set of *Alphabet Cards* in a pile for students to identify - first set in order, second set out of order.

REPETITIONS:
Play once in a session before moving on to other *Alphabet Cards* games.

AGES:
Preschool and kindergarten
Note: Use this game with a new group of students (no matter what their ages) before playing any game which uses *Alphabet Cards*. They will have quick success, and it takes just a moment to play.

MATERIALS:
Alphabet Cards - two colors

PROCEDURE:
As you play this game, keep the atmosphere light. Smile, offer encouragements, relax and have fun. Take charge, but allow the students to be themselves and enjoy the game with you.

With them sitting in front of you, say, "I have some letters here. Can you tell me what they are?"

Toss down the A card.

"A," they will say.

Continue through the first set of *Alphabet Cards*, in order, letting the students say the letters. Toss the *Alphabet Cards* on top of one another. Move at a quick pace but only as fast as the students can identify the letters.

"Good! Here's another set."

Begin with the A card, but after that, toss down the cards out of sequence. Don't worry if there are a few mistakes (unless the students are over the age of 6). They will smile as they realize they were almost tricked.

Make a mental note about how accurate they are, but don't take time for any corrections.

If they miss a few letters, play GAMES 1-2: LEARNING LETTERS and 1-3: FAT SNAKE.

If the second set of *Alphabet Cards* was easy for them to identify, then:

"I thought I could trick you, but your minds are sharp today. This second set of *Alphabet Cards* is really mixed up, isn't it? Let's see if I can lay them out in order."

Since you won't need it anymore, place the first set of *Alphabet Cards* behind you. Lay out the second set, mixed up - A B G E D C F.

You can have a little fun along with them and say, "Oh no! Those aren't right at all! Who can fix them?" The students will all want a turn to fix them. You are now in the middle of another game, GAME 1-4: FIX THE ORDER.

GAME 1-2: LEARNING LETTERS

OBJECTIVE:
Students who don't know some of the letters will pick up a great deal by playing games with students who do know them. However, if you choose to help a child learn the musical alphabet, this is a good game.

IN BRIEF:
Students match and name letters.

AGES:
Preschool

MATERIALS:
Alphabet Cards - two colors

REPETITIONS:
A few times as necessary

PROCEDURE:
Focus only on a few letters the student can learn easily. Save remaining letters for other sessions.

Keep one set of *Alphabet Cards* for yourself. Place the other set in front of the student, out of order and not necessarily in a straight row. Place your A card in front of the student, and give him time to place his A card below it. "This is A."

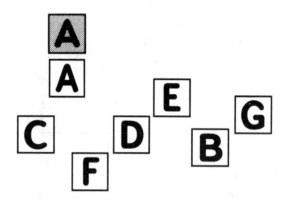

After seeing that the A shapes match, snap your fingers. This is the signal for the student to close his eyes. Rearrange his Alphabet Cards so A is in a different place. Clap your hands twice. This is the signal for him to open his eyes. "Andrew, can you find the A card again?" Repeat this sequence with many words of encouragement and lots of smiles until he finds the A easily. Say A out loud often.

Once A is easy, repeat the same sequence adding B. "I'm adding a B, Andrew. Can you find your B? . . . Very good!"

Continue learning all the letters, in one or more sessions. "Andrew, look at all those letters you found. Wow!"

40

OBJECTIVE:
Besides learning letters, this game lays the foundation for notes going up on the staff. Please include it in your class.

IN BRIEF:
Each child has *Alphabet Cards* to lay out, one at a time next to each other's cards. It's impossible to make mistakes in this game.

AGE:
Preschool and kindergarten

MATERIALS:
Alphabet Cards - six sets of different colors

REPETITIONS:
One FAT SNAKE per session

PROCEDURE:
Deal out all the *Alphabet Cards* so each student has a random mixture of letters and colors. A simpler method if the students are young and you have a small group is to give each student a set of cards. Keep one for yourself so you can provide an example.

"Let's put all our A cards in a row." The students will look through their *Alphabet Cards* to see if they have an A. Help them line up their A cards next to one another.

The students will talk and talk throughout the game. "I don't have an A." "Me neither."

Reassure them. "It's okay, everyone has lots of cards. Maybe you'll have the next letter. Anyone know the letter after A? Right, it's B. If you have a B, can you put it above the A cards? Can you match the colors? It's looking great!" The *Alphabet Cards* should read up rather than down when making a FAT SNAKE. This is because the notes read up on the staff and this game is laying the foundation for that concept.

"What's after B? A . . . B . . . right. It's C! Find your C cards and add them to our FAT SNAKE." If cards are turned upside down, simply correct them. Verbal comments aren't needed; the students will watch and learn. It's also fine if other students fix the cards. This allows them to develop the feeling of working together as a supportive team. Let them do as much as they can.

Continue adding letters one row at a time until the FAT SNAKE is finished. "Colin, you know exactly where to put your card, don't you?"

"Look at the FAT SNAKE we made! Looks wonderful, doesn't it? All the colors and letters are in order. Let's sing Twinkle, singing all the letters of the FAT SNAKE? Follow my finger."

If you use six sets of *Alphabet Cards* you will have twenty-four cards arranged in the musical alphabet. If you sing one letter for each pitch, the notes to "Twinkle, Twinkle, Little Star" will match perfectly. Point to the cards to help the students keep their place. Since this is a popular ABC song, the students will probably sing the regular alphabet, "A B C D E F G . . H I . ."

You can laugh. "Oh my, did I hear H and I? Where do you see H and I? When we sing the musical alphabet, A comes after G. Let's try again, okay?" If this takes a few tries, that's all right. Adjusting from a rote memory to a thinking memory takes practice. However, if someone is being silly to get attention, just continue on singing, politely ignoring the comic, and you will have control of the class once more.

When you're all finished, a nice round of applause is encouraging for the students.

Now it's time to clean up. This is fun and can set an example that cleanup is important. Show them how you can pick up one color of cards and make a neat pile. Assign each student a color. Extra students can rest. Stay with the students on the floor, or they might become silly in your absence.

Very young children may find it too tricky to put the letters back in order, but they may be able to make a neat pile if you ask them to make the corners even. Thank the students as they return the *Alphabet Cards* to you.

It is sufficient to play this game only once in a session even though they may beg to do it again. This will help them look forward to another class.

GAME 1-4: FIX THE ORDER

OBJECTIVE:
To practice fixing the A B C D E F G order. This game is a classic and can be used to reinforce almost any concept covered in this entire book. The students love to close their eyes, anticipate what's getting mixed up and then . . . success! . . . they solve the tricks easily.

IN BRIEF:
Students correct a mixed up set of *Alphabet Cards.*

AGES:
Preschool, kindergarten and elementary

MATERIALS:
Alphabet Cards - one set

REPETITIONS:
5 - 8 per session. It's important for everyone to have a turn.

PROCEDURE:
Lay out one set of *Alphabet Cards* out of order.

"Gosh, are these cards in order?" you can ask.

"Oh, oh. Something's wrong here." "Oh, I know!" "Look at the G! That's not right!"

Call on a student to fix the cards. If help is needed, just call on someone else and praise both of them.

Snap your fingers for them to close their eyes. Switch two of the cards. To encourage confidence, use easy switches.

Clap your hands twice for them to open their eyes. Let someone fix the cards.

Check the *Alphabet Cards* together by pointing and saying them aloud. Snap your fingers and they will get ready for another switch. This game can be repeated until everyone has had a turn. Progress to more difficult switches to keep the game interesting. Soon they will be ready for more than one card to be switched.

OBJECTIVE:
To practice the A B C D E F G order without complete visual reference

IN BRIEF:
Students guess which card is missing.

AGES:
Preschool, kindergarten and elementary

MATERIALS:
Alphabet Cards - one set

REPETITIONS:
5 - 6 per session

PROCEDURE:
Lay out a set of *Alphabet Cards* in order.

Snap your fingers for the students to close their eyes. Remove a card. Leave the space open. Clap your hands twice for them to open their eyes.

They may just raise their hands without knowing the answer so remind them to look at the cards first. "First look. Then think. Then raise your hand when the answer is in your head." After a student correctly names the letter, give it to him or her so s/he has the honor of putting it back in the right spot. It's a nice chance to shine for a moment.

Repeat several times so everyone has a turn.

When this becomes easy, play the game as described above but don't leave the space open. Push the cards together. This makes it a little tricker and more fun.

Occasionally, just for fun, I hide the card under my leg or in an obvious pocket so just a corner is peeking out. It's fun and keeps the class lighthearted.

GAME 1-6: PICK A CARD

OBJECTIVE:
This game helps you know if the students have a mental picture of the musical alphabet. It's a great game for involving parents or introducing the students to team play.

IN BRIEF:
Students randomly draw *Alphabet Cards* and lay them out in order, one card at a time.

AGES:
Kindergarten and early elementary

MATERIALS:
Alphabet Cards - one set for every two players

REPETITIONS:
Back and forth a few times each session

PROCEDURE:
If parents are going to be playing with you, ask them to watch while you play it with the students once.

Hold a set of *Alphabet Cards* in front of the students and ask one to pick a card. "Andrew, can you tell everyone what your letter is?"

"C."

"Right, Andrew. It's a C. Can you put it on the rug?" Hold out the cards and ask someone else to pick a card.

"I got the A!"

"Good. Will it go before or after the C?"

"I can put it right here in front of the C."

"That's exactly right." Let students take turns picking the cards and placing them in order, leaving spaces for the ones still in your hand. Make certain the letters are reading left to right as they face the students.

If a mistake is made it's all right to leave it until someone spots it.

After all the cards are down, point and say them in order. "A B C D E F G." →

If a mistake hasn't been corrected, they will find it now.

"Would you each like your own set of cards to play with your mom or dad?" Invite the parents to join their children on the floor.

Pass out one set of *Alphabet Cards* to each pair of players. They may move wherever they would like in the room, playing at their own pace, following the sequence you demonstrated. After Mom has held the cards, they switch roles. Remind parents to keep the *Alphabet Cards* facing the right direction for their child on all turns.

Unless you are needed as a partner for one of the students, walk around, assisting as needed. If you see an error, casually and nonverbally make the correction.

During the same session, invite the players to play GAMES 1-4: FIX THE ORDER and 1-5: WHAT'S MISSING? or even make up variations of their own.

The players will be relaxed and playful. This game is fun. If anyone (a parent, perhaps?) is too serious, invite him or her to enjoy the play.

Before the game loses the interest of any of the players, compliment them on their good work, and ask them to finish the round they are on. They should put their cards in order and give them to you in a neat pile.

"I made up a new game with my cards today," beams Andrew as he turns in his *Alphabet Cards*.

If you need time to get out materials for the next game, ask them to place their cards neatly on the pile in the center of the floor.

Ah! What would the world be to us
If the children were no more?
We should dread the desert behind us
Worse than the dark before.

Henry Wadsworth Longfellow

SNAKES

Once students have become fluent with A B C D E F G, they are ready to tackle more sophisticated *Alphabet Cards* games. In this chapter you'll have a great time making SNAKES, playing FINE and making scrabble charts. The alphabet will move forwards, backwards and within many octaves. There are long scale passages matched up against short little melodic bits—but all done with *Alphabet Cards* and if desired, demonstrated on the keyboard or with tone blocks. The musical alphabet becomes a place for easy, liberated movement.

As they progress to knowing the musical alphabet forwards, backwards and inside out, their confidence and enjoyment in learning music theory will grow.

In college, I recall freshman classmates pausing to think of the alphabet backwards. It slowed them down a bit to have to think, "What letter is before F? Ummm . . . E."

I want students to be fluent with the musical alphabet when they take dictation or study notes on the staff.

Read on and you'll find many fun games to enhance the joy of learning how to read music.

GAMES IN THIS CHAPTER

GAME 2-1: SNAKE!

OBJECTIVE:
To teach that the musical alphabet doesn't end with G, but continues on again with A B C etc. The SNAKES represent the keys on the piano keyboard and must always read left to right. Making SNAKES may be the first game students play as a group without the teacher being actively involved. Suggestions are included in the text of this game to help insure cooperative play.

IN BRIEF:
Students lay out long rows of *Alphabet Cards.*

AGES:
Elementary ages

MATERIALS:
Alphabet Cards - many sets

REPETITIONS:
10 minutes or so

PROCEDURE:

Mix up two sets of *Alphabet Cards* on the floor in front of the students. "Can you help me put these cards in order?" you ask the students. Use a random assortment of the colors until the cards form one long SNAKE. "What comes after G?"

"Right, A," you smile. "Ah ha! I have another set of *Alphabet Cards* here. Let's mix up all three sets and make another SNAKE."

The students will take on the challenge with glee, "Wow, that will be easy!"

Mix up all the cards, then use a few cards to get them started. Once they catch on, move away and let them continue on their own.

If your class is large enough, it's great for several small groups to be making SNAKES in other areas of the room. Just toss three sets of *Alphabet Cards* on the floor, get them started and away they will go.

Besides helping students learn the musical alphabet, SNAKE making helps classmates learn to work together. Everyone should take part moving the cards around, feel all right if a correction is made and learn how to be kind and help someone else. If you notice someone taking over, hoarding cards or giving orders, step in and remind everyone to join in.

"You know your letters really well, Henry, but be sure to let others make the SNAKE, too." Probably he just got excited and wanted to do them all.

If students get too loud or rowdy you can help them get control by asking them to make their SNAKES without **ANY** talking . . . not even any whispering. This will help them calm down.

On the other hand, if a student is a little reluctant to participate, hand her some cards and help her get involved. "Carrie, your card is next on the SNAKE. Go for it!"

SNAKE making is never to be competitive nor a race. Three or more teams are better than two. This helps eliminate a race situation.

Soon a team will call out, "We're finished! Come look at our SNAKE!" You can smile and help them say their letters in the SNAKE. Then toss in another set of *Alphabet Cards* in a new color and say, "Oh. Look what I have here. I know this pink set would just love to be part of your SNAKE."

Quickly mess up their SNAKE.

"Oh, no! We have to make it again! Hey, let's go! I've got the A. I've got the B!" They will dive into their task.

This game is self-correcting. If a card is left out or put in the wrong place, don't step in. Let them discover and fix it themselves. "Hey, we don't have another E."

"Really," you might answer. "Are you sure?"

"Let's check our SNAKE. Maybe it's in there. A B C . . . ."

"We still can't find our E!"

"Hmmmm. Could anyone be sitting on it? . . . ."

"Hey, look, it's under Polly!"

Continue walking around the room, checking, encouraging, tossing in more cards and mixing up SNAKES.

Ask the students to make SNAKES as long as it's just loads of fun. Before anyone tires, give directions for cleanup.

"Great SNAKE making today. Ok, let's clean up. Please sort your colors and then put your cards in order by seconds (A B C D E F G). I'll take them when you're finished." Cleanup becomes as valuable as making SNAKES.

GAME 2-2: SNAKE VARIATIONS

OBJECTIVE:
To help students be more fluent in the musical alphabet

IN BRIEF:
Students make SNAKES starting with any letter, forwards, backwards or from the middle.

AGES:
Elementary ages

MATERIALS:
Alphabet Cards - many sets

REPITITIONS:
5 - 10 minutes

PROCEDURE:

LET'S START WITH ____: This SNAKE is easy to make. Just begin on a letter other than A.

TAIL FIRST: Another easy but fun version is to make a SNAKE backwards by putting the first card down on the right and working to the left. Make certain the letters read forwards when completed, just like the piano keyboard.

MIDDLE OUT: Begin with any card, adding a card to one side and then the other until it's completed.

MIX-UP: After a group has finished making its SNAKE, snap your fingers to signal them to close their eyes. Mix up the letters. "Guess what I'm doing . . . ," you can tease them.

FACE DOWN: Snap your fingers for them to close their eyes. Turn a few cards face down. Clap twice so they will open their eyes. Let them take turns identifying the letters then turning them over to check.

Always finish each SNAKE with the group by saying the letters together.

GAME 2-3: FINE

Pronounced "fee' nay", the musical term meaning "to finish".

OBJECTIVE:
This is a classic game used throughout **Music Mind Games** to reinforce a concept. It's an ideal game since students play individually while in a group setting. It's lively and fun.

This gives students the opportunity to practice the alphabet with their own set of *Alphabet Cards*.

AGES:
Open

IN BRIEF:
Students hurry to put their own alphabet letters in ABC order.

MATERIALS:
Alphabet Cards

REPETITIONS:
5 - 7 times in a session

PROCEDURE:
It's easiest to show the students one sample game, <u>then</u> pass each one a set of *Alphabet Cards*. If you pass out the cards first, they will fiddle with them rather than listen to you.

Arrange your cards as you talk. "You will put your A card near your left knee. Spread out the other cards on the rug and mix them up until you hear me say GO. Then quickly put your cards in order. A B C D E F G FINE! Everyone understand?"

Give each student a set of *Alphabet Cards*. If you want the class to be a little more peppy, toss the cards to each student. If you want them to quiet down a bit, calmly hand them out. "Okay, put out the A card and mix up the others . . . "

"GO!" They will work as fast as they can to put the cards in order. "FINE!"

Some students will naturally go faster than others. It's important that no one gets hurt feelings by being last. Help this situation by saying:

"When we perform music, is the person who plays the fastest the best musician?"

"No."

"Does it matter if you are the first to say Fine?"

"No."

"Is it more important to finish first or to get your cards right?"

"To get your cards right."

LET'S START WITH ____: Soon it will be easy for the students to play FINE. Then it's time to practice beginning on a different letter. After a round of FINE is finished, ask them not to mix up their cards again. Take someone's A and put it at the end, after G. Ask everyone to do the same thing.

"Now your cards read B C D E F G A. Let's play FINE again only this time let your B card be the first card. Mix up the others . . . . . Ready? GO!"

As soon as it's easy to begin with B, use another letter.

FIND A NEW SET: This version adds a new twist to keep them on their toes. It's fun and not to be missed!

"This time leave your C card out. Mix up the others. Keep mixing. Okay — everyone stand up. Move to a new set of cards . . . sit down and . . . GO!" This version is rather like musical chairs, only no one ever gets left out. Remind them to be careful not to fall on each other as they scramble to find a new set of cards. Repeat this fun variation a few times.

OBJECTIVE:
To help students isolate short segments of the alphabet since music is written in small note patterns as well as long scales

IN BRIEF:
Students fix three sets of three *Alphabet Cards*.

AGES:
Open

MATERIALS:
Alphabet Cards - three sets, three colors

REPETITIONS:
3 - 4 per session

PROCEDURE:
Snap your fingers so the students will close their eyes. Lay out three *Alphabet Cards* from each set. Place the four remaining cards from each set below these cards.

Clap your hands twice for them to open their eyes. Pointing to the first set of cards, A C E, ask:

"Are these three cards right? If you think a card needs to be switched, raise your hand and fix it using these extra cards. Please don't mix the colors, and there is just one important rule. The first card must stay first. You may switch only the second and third cards. Everyone understand? Who would like to try these first three cards?"

Call on someone who has studied the cards before raising his hand.

"Good, Stewart, those are all correct."

Let a student fix just one set of cards so that someone else will get a turn.

Begin this game with easy patterns. If anyone seems confused, say the alphabet aloud, as you point to the cards. Easy patterns to fix are A C B, D F E, C E D and E B G. Harder patterns are A F E, E D G, G B A and F C A.

OBJECTIVE:
To help students develop a quick memory for letters immediately before and after one another

IN BRIEF:
Students add the *Alphabet Cards* before and after one, two or three cards.

AGES:
Open

MATERIALS:
Alphabet Cards - two sets, two colors

REPETITIONS:
5 - 8 patterns per session

PROCEDURE:
THREE LETTERS: Place three consecutive letters of one color (blue) *Alphabet Cards* in front of the students while their eyes are closed. Keep the extra blue cards in your hand. The other set of cards (pink) is mixed up and placed below the three cards.

Clap your hands twice for them to open their eyes.

As you speak, point to the appropriate cards. "Think of the letter that comes before B. If you know it, raise your hand and put it next to the B. You can use these pink cards. Anyone know? Robert?"

"Very good, Robert. Anyone want to put on the letter that comes after D? Linda?"

"Right again!" Snap your fingers for them to close their eyes. Change the three blue cards so there are new ones in front of the students. Mix up the pink set. Clap twice.

"New letters. Oh, I can do it!"

Repeat this several times so everyone can have a turn.

<u>TWO LETTERS</u>: When the students become skillful with three cards, use only two cards. With less visual reference, they will need to rely more on their memories.

<u>ONE LETTER</u>: When they can do two cards easily, use just one card.

This is a good game to switch roles and let the students play the part of the teacher. One group of four and five-year-old students had fun with me. While I closed my eyes I could hear happy whispering as they were arranging the three cards. When I opened my eyes I saw D E F in a new row before me. But when I looked for C and G, I discovered they had hidden them from me!

GAME 2-6: ALPHABET SCRABBLE

OBJECTIVE:
To practice small segments of the alphabet backwards and forwards

IN BRIEF:
This game is a new twist of the classic board game. Rather than words, students write short alphabet sequences. It's self-correcting, loads of fun and can be played with thirds and other intervals.

AGES:
Open

MATERIALS:
Alphabet Cards — <u>many</u>, at least six sets

REPETITIONS:
Once in a session

PROCEDURE:
This is an excellent game to play nonverbally. In fact, you can even introduce it this way. The following description will be without any talking, however, it's fine to play it with talking.

"I have a new game for you today called ALPHABET SCRABBLE. You will enjoy it! It's easy. In fact, so easy that I'm going to teach it to you without talking. Just watch how I lay out the cards. When it's time, you can continue the game by yourselves. The only rule is that you can hold only one card at a time."

"What? How do we do it?" They will be puzzled by this new approach.

"Don't worry. Trust your eyes and you will learn."

Without following a specific color pattern, lay out the beginnings of a scrabble game in the middle of the floor for the students. Make certain your letters read **up and not down** like the regular Scrabble game. This is just like GAME 1-3: FAT SNAKE. Remember, the notes on the staff read up and not down. As you put out your *Alphabet Cards*, put them out in this order, building up and across. You should add notes to any side of any card, just be sure they continue to read **up and across**.

Watch their eyes and when it seems that they've caught on to the idea, toss the remaining cards to one side of the room. It's fun if you make a grandiose gesture so the cards fly across the room, scattering in a table size area. Walk over and pick up <u>one</u> card. Walk back and add it to the scrabble game in an appropriate place.

Gesture for them to continue building onto the scrabble game, adding only one card at a time. If you see mistakes, remove the card and hand it back to the student. This will help everyone catch on. They may also correct cards.

A scrabble game in progress may look like this:

Cleanup can be just as in SNAKES.

Now it's finished!

Never have ideas about children—and never have ideas **for** them.

D. H. Lawrence

LINES AND SPACES

As students play games with *Alphabet Cards* (Chapters 1 & 2) and games with *Blue Jello Cards* and the *Blue Jello Rhythm Puzzle* (Chapter 4) they can be introduced to the concept of lines and spaces. The musical line and space are not what they learned in school. Students are taught to write on the line, but actually they are writing in what in music is known as <u>a space</u>.

The games in this chapter have been developed to help avoid any confusion with lines and spaces and high and low notes for young music students. Although the games may seem appropriate for pre-schoolers, which they are, parts of games are also helpful when introducing the staff to students of any age.

It's important to teach the basics.

Unique staff design The grand staff has only enough space between the bass and treble clefs for B, C and D. The space in printed music is needed for many ledger lines, but this "extra space" can be confusing to students who are learning the staff.

The *Grand Staff Board* has only space for the middle C line. This helps students understand how the two clefs are interrelated.

regular music staff

Music Mind Games staff

After I had taught GAME 3-4: NOTE TOSS during theory class at a workshop in the summer of 1975, an elderly woman came up to talk to me.

"I have been teaching piano for over 25 years. There's one thing I feel strongly about. If not taught correctly, students somehow get the incorrect notion that there's a bass clef and a treble clef, and never shall the two meet. Somehow, they don't see how close the two really are. I think the game you did today teaches this correctly. I like how you've drawn your grand staff."

I was pleased to hear her comments.

No clefs The large *One Staff Board* and *Grand Staff Board* used in this chapter do not have the clef signs printed on them. Instead, students learn how the clefs are placed on the staff. This gives them more awareness for the important information found at the beginning of each line of music.

Before students are asked to learn names of lines and spaces, Chapter 6: GRAND STAFF C'S, they can play the games in this chapter and become familiar with the up and down position of notes on the staff.

Students will bring these games to life in their own unique way.

PART
TWO

3

GAMES
IN THIS
CHAPTER

GAME 3-1: LEARNING TREBLE CLEF

OBJECTIVE:
To introduce the treble clef and the staff

IN BRIEF:
Students learn the treble clef names, pass it around the circle and trace it on the staff.

AGES:
Preschool, kindergarten and elementary

MATERIALS:
1) *One Staff Board*
2) *Clefs Puzzle*
3) *Alphabet Card* G

REPETITIONS:
For 5-10 minutes of a class session

PROCEDURE:
Place the *One Staff Board* flat on the floor between you and the students. Dangle the treble clef in front of them.

"This is a treble clef. Can you all say treble clef?"

"TREBLE CLEF."

"Good. I'll pass it around so each of you can see it. Please say treble clef before you pass it on to the person next to you." With very young students, ages 2 - 4, the unique ways they pronounce "treble clef" will be sweet. If a youngster is too shy to say the names, just let her pass the clef. The students will enjoy feeling the shape of the clef and may be silly, hanging the clef from their noses or resting it on top of their heads. As long as play is lighthearted and not too disruptive, it's fine and you can smile along with them.

After the clef is returned to you, tell them, "The treble clef has another name. It's also called the G clef — just like the letter G." Place the *Alphabet Card* G in the upper left hand corner of the staff board. Pass the clef around the circle again, this time helping them to say, "Treble clef - G clef."

61

To help the students realize that the clef isn't just a random arrangement of lines, they can each take a turn tracing it. The arrows in this illustration show the direction to take.

start

Trace the clef with your finger as you say, "Start at the bottom, all the way to the top, over to the big side, around the circle [pick up the *Toss Note* and bounce along the G line and back saying] G G G G G G G G G G G . . ." Ask if anyone wants a turn. Be ready for eager responses.

Older students can do it on their own, but ages 3-5 do better if they follow your finger around as you say the same words you used when you traced the clef. Place the *Toss Note* next to the clef on the line G.

The students will like bouncing the *Toss Note* along the G line and back while they say "G G G G G G G G G G G G". This reinforces the importance of the G line and introduces its name.

This game can be repeated week after week since the students may forget the names of the clef. Just reteach the same information and feel good about small improvements in their ability to remember the names of the clef and how they begin to trace it more easily.

Every child is born a genius.

R. Buckmister Fuller

GAME 3-2: PLACING CLEFS

OBJECTIVE:
To learn how to place the treble and bass clefs correctly on the staff. This game is a good example of allowing students to discover and learn for themselves rather than "being taught how".

IN BRIEF:
Students work together to discover how the clefs should be placed on the staff, using memory, logic and comparison to printed clefs.

AGES:
Preschool, kindergarten and elementary

MATERIALS:
1) *One/Grand Staff Board*
2) *Clefs Puzzle*
3) Music books or *Dictation Slate*
4) *Alphabet Cards* G and F

REPETITIONS:
Until the clefs are placed correctly

PROCEDURE:
Depending on the age of your students, you can choose to present one clef at a time over several sessions or both in the same session. You may choose to use either the *One Staff Board* or the *Grand Staff Board.*

TREBLE CLEF: "Anyone have an idea how the treble clef is placed on the staff? Yes, Karen, would you like to try?"

Let them take turns arranging the treble clef on the staff. It is amusing to see how they think it should look. Allow them a few minutes to work on it.

"Hmmmm, most interesting. It's almost correct. Let's compare a printed treble clef to ours. Study it carefully to see if you need to make any changes." Give them a moment to get their music books or set out a *Dictation Slate* for comparison.

Give them suggestions, if needed.

"Looking good. But maybe you should check this area over here a bit more."

In case you need guidance on how to place the treble clef:

1.) The curly part on the bottom of the clef faces this way.

2.) The bottom of the clef sits on the line.

3.) There's a little bit of space between the clef and the side line.

In games using the staff boards, let the students place the clefs on the staff rather than doing it yourself. Or for fun - put it on yourself, a little incorrectly. Compliment whoever catches your error.

"David, you're sharp today. You're really watching closely."

BASS CLEF: You may use either the *One Staff Board* or the *Grand Staff Board.*

Hold up the three pieces of the bass clef for the students to see.

"This is a bass clef."

Let the students pass the clef pieces around, saying "bass clef" at the same time. They will enjoy passing all the little pieces.

"Just as the treble clef - G clef has two names, so does the bass clef. Anyone want to guess what the letter is?"

I like to involve the students in conversation rather than just tell them it's called the F clef. This way we develop the understanding that it's all right to make guesses in class. I want them to feel comfortable calling out even an incorrect answer.

I may just let them guess, and whoever calls out F first is told, "That's right!".

Or, I may bend the clef and "attach" the dots so it resembles an F. Then if someone says, "It looks like a silly F," I can say:

"Yes, it does. And many centuries ago when intelligent musicians like you were figuring out how to write down music, they made a clef that looked like their style of F. Anyone ever seen old fashioned writing from long ago?"

Discussions like this take just a few moments and help students feel free to express thoughts in class. Also, this gives them historical perspective about how music developed over the ages. Otherwise, they may think that teachers today made up all of this! If they realize that this is part of evolving history, they may one day jump in, become practicing musicians and help history continue to unfold.

Your students may enjoy seeing this Chart on the evolution of the clefs from **Music Notation** by Gardner Read:

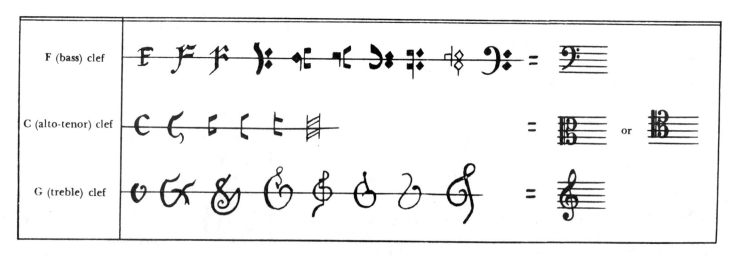

All right, getting back to the game:

"Yes, it is also called F clef. Let's pass it around the circle again. Can you say "Bass Clef - F Clef"?

Handling the clef helps them remember it and gives active little bodies a chance to squirm a bit.

Just as they did with the treble clef, allow the students to figure out how to put the bass clef on the staff. They may compare it to a music book or a *Dictation Slate* to learn exactly how it sits on the staff.

1.) The top part of the clef touches the top line.

2.) There is a little space between the clef and the side line.

3.) The dots are in the spaces.

Both clefs are equal distances from the side line. →

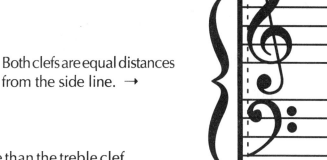

The shape of this clef is easier to trace than the treble clef. "Let's take turns tracing the bass clef." Pointing to the treble clef ask, "Remember what letter we said as we touched this line?"

"G G G G G G G G G G G," they will remember.

"Right. So what will we say for the bass clef?" you ask them.

"F F F F F F F F F F F," they figure out. Place the *Alphabet Card* F near the clef.

"Yes, you're right! Now for the big music mind question. Where is that line F?"

Give them time to look at the clef and someone may tell you that it's between the dots. Place the *Toss Note* near the clef on the line F.

The students will enjoy saying a quick "F F F F F" as they move their fingers around the clef (start from the "ball") and "dot dot" as they tap each dot. As they bounce the *Toss Note* along the line, they can say "F F F F F F F F F F F . . ."

Snap your fingers as the signal for the students to close their eyes. Move the clef (or clefs if you are using the *Two Staff Board*) around. Clap your hands twice for them to open their eyes and let them take turns fixing the clef(s).

Before putting the materials away, ask them one more time the name of the new clef. If they've forgotten you can help them with:

"Maybe it will help you to think 'baseball - bass clef'. And these two dots can be the two balls. Bass clef. Baseball."

This idea will make them smile. However, I don't recommend saying this more than once or twice. It's a catchy little saying, not to be overused. It's best if the students remember the bass clef name because they hear "bass clef" repeatedly.

GAME 3-3: LINES AND SPACES WITH FACES

OBJECTIVE:
To teach the difference between lines and spaces using the *Bingo Cards* and *Bingo Dots*

IN BRIEF:
Working as a group around a pair of *Bingo Cards*, students place the *Bingo Dots* faces on either lines or spaces. Seeing that a line note has a line going through the middle of the face makes lines and spaces easy to understand.

AGES:
Ages 3 & 4 and older

MATERIALS:
1) *Bingo Cards*
2) *Bingo Dots*

REPETITIONS:
Use several cards in the session. Game probably needs to be played just once.

PROCEDURE:
Divide the *Bingo Cards* into one or two piles and place them between the students and yourself.

Place a handful of *Bingo Dots* in your hand, face side up, and hold out your hand to the students, saying, "Please take any note you like and place it on top of a black note on the cards."

66

After all the notes are covered you can point to a line note and say, "You see this note here? He has a line going right through his head so we call this a line note."

Point to a space note. "This note is in between the lines so we call it a space note."

Let the students look at the notes for a moment. "Let's take off just the space notes. Put any notes that are in spaces back in my hand." The students will cooperatively take turns placing the notes back in your hand.

Guide them if needed by saying, "Yes, that's a space note. Very good . . . . . hmmmmm, that's a line note. Let's leave it on the card right now."

After they have placed all the space notes in your hand ask them to take off all the line notes.

Repeat this procedure over and over with new cards.

Once you think they are catching on, ask them to put the faces on just the line notes.

Then let them cover the remaining notes, pointing out that they are space notes.

Let them remove the *Bingo Dots* by placing the space notes in your hand, then repeat with the line notes.

Use new cards until the concept is easy for them to understand.

"Good game. Your minds did very well today. Thank you."

GAME 3-4: NOTE TOSS

OBJECTIVE:
To teach the difference between a line and a space

IN BRIEF:
Students toss a note on the staff and call out if it's on a line or space. For young students, the class can call out if the child tossing the note is shy.

AGES:
Preschool, kindergarten, elementary

MATERIALS:
1) *One/Grand Staff Board* - either
2) *Clefs Puzzle*
3) *Ledger Line Sheet*
4) One BLUE from the *Blue Jello Rhythm Puzzle*

REPETITIONS:
If possible, let everyone have one or two tosses.

PROCEDURE:
Ask the students to sit in front of you on the rug with the *Staff Board* between you. Try to arrange for them to sit across from you. If they are right next to you, the staff will be completely upside down for them.

This game doesn't require verbal instruction.

Place the *Toss Note* on a line and say "line". Move the *Toss Note* to other lines, saying "line" each time. The students will join in and say "line" along with you.

Move the *Toss Note* to a space and say "space". Move it to other spaces and say "space". Again, the students will join in and say "space" with you.

Move the *Toss Note* to either a line or a space, saying the appropriate name each time. After a few turns, they will have caught on and can say "line" or "space" so you should remain quiet. They easily learn the difference.

Ledger lines are easy and should be introduced in this session in the same manner. Just move the *Ledger Line Sheet* into place either above or below the staff and say "ledger line" or "space".

Place the one BLUE a foot or so below the *One Staff Board*. Let the students stand behind the BLUE and take a turn tossing the note. The *Toss Note* will "plop" on the *Board* nicely if it's tossed a little like a frisbee.

It's fine if the whole group calls out where the *Toss Note* landed rather than only the student who tossed it. In case someone is shy, this allows him to participate by tossing but not having to speak alone. It also keeps the whole group involved.

If the note doesn't land directly on a line or a space, move it a little. If the *Toss Note* lands above or below the staff, insert the *Ledger Line Sheet* under the note.

Occasionally someone tosses too hard and hits you (that's one reason why it's soft!). Join the laughter and hand the note back to the student. "Do I look like a line or a space? A bit gentler this time, okay, Jenny."

Now and then someone will deliberately toss the note off the staff to get attention. Give him or her another chance with the exact instructions as before. If this continues, hand the note back to him, look directly into his eyes and say, "One more chance, Brad." If he persists, hand the *Toss Note* to the next player. "Please have a seat, Brad."

For turns, you can either go around the circle or select students randomly. Another idea is to let the student who just had the turn choose the next person. As s/he glances around at classmates I suggest choosing the person who's being the quietest. This simple idea keeps everyone's attention on the game and everyone settles down rather than calling out, "Me! Please, me next!"

If a child is to keep alive his inborn sense of wonder, he needs the companionship of at least one adult who can share it, rediscovering with him the joy, excitement and mystery of the world we live in.

Rachel Carson

GAME 3-5: MUSIC BINGO

OBJECTIVE:
To help students recognize high and low on the staff

IN BRIEF:
Students match notes from the *One Staff Board* to their own *Bingo Cards*. Game is played until every student's card is filled so that everyone wins.

AGES:
Kindergarten and elementary

MATERIALS:
1) *One Staff Board*
2) *Clefs Puzzle*
3) *Ledger Line Sheet*
4) *Bingo Cards*
5) *Bingo Dots*

REPETITIONS:
One game per session, even if they beg for more! With some pre-school students, I've found they enjoy playing this game at every theory class for months. It's the perfect game to conclude a class.

PROCEDURE:

PRE-BINGO STUDY (Version with parents present):

"Parents, how are your musical minds? I need you for a game today. Please watch while we learn about high, low and middle."

Explain to the students and their parents that only the note on the middle line is the "middle". All the other notes are either "high" or "low".

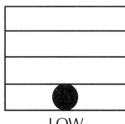
LOW

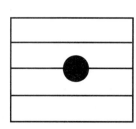
MIDDLE

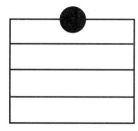
HIGH

Although it's not difficult, understanding high and low on the staff is a sophisticated concept for young children. Some confusion is usual. For example, this letter A is still an A even though the card is upside down. But when this note is turned upside down, it's a different note.

  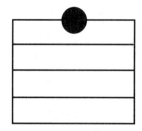 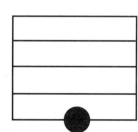

"Students—please come get a *Bingo Card*. Then walk back to your moms and dads. Tell them if the notes on your card are lines or spaces and if they're high, low or middle." Students can work at their own pace. After telling their moms or dads about the notes on their card, they can bring it back to you for a new one. Collect and hand out

Bingo Cards until each student has seen about five to seven cards. Cards will be coming in and going out quickly .

Observe if everyone is doing all right and understanding the concept. Students love this game. It provides them with a chance to move around a bit, and they will be lively, laughing throughout.

(Version without parents present):

Place the *One Staff Board* in front of the students. Place the *Toss Note* on the middle line and explain that a note on this line will be called "middle". Lines or spaces above the middle line will be called "high" and those below will be called "low".

Place the *Bingo Cards* in a pile in front of the students. "Can you tell me if the notes on our *Bingo Card* are high, low or middle?" Go around the circle giving each student a turn choosing a note on the card and saying if it is "high", "low" or "middle". Continue through the pile of *Bingo Cards*, giving everyone several turns.

Repeat this with different notes and different cards until you're convinced the students understand how to relate the notes printed on the cards to the *Toss Note* on the *One Staff Board*.

PROCEDURE FOR THE MUSIC BINGO GAME

Seat the students on the floor so they can see the *One Staff Board*. Give each one a *Bingo Card*. You have a choice as to how you hand out four *Bingo Dots* to each student. If you want them to settle down, gently hand them their *Bingo Dots*. If you want them to loosen up and have more fun, toss them their *Bingo Dots*. Ask them to hold the *Bingo Dots* in their hands.

If parents are present, invite them to join the children on the floor, sitting behind their child. If you have more than eight players, you may want to have two students share a card.

Make certain that the students turn their *Bingo Cards* so the lines on their staffs are facing the same direction as the lines on the *One Staff Board*. A young student could get confused if her card is turned sideways.

If you have a large class and students are seated all around you, remove the clef sign and let the top of the staff be relative to where each student is seated.

"This game is simple. Just match the notes I put on this staff board to the notes on your *Bingo Card*. If I have a note on my staff that you don't have on your card, just wait for another turn. When you cover all four notes, call out 'BINGO'. Okay — everyone ready?" Once you start the game, the students shouldn't turn their cards around.

Place the *Toss Note* on a line or space on the *One Staff Board*. The students are to look for that note on their *Bingo Card*. If they have it, they can cover it with a *Bingo Dot*. If they don't have it, they can wait for another turn. Continue placing the *Toss Note* on a note, one at a time, giving the students a chance to check their cards for the note.

<u>IMPORTANT!</u> If you see a student who doesn't have as many notes, use one of the notes on his or her card next. As the game progresses, try to keep things even so everyone has about the same number of notes covered. The students are very sensitive about this.

Parents may gently guide their children as needed.

If the PRE-BINGO STUDY was done well, the students shouldn't have too much trouble finding their notes. If errors are made, make a mental note of the student(s) who may need more practice. If you try to help him or her during the middle of the game, the flow of the game will be interrupted, students may loose concentration and the one you try to help will be put on the spot. It's all right to offer a word or two of help if that's all. This game will be easier when it's played again in later classes.

IMPORTANT:

By keeping a careful eye on the cards while the game is progressing, it is possible to "fix" the game so several students will BINGO at the same time. Also, always be careful not to let just one student be last. Then no one's feelings get hurt, and it's more festive for several students to finish together.

If a particular student needs a boost, make sure s/he bingos first.

The object of the game is for all students to cover all four notes on their *Bingo Cards*. As that happens, each student calls out "BINGO!".

"A bingo! Very good!" Without missing a step, continue to put notes on the staff for the students to match. The game ends only when <u>everyone</u> has said "BINGO".

"Look at that! All those bingos. How smart you all are today." A round of applause will bring even more smiles to the students' faces.

They will love helping you clean up.

It is true that a child is always hungry all over; but he is also curious all over, and his curiosity is excited about as early as his hunger.

Charles Dudley Warner

BLUE JELLO
INTRODUCING RHYTHM

If melody brings soul to music, it is rhythm that gives it life. Rhythm creates the feeling, the mood, and uniquely transforms the melodic and harmonic sounds. Why then, did so many of us learn about rhythm by hearing "Two quarter notes equal a half note and two half notes equal a whole note."? Suddenly this energy of sound, this rush of life is reduced to a simple math problem.

If rhythm is sound, then students will gain the most by learning about it by listening, a vital step in expanding a vocabulary of rhythms. But is sound enough? We all can turn on a radio station, put in a cassette tape or slip in a C.D.

What's needed is an organized visual/aural system to learn what those sounds are and how they relate to each other. Values and relationships must be thoroughly explored in a fascinating manner. Later, rhythm can be combined with melody, pulse and tempo.

What can be used to give rhythm pedagogically, meaningful sound?

BLUE JELLO.

"Blue what?" you ask.

Well, it's students we are teaching. And their interest is captured by clever things that also make sense.

What is BLUE JELLO?

Here's how it works. Students are introduced to rhythm with sound but without bar lines, time signatures or any explanation of relative value. *Blue Jello Cards* and a *Blue Jello Rhythm Puzzle* give students words for specific rhythmic patterns using simplified rhythmic symbols.

BLUE JELLO represents a quarter note and a pair of eighth notes.

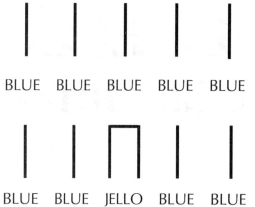

BLUE   BLUE   BLUE   BLUE   BLUE

BLUE   BLUE   JELLO   BLUE   BLUE

There are words for the other note and rest values, too. In a rhythmic setting, words like "purple, huckleberry, gooseberry, berrygoose and celery" make students smile and instantly understand all sorts of rhythm patterns.

A full vocabulary of rhythms

Using *Blue Jello Cards*, beginning students are soon saying words representing all varieties of rhythms that have been considered much too complicated for them. However, not only is it possible to start with a full assortment of rhythmic patterns, it's fun, interesting and pedagogically superior.

This is based on a very simple fact. Parents don't limit their vocabulary when talking with their youngsters. Although "Mama, Dada, ball, wawa," are common first words, parents worldwide use their full word power in expressing themselves to their children, not just these first simple words.

Ever watch a mom or dad out with their baby shopping for groceries? "Well, Michael, what should we have for dinner on Friday? How about teriyaki chicken, rice and zucchini . . . or would you rather have fettucini and broccoli. Hmmm. Oh, and apple pie a la mode or chocolate mousse for dessert?" At all levels parents just talk, and their children absorb it all. And this goes on for years, naturally.

The same can be true of rhythm. All students are intrigued by the variety of rhythms I present. They are eager to learn more. They are capable of learning it all.

BLUE JELLO materials

Blue Jello Cards are large cards with visually simple rhythmic patterns. These are shown to the students as "information gifts." They are not used as testing tools — like flash cards. By imitating the teacher, students soon say the cards, in rhythm.

An innovative *Blue Jello Rhythm Puzzle* allows students to create rhythm patterns themselves. After a short time with BLUE JELLO patterns even preschoolers are reading, clapping and writing rhythms.

The pieces of the puzzle are easy to move around so there's an open invitation for creative rhythm patterns. To simplify matters, we don't use bar lines, so time signatures aren't important, just yet. It's nearly impossible to make mistakes, but it is possible to do rhythmic dictation after just a few sessions.

Both materials are versatile and used in a variety of games.

BLUE JELLO history

I'm often asked where the words BLUE JELLO came from.

Since my goal was for absolute understanding from the very first lesson, I wanted to use words with just the right number of syllables for a particular note. For example, I could never understand why some teachers ask their students to say:

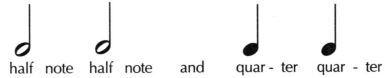

half note half note   and   quar - ter quar - ter

since the beat spoken is really:

and

I prefer a one syllable word like "too-oo" for the half note. With a slight emphasis on the "oo", students learn to feel the pulse. The one syllable word "blue" is used for the quarter note value.

too-oo - too-oo   blue   blue

When I began teaching, I had not studied the "Ta and tee tee" from the Orff/Kodaly system so I made up the words as I went along.

The first words to take life were "blue yellow" for the quarter note and pair of eighth notes. But after a few classes I noticed that "yellow" didn't have enough emphasis on the first syllable. Always intrigued with Dr. Seuss semantics, I chose "jel-lo". BLUE JELLO is unique, so the words were easy and fun for the students to remember.

Once in the 1970's I was teaching at a five day workshop in Ithaca, New York. Mid-week I happened to walk by the director's office and overheard him lamenting about the complaints and requests from various parents and teachers.

"A mother staying on the 3rd floor wants another pillow. The one in her room is too soft. Someone else wants me to find a bus schedule back to Baltimore. And this is the clinker — would you look at this? Someone wants the cafeteria to serve blue jello at dinner tonight. Of all the crazy . . . . " I poked my head in to explain and laughingly invited him to visit our class the next day, which he did.

I remember adding two words while I was teaching in Ottawa, Kansas. It happened that I had to step over masses of squashed tree berries on the sidewalk each day as we walked from our dorm. Since I grew up in Arizona, I'd never seen this tree before. "It's a gooseberry tree," I was told. "Gooseberry . . . gooseberry . . ." I thought. "Wow! That's just the word I'm looking for."

GOOSEBERRY

BERRYGOOSE

PUR-PLE comes from a teacher in Europe who called to tell me how pleased she was to use my theory games. "Did you come up with any ideas of your own?" I asked her.

She told me about using PUR-PLE for the dotted eighth and sixteenth notes. I liked it right away and shared it with my class of 10-and 11-year-old students that afternoon. It was a big hit!

PUR-PLE

We studied lots of rhythms that day. "What about this sixteenth note triplet?" they asked. "What should we call it?"

"What about . . . CELERY?" I suggested off the top of my head.

We tried it and liked it. Celery is a three syllable word that moves very fast when you say it . . . perfect for a sixteenth note triplet. Try it as a pick-up to a down beat: " . . . CELERY BLUE."

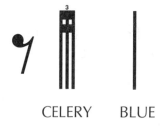

CELERY   BLUE

Pulse is vital

Without pulse, music is uncertain and halting. The pulse must be steady, like the ticking of a grandfather clock or your own heartbeat. Within the framework of a time signature, there's a subtle emphasis on the first beat. Once I had the opportunity to watch a friend playing BLUE JELLO with a group of students. I was taken aback for although they were saying the correct words to match the rhythms, a steady pulse was absent. The JELLOS were said like sixteenth notes, and there were numerous small pauses interspersed in the rhythms.

Before beginning any pattern, be sure to establish a tempo first. "Ready go" in time works well. If the teacher respects the pulse, the students will also.

Sequence of study

The games in this chapter are presented in a progressive sequence. You will find success if you follow it. How quickly you advance through the games depends on your students. You may find yourself improvising with the materials, and that's just fine. It's fun, and the students will enjoy the spontaneity.

Since the ability to read and understand rhythms is essential to reading music in any form, it's a good idea to include rhythm games in nearly every theory class.

GAMES IN THIS CHAPTER

GAME 4-1: *BLUE JELLO CARDS*

OBJECTIVE:
To familiarize students with a variety of rhythmic patterns, a steady pulse and the words used for various note values

IN BRIEF:
Students watch the cards while the teacher says the rhythms and points with the pulse. Soon students join in. Cards are used repeatedly over many classes. Clapping is used. Unlike flash cards, the *Blue Jello Cards* are never to be used for testing.

AGES:
Open

MATERIALS:
Blue Jello Cards - some or all

INTERMIX:
Use simultaneously with the *Blue Jello Rhythm Puzzle* and the early games in Chapter 7: NOTES & RESTS, although not necessarily in the same session.

REPETITIONS:
Once through 12 - 15 patterns in a session

PROCEDURE:
These cards are for the purpose of sharing information, not for testing. Please use them in this way, and they will be enjoyable and educational. Feel free to mix easier rhythms in with more complex rhythms.

WORDS TO USE: (say in correct rhythm)

❘ = BLUE	♫ = GOOSEBERRY	♪ = OH or JEL (depending on where it occurs in the beat)
♫ = JEL-LO*	♫ = BERRYGOOSE	
♩ = TOO-OO	♫. = PUR-PLE	❘. = BLU - UE
♩. = THREE-EE-EE	❘. ♪ = BLUE — O	♫. = COOKIE
○ = FOUR-OR-OR-OR	❘❘❘ = JELLO JELLO	
³♫❘ = PINEAPPLE	♫ = CELERY	
♫❘ = HUCKLEBERRY		

* Since JELLO represents a pair of eighth notes, it's important to say it evenly, without an accent on the JEL. If you say it with equal accents on both syllables, the students will imitate you.

For rests, whisper with a steady beat. The shorter rests should be said in the appropriate rhythm.

𝄽 = REST	𝄾 = REST	
▬ = REST REST	𝄿 = REST	
▬ = REST REST REST REST		

WITHOUT CLAPPING: It is easy to use these cards. You need not provide any instructions or explanations other than, "I have some cards to show you today. You'll hear some interesting words. When you're ready to say them with me, please join in."

Hold the cards in one hand as you face the students, all of you sitting on the rug. Point along the top of the cards with your other hand as you say the words in a clear voice.

Keep a perfectly steady pulse and use a tempo of approximately mm = ♩ = 72. Point with an emphasis on the quarter note pulse rather than subdivisions of the beat.

When you finish a card, bring a new one over the top from the back of the pile. The tempo of the cards is really steady. Allow one beat to move the new card in place and don't interrupt the flow to say "ready go". As the students feel comfortable with what you are saying, they will join in.

After you say all the cards once, flip the pile over and go through the rhythms found on the back.

Encourage them with smiles and say "good". Please do not interrupt yourself to correct, explain or otherwise teach the students. Just let them absorb the information.

That's all there is to it.

WITH CLAPPING: As soon as they are able, invite the students to clap along as you say the *Blue Jello Cards* together. So they can watch you clap, rest the *Blue Jello Cards* on the rug, leaning up against your feet.

Rests: A rest has no sound, only space. So rather than a clap, open your hands when you whisper REST. For a half note, open your hands twice and whisper REST REST in time. For a whole note, open your hands four times and whisper REST REST REST REST.

Half, dotted half, whole: In order to feel the half note pulse, clap normally as you say "TOO" and raise your hands to chin level. As your hands return downward, finish the word, "-OO". It is a very easy movement, and the students will pick it up quickly. Doing the cards with you will give them practice. A dotted half note is "THREE-EE-EE" with one clap and two hand pulses. A whole note is "FOUR-OR-OR-OR" with one clap and three hand pulses.

You may show the students these cards for many months. Depending on the age of your students and how often you see them for class, you may do this weekly (it takes only a few minutes).

Continue this game even after the students have moved on to the rhythm games using the *Real Rhythm Cards* (Chapter 13). This provides a comfortable opportunity for review.

Children have neither past nor future; and that which seldom happens to us, they rejoice in the present.

Jean de la Bruyere

GAME 4-2: BLUE JELLO

OBJECTIVE:
To let students and you create rhythms

IN BRIEF:
Puzzle pieces are moved into many patterns which students read and clap.

AGES:
Open

MATERIALS:
1) *Blue Jello Rhythm Puzzle*
2) The blank side of the *Notes & Rests Game*

REPETITIONS:
Several patterns in each session

PROCEDURE:
Place the blank side of the *Notes & Rests Game* in front of the students. Place about six BLUES on the board in a row, spaced evenly. They represent quarter notes.

"What color are these?" you can ask.

"Blue."

"Right. That's what you say for each one. BLUE . . . BLUE . . . BLUE. . . . ." Point to the top of each one as you say the words. A tempo of mm = ♩ = 72 is a good speed for this exercise. Then ask the students to join you in saying the words.

"Very good. I have a shorter one, too." Show the students the shorter JELLO, laying it next to a BLUE so they can see easily see that it's shorter.

Then place it across the top of two BLUES. "It makes these BLUES a . . . "

"A JELLO!" They know this from the *Blue Jello Cards*.

"Right! Let's say it. Ready - GO — BLUE . . JEL-LO . . BLUE . . BLUE . . BLUE."

Reinforce that JELLO is said with equal emphasis on the two notes. "Have any of you ever eaten Jell-o?"

"I have." "I have," they will answer.

You can ask them, "Have you ever eaten <u>Blue</u> Jell-o?"

"Yes, it's delicious!"

Holding one up, ask, "Would anyone like a bite?"

"No! No!" they will laugh.

"Don't worry. We won't eat these. Remember that the Jell-o you eat is called Jell-o. The word we use for our rhythms is JEL-LO. Can you all hear the difference?" Practice several times. Say your words clearly and they will understand.

"I can move the JELLO to make a new rhythm. Let's try this one together."

Even preschoolers are able to say these rhythms after a few minutes. Give them lots of praise.

"I have another JELLO."

"Oh boy!" they will smile.

Write a few rhythms using two JELLOS. Point and say the words with the students so they learn correctly. You can continue adding more BLUES and JELLOS to make the patterns longer. Be kind and introduce the material in small steps. Using a moderate tempo, they will be able to say each new rhythm pattern. This is the first session, so don't worry if it's not perfect. Just help them get the idea.

Now comes your chance to build their confidence. If traditionally taught, students may think that rhythm is hard. When introduced with BLUE JELLO, rhythm is easy. So I play around a bit until the students are saying to me, "This is easy!"

Add a few more BLUES and JELLOS and write out a new rhythm pattern. It shouldn't be any harder than the previous ones, just a new combination. "All right, here's a new rhythm for you. I think it's pretty tricky. Does it look too hard?"

"No, it's easy! This will be a cinch!"

"All right, are you ready? GO." Point and say the words with them.

"My, that was good. But, I bet you can't do this one."

"Oh, really? You can't fool us!"

Write a few more patterns for them until, "I can't think of anymore hard ones. You were all terrific today. Wasn't this hard for you?"

"No, not us!"

"Well, I will think all week and figure out something tricky for our next class. Just you wait!"

OBJECTIVE:
To learn to clap rhythms using additional patterns

IN BRIEF:
As the students are able and as interest warrants, you can add other patterns. Remember — nothing is difficult if it's presented clearly and without making it appear to be hard.

AGES:
Open

MATERIALS:
1) *Blue Jello Rhythm Puzzle*
2) Blank board (optional)

REPETITIONS:
Depends on ability and interest of students

PROCEDURE:

<u>Triplets:</u> PINEAPPLE is a favorite. Say the triplet correctly, and the students will imitate you.

<u>Rests:</u> Rests are easy to add since they were learned with the *Blue Jello Cards*. Hold up a quarter rest, smile and say, "Look at this shape, would you? What is it?"

"A rest," they will whisper.

Substitute the quarter rest for a BLUE and clap the pattern together.

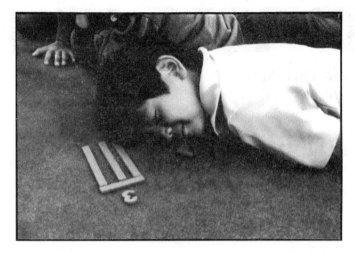

This clever student decided to take a rest on the rest!

When teaching the half rest, substitute it for two quarter rests.

Half note - step one: This activity is done so they will always remember the note "with the hole in it". Holding up an index finger, ask the students, "Can you hold up your finger like this? Good."

Take a TOO-OO from the *Blue Jello Rhythm Puzzle*. Slip it on your index finger.

Turn to the child sitting to one side of you and gently slip the TOO-OO onto her finger by touching finger tip to finger tip.

"Can you pass the TOO-OO clear around the circle?" Encourage the students to keep their fingers pointing straight up if they are receiving the TOO-OO and to invert their fingers when they are passing. They will love this!

The students will try to pass the TOO-OO around the circle without dropping it. But if a child drops it, smile and reassure him.

If you have a larger group (over 12 or so,) pass another TOO-OO around the circle in the other direction at the same time. Everyone will have two turns and will not have to sit idle.

<u>Half note - step two:</u> When the TOO-OO is passed back onto your finger, tell the students, "That was great. Now, this BLUE is changed into a TOO-OO." Gently drop the TOO-OO so it lands at the bottom of a BLUE, making certain it is touching the BLUE. "The TOO-OO lasts twice as long as the BLUE or JELLO. So, we need to take away the BLUE right after it."

Point with your finger and say the rhythm. When you say the "OO" beat of the TOO-OO, move your finger to the space you just created.

Let the students remove the beat following the TOO-OO, whether it's a BLUE or a JELLO. They will quickly learn this important but easy concept.

Teach dotted half notes (THREE-EE-EE) and whole notes (FOUR-OR-OR-OR) in the same way. Always let the students remove the beats following these notes so they are aware of the length of these longer notes.

<u>Eighths and sixteenths:</u> Since they've seen the rhythms on the *Blue Jello Cards*, the students may be able to show you how to write " Gooseberry, berry goose, huckleberry, cookie and purple" if they're given the correct puzzle pieces. They can learn how to modify a jello to make these rhythms.

Write lots of patterns. Let the students be creative, too.

The child must teach the man.

John Greenleaf Whittier

GAME 4-4: I CAN WRITE IT

OBJECTIVE:
To let students create rhythms. They love this version of BLUE JELLO.

IN BRIEF:
If parents are present, invite them to clap a rhythm the students write. Advise parents beforehand to have fun and make a mistake or two. Watch how much this improves class spirit.

AGES:
Open

MATERIALS:
1) *Blue Jello Rhythm Puzzle*
2) Blank board (optional)

REPETITIONS:
Enough patterns to involve each parent and child, or students can work in groups

---

PROCEDURE:
Before playing this game, it's imperative that parents be told how to play. Although many will be perplexed at your request, ask them to make mistakes — on purpose. The reasoning is this: if they simply clap the rhythm correctly, the students will soon lose interest.

On the other hand, if the parents act confused, mix up the pattern and generally mess up, the students will be totally absorbed and involved. They will laugh and watch carefully, trying to catch the parents' mistakes. Then to prove their abilities, they will try hard to do it well. It's great.

During a previous game, perhaps when the students are making a SNAKE or something, walk around to the parents whispering, "When I invite you to join us for a BLUE JELLO game, make mistakes when you clap the rhythm."

"Oh," laughs a dad, "that will be easy for me!" This gives parents who haven't studied music an "out". They can relax and fit in perfectly.

If you don't have enough time, whisper it to one parent and ask the message to be passed around to the others.

<u>One student:</u> "Would anyone like to write a BLUE JELLO rhythm for your mom or dad?"

"Close your eyes, Mom. No peeking!" says Mary.

"Peeking wouldn't help me, Mary," laughs her mom.

Mary takes her job seriously and carefully writes a rhythm pattern for her mom. She claps her hands twice. "Open your eyes, Mom."

All the students are eager to see what happens.

Mary's mother moves closer to the board. "Oh my, Mary. This looks awfully tricky." The students laugh.

"BLUE BLUE JELLO JELLO BLUE BLUE," claps Mary's mother.

Mary looks at her mother with amazement. "Oh no. Did you hear that? I only wrote one JELLO. The JELLO is here, not there!" The students become more excited.

"Oh, may I try again, Mary?" asks her Mom calmly.

86

"All right. Watch carefully now," encourages Mary.

"BLUE BLUE JELLO BLUE BLUE."

"Oh, not again! You forgot the last two BLUES! You have to try harder." Mary's mother will get all sorts of advice.

"Want me to point for you, Mom?" asks Mary kindly.

"That might make the difference. Please do, Mary."

"BLUE BLUE JELLO BLUE BLUE BLUE BLUE," tries Mother again.

"You did it. Yeah!" Mary gives her mother a big hug.

You can ask, "Anyone want to be next?"

"I do. Oh, please, me. Mom, raise your hand." Everyone will beg you for a turn at once.

All the students: You can also make this a class effort and let the students write a rhythm for all their parents. They will go wild! How exciting to be creative with something you understand.

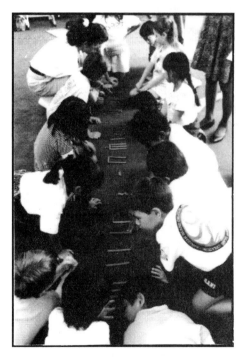

Make adjustments as necessary.

The students will laugh as the parents stand over them and try to clap their long rhythm.

Smiling, help the parents out by clapping along with them.

After the parents have it right, most likely with student help, ask everyone to clap it together.

This is an eager, happy bunch of students!

The major obstacle to learning is fear: fear of failure, fear of criticism, fear of appearing stupid. An effective teacher makes it possible for each child to err with impunity. To remove fear is to invite attempt. To welcome mistakes is to encourage learning.

Dr. Haim G. Ginott

GAME 4-5: FIND THE JELLOS

OBJECTIVE:
To introduce rhythmic dictation, students write a pattern clapped by the teacher. This game is fun, easy to do and invaluable.

IN BRIEF:
As a simple pattern is clapped, students watch six or more BLUES to see where the JELLO is. A JELLO is added to write the rhythm.

AGES:
Open

MATERIALS:
1) *Blue Jello Rhythm Puzzle*
2) Blank board (optional)

REPETITIONS:
4 - 6 patterns per session

PROCEDURE:
Place the blank board in front of the students. Lay out six BLUES. Place one or two JELLOS near the BLUES.

"I'm going to clap a rhythm for you. Listen carefully, and see if you know where the JELLO should go."

Without saying the words, clap clearly at a moderate tempo. Students will be excited, raising their hands to give the answer.

Rather than just saying, "Yes - that's right" or "No, try again" after Colin adds the JELLO, you can say:

"Good, Colin. Everyone, I'm going to clap my rhythm again. See if it matches the one Colin has written." This gives the students a chance to hear the rhythm and compare what they are reading.

Give everyone a turn. They enjoy this game.

As students become competent with this game, without warning, clap a rhythm with two JELLOS. See what happens. Some students will catch on and ask for another JELLO. This keeps them on their toes, and they gain confidence as they realize they can catch you at your tricks.

GAME 4-6: FIX THE RHYTHMS

OBJECTIVE:
To practice rhythmic dictation. Students love this game. It's hard for adults but easy for students.

IN BRIEF:
Rhythmic dictation patterns will be longer than in GAME 4-5: FIND THE JELLOS. It's visually more challenging to have to change a rhythm pattern than to just add a JELLO.

AGES:
Open

MATERIALS:
Blue Jello Rhythm Puzzle

REPETITIONS:
4 - 6 patterns per session

PROCEDURE:
Write out a rhythm pattern.

"I'm going to clap this for you, but I just might change something. Listen to the whole rhythm then raise your hand if you think you know what was different. Should you watch me or the BLUE JELLO?"

"The BLUE JELLO!"

"Right. Here's the first one." Remember to clap patterns you know they can solve. They will be encouraged and learn faster.

"I know! It's easy." Call on someone who is quiet. After it's fixed, let everyone clap it together.

As students are able, make more changes to keep it challenging and interesting.

GAME 4-7: NOTE AND REST HUNT

OBJECTIVE:
To relate the BLUE JELLO concept to real printed music. Parents and students feel their music books are more user friendly after this game.

IN BRIEF:
Students find notes and rests in their music books and identify them by name. The *Blue Jello Cards* are used as reference.

AGES:
Kindergarten and early elementary

MATERIALS:
1) *Blue Jello Cards*
2) *Magic Notes* and *Magic Wands*
3) Students' music books

REPETITIONS:
Once

PROCEDURE:
Lay the *Blue Jello Cards* out in a square formation so all possible notes are facing up. Pass out music books or ask

the students to get theirs. Hold a handful of *Magic Notes* in your hand. Invite the students' parents to sit with them if they are present.

"Please look through your music books for any of these notes and rests. When you see one, let me know and I'll put a *Magic Note* on the card. Just keep flipping through the music. You'll see that there are many interesting ones on every page."

Soon someone will call out, "I have a THREE-EE-EE right on this page. Look!" Toss a *Magic Note* onto a THREE-EE-EE on one of the cards.

They will be excited as they hunt through their music books for notes and rests. You'll soon be flipping *Magic Notes* on the cards faster than you can keep up with. If a particular note or rest has no more spaces on the cards, simply toss two on the same spot.

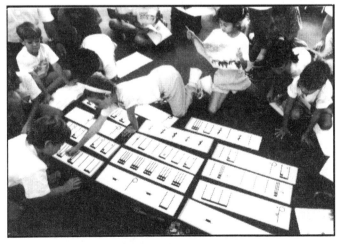

"Looks as if we've found all the JELLOS. Try to find the ones without *Magic Notes*. Anyone see a HUCKLEBERRY?"

91

GAME 4-8: *BLUE JELLO CARDS BINGO*

OBJECTIVE:
Students to practice identifying short rhythmic patterns

IN BRIEF:
Blue Jello Cards are placed in a bingo arrangement. As cards are clapped, students find them, marking them with *Magic Notes.*

AGES:
Pre-K through elementary

MATERIALS:
1) *Blue Jello Cards*
2) *Magic Notes* and *Magic Wands*

REPETITIONS:
Until bingo or until all the cards are marked

PROCEDURE:
Let the students help you place the *Blue Jello Cards* in a bingo card arrangement. Give each student a handful of *Magic Notes.*

The game is simple. Clap the rhythm on one of the cards.

The students are to find it and put one of their *Magic Notes* on the card.

It's not a race to find the card first. They work together, copying each other. Since the students have their own *Magic Notes* to put on, they pay attention and try their best.

You can play until you have achieved several completed rows, or until all the cards are marked. Enjoy!

They will enjoy picking up the *Magic Notes* with the *Magic Wands.*

GAME 4-9: *RHYTHM BINGO* NOTE HUNT

OBJECTIVE:
For students to become familiar with the *Rhythm Bingo Cards* and their patterns

IN BRIEF:
Students locate notes within the patterns found on their *Rhythm Bingo Cards*. *Real Rhythm Cards* introduce students to relative values and help them keep track of patterns already used.

MATERIALS:
1) *Rhythm Bingo Cards* - side 1
2) *Magic Notes* and *Magic Wands*
3) *Real Rhythm Cards*

AGES:
Pre-K through elementary

REPETITIONS:
Until each student has found all the notes

PROCEDURE:
Pass out one *Rhythm Bingo Card* and a handful of *Magic Notes* to each student.

Depending on your students' ability, you have two choices on how to present the information.

1. Say the name of the note(s) and clap it:

The students will have a delightful time finding the notes you call out. Their chatter will be light and happy as they discover new notes with each turn.

"I have that one."

"Look! I have one, two, three, four, five, six . . . I have six huckleberries on my card!"

"I've found every one so far!"

2. Identify the note(s) by clapping only:
To help them understand the notes and rests they are hearing and seeing, lay out *Real Rhythm Cards*.

Continue until the students have filled up their *Rhythm Bingo Cards*. "You were terrific with that game. All your cards are covered!"

93

They will enjoy cleanup using the *Magic Wand*.

I am certain that children always know more than they are able to tell, and that makes the big difference between them and adults, who, at best, know only a fraction of what they say. The reason is simply that children know everything with their whole beings, while we know it only with our heads.

Jacques Lusseyran

GAME 4-10: *RHYTHM BINGO*

OBJECTIVE:
To identify (and clap) short rhythmic patterns

IN BRIEF:
Students match patterns on their cards as they hear them clapped. Students clap a rhythm on their card for the others to find.

MATERIALS:
1) *Rhythm Bingo Cards* - side 1
2) *Magic Notes* and *Magic Wands*

AGES:
Pre-K through adult

REPETITIONS:
Until each student has several bingos

PROCEDURE:
Hold out the *Rhythm Bingo Cards*, letting each student take one. Also give out handfuls of *Magic Notes*.

"This game is fun and so simple. I'll clap a rhythm for you. If you have that pattern on your card, cover it with a *Magic Note*. Please put your cards flat on the rug."

Clap the pattern at a moderate tempo. It's best if they are able to find the patterns without hearing the words, but depending on the ability of your students you may have to work toward this goal.

As with all the bingo games, continuously survey the cards so you can notice if one student has fewer patterns covered than the other students. Then clap a pattern found on his or her card. Keep a smile on everyone's face.

Play until everyone has several rows of bingo.

VARIATION: To provide variety and give students practice clapping rhythms ask:

"Ann, could you please clap one of the rhythms on your card for everyone else to find?" Ann will survey her card and select a rhythm she knows she can clap.

Give other students a turn. Help them steady the pulse or correct the clapping if needed. Be encouraging rather than putting them on the spot to perform. However, if this is something they are comfortable with, they will enjoy the chance to shine for a moment.

I played this game with a diverse group of 8th through 10th grade piano majors at Douglas Anderson School of the Arts, a magnet arts high school in Jacksonville, Florida. Even though I'd just played this game at my son David's Montessori preschool, I decided to use it to teach these older students the words I use for the various notes. We had to use cafeteria tables so this was easier than the *Blue Jello Cards* or the *Blue Jello Rhythm Puzzle*.

They loved the game! Outside of Ann, a former student of mine, none of the students had ever approached music theory in this way. They felt having the words to match the rhythms made it all so much clearer. By the second day, we turned the cards over to Side 2 and they had terrific success with the more complicated patterns. It was fun for all of us.

GAME 4-11: GROUP *RHYTHM BINGO*

OBJECTIVE:
To play bingo in groups rather than individually. This version enables students to work together. The need to survey many cards simultaneously develops the ability to look at short rhythm patterns as if they were words. This is helpful in music reading where one must take in much information quickly.

IN BRIEF:
Several students play with several cards

MATERIALS:
1) *Rhythm Bingo Cards* - side 1
2) *Magic Notes* and *Wands*

AGES:
Open

REPETITIONS:
For 5 - 8 minutes

PROCEDURE:
If you have a large class, use teams. Have the students sit with the *Rhythm Bingo Cards* spread around so they can see all of them. Give everyone a handful of *Magic Notes*.

As you clap rhythms, they look over the cards, finding the patterns. Since each pattern occurs a minimum of five times, they should find several on each turn.

With so many cards, it may be hard to get a bingo on any one card. To give the game a feeling of conclusion ask them to choose one card and place the *Magic Notes* from all the cards on it, matching the corresponding spaces.

Variation: Layer a simple melodic pattern on the rhythm rather than just clapping the pattern. For example: for this rhythmic pattern, play this on the piano.

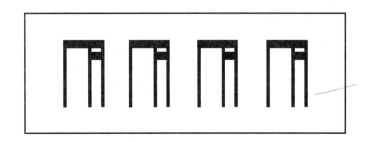

I CAN HEAR THAT
DICTATION PART 1

The ability to take melodic dictation is considered an advanced concept to many music teachers. Although I had studied music for years, attended music camps and won piano concerto competitions, I'd never tried it until my first week at college. I felt bewildered and overwhelmed with the phrases the professor played for us. I really concentrated to keep the pace expected of my ears. Is it possible to begin dictation earlier?

Yes. Much earlier.

Preschool students can easily hear the melodic direction of notes. First we sing numbers to match short five note melodies. Since they are often too young to write their numbers, amazed moms and dads write for them. (Or we use *Number Cards*.)

Instead of paper, we use *Number Slates*, made from magic slates found in toy stores. To change answers, students simply pull up on the plastic and the page is clean. Since they love these magic slates, dictation starts off on a happy note.

Dictation should begin <u>before</u> students learn to read music. Hearing and writing music patterns is an excellent pre-step to reading. Students learn to trust their ears and discover first hand how sound translates into written notes. Students become better readers when they have this dictation experience.

The games involving dictation can also serve to quiet a class that is too excited. It's a calming experience to listen to a short melodic pattern and write it. Since there is little interaction between students, everyone stays quiet and respectful of each other's space.

With the early singing exercises I use middle C since it is a comfortable range for most voices. When using the staff, we begin on G, a fifth above middle C. This five note scale doesn't contain sharps or flats or require any ledger lines, thus making the process easier.

The dictation games in this chapter deal with pitch only and not rhythm. Separating the two definitely contributes to the success of these dictation games.

Students of any age can be introduced to dictation using these games. If they are at an age where they won't be turned off by singing, I would begin here. However, if you suspect that singing will not go over so well, just begin with the games. With older students, it's entirely possible to spend a few moments with concepts from <u>this chapter in one session</u>.

Other games in this chapter teach the black note/white note pattern and the names of the keys on the piano.

PART
TWO

5

GAMES IN THIS CHAPTER

OBJECTIVE:
To introduce melodic dictation by singing and writing numbers

IN BRIEF:
Simple five note patterns are played for students, who sing them using a number for each pitch. Once this concept is understood, they write the pattern on *Number Slates* or with *Number Cards*.

AGES:
Pre-school and early elementary

MATERIALS:
1) Piano
2) *Number Slates* and pencils
3) *Number Cards*

Simple directions to make *Number Slates* and *Number Cards* are found in the Appendix.

REPETITIONS:
5-7 patterns
One or more sessions

PROCEDURE:

Step one: Ask the students to gather around you at the piano, sitting comfortably on the floor. "Let's do dictation today. I'm going to play a few notes on the piano. We'll use numbers to match the notes."

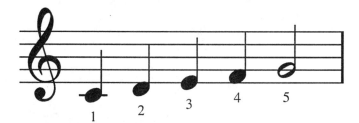

Play along as you explain. Use middle C as your starting note. "This is one. This is two. This is three. This is four and this is five. It's easy, isn't it? I'll play a pattern, then you sing the numbers with me. Ready?"

Play something simple like:

"Please sing with me." Play along as they sing with you. "1 2 3 4 5. Good. Very good. Here's another one."

"Sing: 1 2 3 4 5 5 5. Good. Please listen."

"Sing: 1 2 3 4 4 5. Right. This is easy, isn't it?"

Although watching your fingers as you play may help them to understand what's happening in the beginning, it's best to discourage them from looking at the piano. Instead, encourage them with compliments on how well their ears work. Closing their eyes while you play the patterns can direct their independence and sharpen their concentration.

Play the patterns clearly and evenly at about mm = ♩ = 84. Progress to other patterns only as students are able to understand this completely. Use short, stepwise patterns.

Let them practice singing patterns during one or more sessions. Once they are able to sing patterns easily, progress to step two.

Step two - *Number Cards*: If you teach young students who may not write their numbers very fast and there are no older students or adults available to help them, you can use *Number Cards*. Place the cards in five piles in front of the students. Play the pattern twice.

Call on a student to write out the pattern with the *Number Cards*.

Cards should be returned to their piles between patterns.

Step two - *Number Slates*: Give each student a *Number Slate* and pencil. If you teach young students, let them tell their parents which numbers to write.

Continue to use middle C as the starting note since they will sing the patterns before writing them on their *Number Slates*.

"Please put your pencils and *Number Slates* on the rug in front of you. Here's the first pattern. I'm going to play it two times."

"Let's sing it together. 1 2 3 3 3. That's right. Now you may pick up your slates and pencils and write the numbers."

It helps if you play the pattern again after a few moments. They can refresh their memories and check their work at the same time.

As they finish writing they will hold up their slates so you can tell them if their numbers are correct. Since some students may still be writing, this should be done without any talking. If correct, an encouraging smile makes a student happy. If it's not quite correct, I will shake my head a bit and mouth "almost" to them. They smile and listen while I play the pattern again.

Before saying, "Let's check our work," you may have played the pattern 3-5 times.

As you work with the students, you'll be a able to tell what kind of patterns to play. Remember that they will try their best to write these correctly. If the steps are small with plenty of repetition, they will feel the most confidence. Measure the difficulty of the patterns so they can write them out correctly in a few playings. If they make errors or ask you to play the patterns again and again, the patterns are either too long or too complicated.

Ideas for beginning patterns:

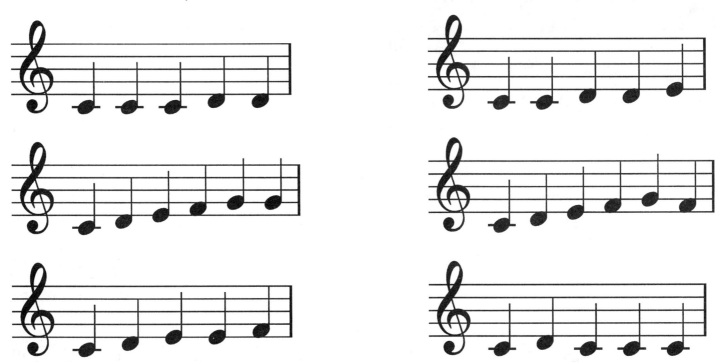

When patterns like these become easy, they may be ready to try dictation with notes.

GAME 5-2: DICTATION WITH *ONE STAFF BOARD*

OBJECTIVE:
To take melodic dictation using the staff

IN BRIEF:
Using blank *Notes With Letters* and the *One Staff Board*, students work together to learn how to write simple patterns. They have their own *Number Slates* on which to first write the pattern.

AGES:
Kindergarten and older

MATERIALS:
1) Piano
2) *Number Slates* and pencils
3) *One staff board*
4) *Clefs puzzle*
5) Blank side of *Notes & Rests*
6) *Dictation Slates*
7) *Magic Notes* and *Magic Wands*

REPETITIONS:
5-10 patterns

PROCEDURE:

Use the G above middle C as the starting note since the five note scale needs neither sharps, flats nor ledger lines. It also fits comfortably in the middle of the staff.

Ask the students to sit around the *One Staff Board* and place the treble clef correctly. Place the *Notes* on the *Board*, ready for the first pattern.

"First let's practice writing out patterns without any sound. Our starting note will be G." Let a student put G on the staff. "The first pattern is 1 2 3 4 5 5. Who wants to try writing it?"

There are several common misconceptions students might have when transferring sound into notes on a staff.

1) They may want to write only on the lines.

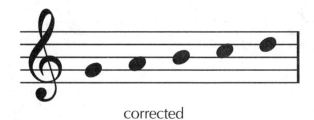

corrected

102

2) Descending patterns may look like this:

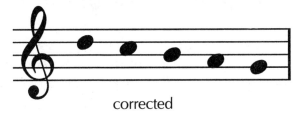

corrected

3) They may want to write a pattern the way it's played on the piano, beginning on a note then returning to the same note.

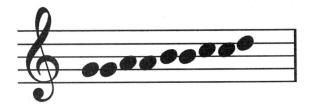

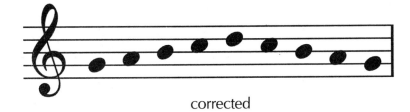

corrected

4) They may put notes underneath each other.

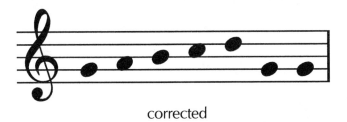

corrected

5) They may want the notes to touch each other since the sound is legato. Smile and say, "Even though the sound is touching, the notes need to be separated, otherwise the ink used in printed music will keep running together."

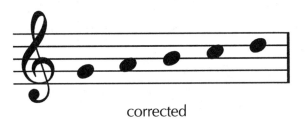

corrected

"Ready to write a pattern I play for you? Place your slates and pencils on the floor and we'll be ready to go. Here's the first pattern. I will play it twice."

First they should write the pattern on their *Number Slates*. After everyone has written it correctly, call on someone to write it on the *One Staff Board* using the *Notes*. If necessary, let several students help write it.

Repeat using different patterns.

Step using individual *Dictation Slates*: In this session or a later one, students may be ready to write patterns on their own *Dictation Slates* with *Magic Notes*.

Play the pattern twice. If needed, they can write it first on their *Number Slates*, then write it on their *Dictation Slates*. A student who wrote the pattern correctly can write it on the staff slate.

GAME 5-3: REPEATED NOTES AND INTERVALS

OBJECTIVE:
To help young students visually recognize repeated notes and intervals on the staff

IN BRIEF:
As a group, students place magic notes on repeated notes or selected intervals.

MATERIALS:
1) *Melodic Bingo Cards*
2) *Magic Notes* and *Magic Wands*

AGES:
Preschool

REPETITIONS:
Usually several cards of one interval per session

PROCEDURE:
"I had two boy dolls when I was little. One was named Pete and the other was named Repeat. Can you tell me how my dolls looked?"

"I bet they were just alike. We're they twins?"

"Exactly. Want to learn about repeated notes today? Can you all say `repeated notes'?"

Place the *Melodic Dictation Cards* on the rug between you and the students and hold some *Magic Notes* either in your hand or on the wand. Pointing to a pair of repeated notes say:

"Can you see how these notes are in a row on the same line? They are just the same. And since they are in a row, we call them repeated notes. Look at the patterns on this card. Can you find other repeated notes? When you do, raise your hand and you may take a *Magic Note* and place it on top of the two notes. Can anyone see any repeated notes?"

"Oh, here's a repeated note!" discovers Michelle. She takes a *Magic Note* and places it on top of the notes. Sing the pattern together as you point to the notes on the card.

Everyone is busy looking for repeated notes. Help each child have a turn finding repeated notes. Let them sing the patterns. Soon they will like taking turns pointing to the notes.

Repeat with another card.

Another session: Repeat the game as described except use a different interval such as a second or third, either up or down.

GAME 5-4: *MELODIC BINGO COPY GAME*

OBJECTIVE:
To help students understand how melodic patterns are written on the staff

IN BRIEF:
Students copy patterns from the *Melodic Bingo Card* onto the *Grand Staff Board* or individually using *Dictation Slates*. Patterns are sung after being written. A favorite game.

AGES:
Pre-school and older

MATERIALS:
1) *Melodic Bingo Cards*

Group play: 2) One *Alphabet Kid*
3) *One Staff Board*
4) *Clefs Puzzle*
5) Blank sides of *Notes With Letters*
Individual: 2) *Alphabet Kids*
3) *Dictation Slates*
4) *Magic Notes* and *Magic Wands*

REPETITIONS:
4 - 5 patterns in a session

PROCEDURE:
Group Play: Place the *One Staff Board* between you and the students and let them place the clef correctly. Choose a pattern and let a student copy it using the blank notes. Place the *Alphabet Kid* on the chosen pattern to help the student keep his place.

It is helpful to sing the pattern as new notes are added. When completed, encourage the students to sing with you.

105

Individual play: Let each student take a *Melodic Bingo Card*, a *Dictation Slate*, an *Alphabet Kid* and *Magic Notes*. The game is played the way it was described except students copy patterns from their cards onto their slates.

"Cleanup is fun. I'm going to play someone's pattern. If I didn't play your pattern, you may look around to see whose pattern I did play. Here's the first one."

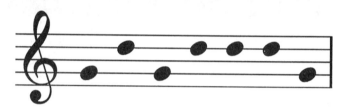

"Hey, that's mine! Here it is right here!" calls out an excited Andrew.

"Right you are. Andrew, you can clean your notes off. Who's next? Listen, here it is.

GAME 5-5: TWO FINGERS - THREE FINGERS

OBJECTIVE:
To teach the black note pattern on the piano. To teach up and down on the piano.

IN BRIEF:
Lining up next to each other at the piano, each student places five fingers on five black notes. Playing one note at a time they first play up the keyboard, then down.

AGES:
Open

MATERIALS:
Piano

REPETITIONS:
Once through the game

PROCEDURE:
Ask them to hold up two fingers with their left hands and three fingers with their right hands.

"Everyone remember how many fingers you are holding up because we're going to play a game with them. All right, put your hands in your lap and make a fist. Great. When I call out GO, see how fast you can put the correct fingers back up in the air. " . . . GO!" Check around and help anyone who needs it.

"Okay, hands in your laps. . . . GO!" Repeat this fun game a few times. It's easy but important.

Ask seven students to keep their fingers out and line up, shoulder to shoulder at the piano keyboard.

"Without playing the keys, please place your fingers on the black notes. Stand close together so all the black keys, except the extra one at the bottom are covered."

Explain that everyone is going to get a turn playing the black notes. First is the student at the lower end of the keyboard. Starting with the lowest note, s/he should play each key, one at a time and in order.

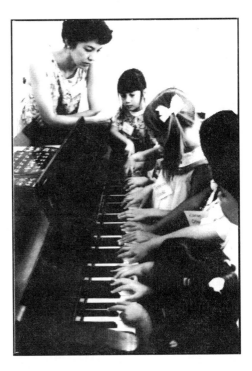

Ask them to play their notes, one at a time, in order up the keyboard. This pentatonic scale will have an appealing sound. "This is going UP the keyboard."

"Let's go back DOWN the keyboard." They can reverse the pattern and play a descending scale together.

Ask them to listen as the pitch of the notes gets higher or lower. Keep reinforcing what is up and what is down on the keyboard.

Everyone may enjoy learning a new word. "The scale you have been playing has five tones (the five black keys) and is called a pentatonic scale. A pentagon has how many sides? . . . Right, five sides. Pentatonic and pentagon both mean five."

Give waiting students a turn to play the pentatonic scale and learn about UP and DOWN.

GAME 5-6: C KEYS ON THE PIANO

OBJECTIVE:
To teach the names of the C keys on the piano

IN BRIEF:
Students place *Alphabet Kids* on the piano, first finding all the C's then each note in turn.

AGES:
Open

MATERIALS:
1) Piano
2) *Alphabet Kids*

REPETITIONS:
One or more sessions
Play until all seven notes are learned.

PROCEDURE:
Once the students have become familiar with the "three black, two black" note pattern on the piano they can learn the names of the keys easily.

Someone in the class may already know which keys are named C. Ask if anyone does. Let her place an *Alphabet Kid* on the C note.

"Right. That is a C. Notice how C is just below these two black notes. Can anyone find another C?"

"Right again." Let students find all seven C's on the piano. You can either keep moving C *Kids* or turn the *Alphabet Kids* backwards so their letters don't show.

Snap your fingers so they'll close their eyes. Mix up the *Alphabet Kids*. Clap twice so they open their eyes.

"Oh, look at how mixed up all those people are! Raise your hand if you can fix one. Please fix only one kid."

They will enjoy this game. It's important, but easy, and the little *Alphabet Kids* are cute for the students to play with.

So, like a forgotten fire, a childhood can always flare up again within us.

Gaston Bachelard

GAME 5-7: INTRODUCING CARDBOARD KEYBOARDS

OBJECTIVE:
To orient students to the *Cardboard Keyboards*

AGES:
Open

IN BRIEF:
Students practice finding notes on the *Cardboard Keyboards* using *Magic Notes.*

REPETITIONS:
Several times until keyboard orientation is understood

MATERIALS:
1) *Cardboard Keyboards* - one per student
2) *Magic Notes* - 4 or 5 per student

PROCEDURE:
Place the *Cardboard Keyboards* in a pile on the rug between the students and you. "You have done a good job finding the C's on the piano. Would you like a turn finding the C's on your own *Cardboard Keyboard*? First let's try it together. Would anyone like to place a *Magic Note* on a C on this *Cardboard Keyboard*?" This should be easy for them to do.

"Exactly right. Can you find another C? . . . Good. How about the other C?"

"Would you each like a keyboard and three *Magic Notes* so you can do this yourself? Great!" Give everyone a *Cardboard Keyboard* and a few *Magic Notes*. Ask them to spread out in a circle with their *Keyboards* on the rug.

"Okay. Please find one C on your *Keyboard*. Very good. Can you find the other C's? Looks great."

"That was very good. Please clean off your *Keyboards* and find all the C's again . . . . You did it. Ready to play a game now? Move your *Magic Notes* so they aren't on any C's. All right, when I say GO, stand up and move to a new *Keyboard*. When you sit down, fix the notes on your new *Keyboard*. Remember to walk gently after I say go . . . ready . . . GO."

Later session: After students can easily find the C's, let them practice finding C and D. In later sessions, continue adding notes until they can find any note.

109

GRAND STAFF C's

Studying the names of the lines and spaces is a basic part of every music student's education. Although reading music is more than just memorizing the names of the lines and spaces, knowing the staff is indispensable to reading music and understanding music theory. Teachers will agree on the importance of learning the staff . . . it's how to do it that's open for discussion.

Unfortunately, the most common way to memorize the staff is to teach students to recite jingles.

> **E**very **G**ood **B**oy **D**oes **F**ine
> **A**ll **C**ows **E**at **G**rass
> **A**ll **C**ars **E**at **G**as
> **FACE**
> **A**my **C**arter **E**ats **G**rits
> **G**ood **B**oys **D**on't **F**ight and **A**rgue
> **E**mpty **G**arbage **B**efore **D**ad **F**lips

These jingles may work at first but here's what is happening. The student is trapped into relying on the silly jingle to figure out each note . . . one at a time. If the student counts correctly, s/he will be able to name notes on a music theory exam and perhaps mistakenly assume this is reading music.

But, it's not. How can anyone learn to read music by saying a jingle to figure out notes, one at a time? It is a slow system which doesn't lead to understanding what the musical staff really represents.

Once a fine musician friend of mine admitted that she can't get rid of those jingles even though she doesn't need them. She says they just pop into her mind without invitation. Perhaps there are others like her.

So. I suggest you toss those jingles out with other outdated ideas like sack dresses, poodle skirts, Brill Cream and tail fins. Times have changed.

Educational ideas have certainly changed.

What can replace this system?

A quick, reliable one that ties together note recognition on the staff, on the keyboard and with the ear at the same time.

Several years and many, many games ago I began developing a system that works superbly. The games are fun and the memories of the students are quick and secure. In no time at all, the staff makes sense and students can begin reading music. And, as you might expect, the ability to read develops at a steady pace.

The procedure is simple. Students learn the location of all the C's on the grand staff. Ledger line notes are included right from the beginning. They can memorize all these C's almost as easily as one. The location of the C's on the piano is introduced at the same lesson using the *Alphabet kids.*

The familiar *Grand Staff Board, Clefs puzzle, Ledger Line Sheets* and large *Notes with Letters* are used to introduce the notes. Students play fun games moving the *Notes* around the staff, learning their placement.

After C is secure, they study D, the note one second up from C. Just as before, they learn all the D's on the grand staff.

Then we study all the B's. After that, the concept takes hold and the rest of the notes don't take much time at all to figure out.

My students are usually in kindergarten when they begin learning where C's are found on the staff. They thoroughly learn the placement of the five C's using a variety of games. It's vital to continue checking their memories before studying any other notes. Take your time. Rather than be impatient to move on to learn the other notes, it's wise to play a few more games with C to lock in a student's instant recognition.

Students should be able to look at a note and immediately know if it's a C. That means there's absolutely no time to count up from another note. Remember . . in reading, there's no time to count lines and spaces. It must be instant.

If the memory of the C's is automatic, then the others are learned without much effort. However, if the C's are confusing in the slightest, then the entire staff could be in question.

Unique staff design: The *Grand Staff Cards* are not like other musical staff cards. Each note is on a card with the entire grand staff. Seeing both clefs for each note allows students to visualize the whole staff and ultimately read

PART TWO

6

111

from both clefs more easily. This simple idea goes a long way in helping students form a secure memory and total understanding of the staff.

Each clef has its own color. The green cards show notes in the bass clef, and the blue cards show notes in the treble clef.

As with the *Grand Staff Board*, there is only enough space between the treble and bass clef for B, C and D. If the normal space found in printed music is used between the clefs, students will certainly wonder, "Why is all that space there for just C?"

There are eight *Grand Staff Cards* which enable students to study and learn the middle ledger lines. All the notes are found in both the treble and bass cards to help clarify how the two clefs overlap. The two cards of the same note are printed alike except for two points: 1) one card is green and one is blue, and 2) the stem on the bass clef goes down and the treble clef goes up.

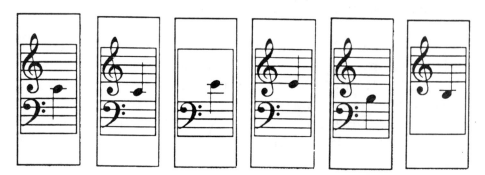

As with all the **Music Mind Game** materials, these are never used as flash cards. Flash cards are held up in front of a student to identify, like a test. Not these cards. They are used in lively, noncompetitive, cooperative games.

Your students will enjoy these games because the learning steps are designed for success and happiness. Students will be pleased with their knowledge and quick ability. Remember, if you take the time to learn something thoroughly and correctly, you will have that information for life. However, if something is learned in haste, it may be forgotten or cause unnecessary confusion for years to come.

GAMES
IN THIS
CHAPTER

GAME 6-1: THESE FIVE C'S

OBJECTIVE:
To teach where five C's are found on the grand staff and the piano

IN BRIEF:
Using a *Grand Staff Board* and the *Alphabet Kids* on the piano, students find the five C's from two ledger lines below the bass clef to two ledger lines above the treble clef.

PREGAMES:
5-5: TWO FINGERS - THREE FINGERS
5-6: C KEYS ON THE PIANO

AGES:
Open

MATERIALS:
1) *Grand Staff Board*
2) 3 *Ledger Line Sheets*
3) *Notes With Letters*
4) *Clefs Puzzle*
5) Piano
6) 5 *Alphabet Kids* - if you don't have five C *Alphabet Kids*, just turn them around so the letter isn't showing.

REPETITIONS:
Once through the game

PROCEDURE:
Place the *Grand Staff Board* in front of the students and let them place the clefs correctly.

Review the names of the clefs and let the students remember where the treble clef line G and the bass clef line F are located.

To give them a perspective of how the clefs influence the names of the lines and spaces, move the clefs and let them place the notes correctly.

Reassure them that although the clefs are moveable and it is possible to write music this way, they can depend on the clefs staying put in their music.

"Let's learn where the C's are found on the grand staff and where they are on the piano. There are five C's. And they are easy to remember.

"The first one is in the middle of the staff and is called . . . middle C." Place one of the notes on middle C. "Remember that this note is on a line, right between the bass and treble clefs."

Place a *Ledger Line Sheet* under the C so it is indeed on a line. Let the students take turns placing middle C.

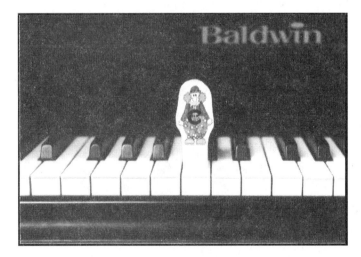

"Now I'd like you to show me where middle C is on the piano." Either they already know this, or they will look for the C in the middle of the piano. Let someone place the *Alphabet Kid* C on middle C. Leave it there as reference.

"Next let's learn which two spaces are named C." Place a note on the treble clef C space and a note on the bass clef C space. Help the students notice how both C's are one space from the top and bottom. Using your hand as if you were playing an octave on the piano, show how they are both equally spaced from middle C.

Although it's not incorrect to count "1 2 3 4 5 6 7 8" to show them that they are eight notes apart, it's of greater benefit for the students to visually see the distance between them. Remember that when we read music, we can't take time to count to see if two notes are an octave apart. Instead, we learn by recognizing the distance separating them.

Give each student a turn placing all three C notes correctly.

"Who can find the treble C on the piano? Is it higher or lower than middle C?" Hand a willing student an *Alphabet Kid.*

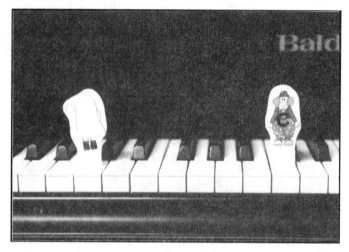

"Right. Now who would like to find the bass clef C?"

"There are two more C's to learn today." Place one C on the second ledger line in the treble clef and one in the bass clef on the second ledger line below the staff. Ask the students if they can tell you what these two notes have in common.

As you talk, point to the staff to illustrate what you are saying. "It's really so easy if you notice that the middle C is a line note, exactly in the middle of the staff. The next C notes are both spaces and the outside C's are both ledger line notes, with one ledger line between them and the staff. Octaves are always found as a line, space, line, space, etc."

I like to have a bit of fun and also make certain the students understand that last comment.

"I know there's not room on the board, but will the next C after this high C be a line or a space?" I indicate its position on the rug up an octave from high C. The students use their imagination to "see" this note.

"A space," they answer with a smile.

"And this one?" I keep moving my hand up by octaves. "Now we're up so high only the dogs can hear us!"

"Now let's move over to the piano again. Who would like to find the very high C on the piano? Good. And the very low C on the piano? Right."

Give each student a chance to place all five C's on the *Grand Staff Board.* Most likely, this will be easy. But if anyone forgets where a note goes, kindly show him or her. With practice, everyone can do this and will feel encouraged about learning the staff notes.

GAME 6-2: FIX THE C'S AND PASS OUT

OBJECTIVE:
To practice remembering where the five C's are found on the grand staff

IN BRIEF:
FIX THE C'S: You mix up the C notes for students to fix after they open their eyes.
PASS OUT: You pass out the notes for them to put on the staff correctly.

AGES:
Open

MATERIALS:
1) *Grand Staff Board*
2) *Notes With Letters*
3) 3 *Ledger Line Sheets*
4) *Clefs Puzzle*
5) Piano

REPETITIONS:
5 - 7 repetitions per session

PROCEDURE:
Place the *Grand Staff Board* in front of the students and let them place the clefs, the *Ledger Line Sheets* and the five C's on the staff.

FIX THE C'S: Snap your fingers once for the students to close their eyes. Rearrange some or all of the notes depending on the abilities of your students.

Clap twice as the signal for them to open their eyes.

"I made it pretty tricky, didn't I?" you can tease.

"No, this is easy! You can't trick us."

Call on several students to fix the notes. Repeat several times for fun and reinforcement.

It's also great to ask them to fix only one thing when it's their turn. If they slide a ledger line sheet with a note on it say, "Oops, that's two things!" Everyone will keep their interest focused on the notes longer when you play this way and the correct placement of the C's will be more firmly etched in their memories. You can also move the clefs slightly and wait for someone to notice.

PASS OUT: Pass out the C notes for students to place on the staff. Remember, learning means doing it yourself.

Let each student go to the piano and find the C s/he just placed on the staff. Pass out the notes again.

GAME 6-3: C TOSS

OBJECTIVE:
To practice naming C's using a fun toss game and to introduce the concept of intervals.

IN BRIEF:
Students toss a note on the *Grand Staff Board* hoping it lands on a C. If it doesn't land on a C the student moves the note to the closest C. S/he receives a *Magic Note* for each second the note must be moved to be on a C.

AGES:
Open

MATERIALS:
1) *Grand Staff Board*
2) *Clefs Puzzle*
3) *Ledger Line Sheets*
4) *Magic Notes* and *Magic Wands*
5) One BLUE from *Blue Jello Rhythm Puzzle*
6) *Notes With Letters*
7) *Gold Coins*

REPETITIONS:
Several tosses per student

PROCEDURE:
Let the students arrange the clefs on the *Grand Staff Board*. Review where the C's are found using the *Notes With Letters*.

If it lands on a C, they may leave it there. If not, also leave it where it landed. Ask a student to put a *Note with Letter* on the nearest C so the students can see the interval created.

Place the BLUE a few feet below the board. The students take turns tossing the *Toss Note*.

To help in the study of intervals, let the student figure out how far the note "is from one of the C's. Everyone around the circle gets a *Gold Coin* or *Magic Note* on each others' turns."

lands on C	= one *Gold Coin*
a second away	= 2 *Magic Notes*
a third away	= 3 *Magic Coins*
etc.	

118

GAME 6-4: GRAND STAFF CARD C'S

OBJECTIVE:
To locate the grand staff C's using the *Grand Staff Cards*. Played as a group with one set of cards after C's are located on the *Grand Staff Board* using the C *Notes With Letters*

IN BRIEF:
One at a time, *Grand Staff Cards* are passed around the circle. When a student recognizes a C, it is placed on the rug to form a line of six C cards.

AGES:
Elementary and older

MATERIALS:
1) *Grand Staff Cards*
2) *Grand Staff Board*
3) *Clefs Puzzle*
4) *Ledger Line Sheets*
5) *Notes With Letters* - the five C notes

REPETITIONS:
Until all the C cards are located — may be repeated in later sessions

PROCEDURE:
Place the *Grand Staff Board* in front of the students and ask them to place the clefs, *Ledger Line Sheets* and five C *Notes With Letters* correctly. Give them time to work together to get everything right.

"Looks good. You're remembering this well. I have some new cards to show you today." Show the students the *Grand Staff Cards* and let them comment on what they see.

"Let's see if you can find the C's on these cards."

Move the *Grand Staff Board* to the side, a little away from the group. Keep the middle area between you and the students clear. Pass each student a card.

"If you have a C in your hand, please put it on the rug. You may keep the other cards in your hand."

Pass out another round of cards, one to each student.

As the C cards are placed on the rug, put them in order from lowest to highest so it's easy for the students to know what C's they are still looking for.

If an error is made in any way, gently point it out to the group as a whole. "Ahhh. Here's a B." Or . . . "This is an E, not a C." Then put that card back in the pile in your hand. It will be passed out again and hopefully played correctly.

119

Continue passing out cards, waiting between rounds for the students to study their cards and take out the C cards. After all the cards are passed out, you should have all the C cards on the floor, laid out in order.

If you don't then here's a way to find the C without having to look through each student's cards yourself and put that student on the spot.

"All right, let's help each other find the missing C. Please pass your stack of cards one person to your right. Now, look through these cards and if you can find the C, put it on the rug." This will help the missing C turn up.

Most likely a student will notice that there are two middle C cards and point this out. "Right, Joseph, there are two middle C cards. One belongs to the bass clef and one belongs to the treble clef, but they're the same note. For our game, let's place them side by side."

Grading cannot be done by test. Tests can only determine how much the children have understood and whether there are any who have not understood. Actually, these results would show the teacher's ability rather than the child's.

Shinichi Suzuki

GAME 6-5: FIND THE C'S

OBJECTIVE:
To practice quick recognition of the C's using *Grand Staff Cards*

MATERIALS:
Grand Staff Cards - one set for each student. If you have a large class, two or three students can share a set.

IN BRIEF:
Each student looks through his or her own set of *Grand Staff Cards* one at a time, taking out the C's.

REPETITIONS:
Once or twice through the cards per session

AGES:
Elementary and older

PROCEDURE:
Pass out the *Grand Staff Cards*.

"I want to you find the C notes using your cards." Ask the students to line up their C cards on the floor in order from lowest to highest.

Sometimes students won't know how to work with thirty cards and will spread them all out on the floor and try to locate what they are looking for.

Teach them to hold the pile of cards and go through them one at a time. Whenever a C card appears, they should remove it and place it in a special stack. Not only does this help them work more efficiently, it helps them organize and sharpen their memories.

"Be sure to line up your cards from the lowest C in the bass clef to the highest C in the treble clef." Move around the class offering help as it is needed. Remember that this is a learning game, not a testing game.

GAME 6-6: GRAND STAFF CARDS AND THE PIANO

OBJECTIVE:
To relate the staff cards to the piano. This provides a cross check to see if the students do understand how the notes are placed on the piano.

IN BRIEF:
First, as a group, students place *Alphabet Kids* on the piano to match the *Grand Staff Cards*. Second, one at a time, students identify a *Grand Staff Card* by placing an *Alphabet Kid* on the correct C.

AGES:
Elementary and older

MATERIALS:
1) Piano
2) *Grand Staff Cards* - six C cards
3) *Alphabet Kids*

REPETITIONS:
Once through a set of cards

PROCEDURE:

STEP ONE: Ask the students to help you line up the staff cards on the piano music stand, in order from lowest to highest.

Place the *Alphabet Kid* C in front of the treble clef middle C card. "Can anyone find where this kid belongs on the piano?"

"I can, watch me," says Bruce.

"Absolutely right. How did you do that?" They will laugh. "Okay, now the tricks begin," you can tease. Place the *Alphabet Kid* C in front of the bass clef middle C card. "Who can find where this note is on the piano?

"Ah ha! I thought I would fool you, but you're too smart."

Continue in this manner, giving students a chance to match the notes on the cards to the notes on the piano.

STEP TWO: Take the *Grand Staff Cards* off the music stand.

Ask them to line up near the piano. If possible, position them so they can see the keyboard and learn from each other. They will also be less likely to misbehave if they can see.

Give the first student a *Grand Staff Card*. S/he places the card on the music stand and the *Alphabet Kid* on the matching piano key. They will enjoy taking turns matching notes to keys and will gain much understanding of the keyboard.

NOTES AND RESTS - PART 1

The rhythm games found in this chapter are grouped together because they use the *Notes & Rests Game.* They vary in difficulty from a matching game for pre-school students to making a Card Chart to learn the relationship of 23 basic note and rest values. In Chapter 15: NOTES AND RESTS - PART 2 there are advanced rhythmic games that can challenge even an accomplished musician.

This clever series of games allows the players to mathematically study rhythm without the intervention of melody or harmony. These games are loads of fun. They clarify the study of rhythm as logical steps that anyone can learn and thus become rhythmically literate.

Rhythm is important. Along with dictation, every music teacher must take an active interest in thoroughly teaching rhythm. The musical alphabet, lines and spaces and even scales and chords are basically memory work, but rhythm and dictation involve a sensitivity to pulse, tempo and note relationships.

A teacher can easily become well versed in these enjoyable, stimulating games and can introduce them when it is appropriate. As with other subjects in this book, it is all right to improvise with these materials for individual needs.

I want to thank Penny Kunkel and Evy Olson of Lincoln, Nebraska for showing me their game in 1978 which inspired *Notes & Rests.*

The games in this chapter must be played simultaneously with those in Chapter 4: BLUE JELLO and Chapter 13: REAL RHYTHMS.

Rests cards used in these games:

Note cards used in these games:

During all of these games try to refer to the notes and rests by name rather than saying, "These notes are in the right place now." Instead refer to them by name, i.e. as two eighth notes or a jello. Remind students to do the same. Names will become automatic and easily used in their vocabulary.

GAMES IN THIS CHAPTER

GAME 7-1: MATCH

OBJECTIVE:
To learn the various shapes and subtle differences between 23 different notes and rests.

IN BRIEF:
Students match cards onto the game board

AGES:
Preschool and older - this game should be played with any age group to provide an introduction to the games in this chapter.

MATERIALS:
1) *Notes & Rests Board*
2) *Notes & Rests Cards*

REPETITIONS:
Play once in a session. May be played week after week for preschool age students.

PROCEDURE:
Place the *Notes & Rests Board* in front of the students and ask them to sit around it. You can sit at the top of the game board.

"Can you help me match these cards?" you can ask the students. Show one card to the students. Let's say you choose the <u>dotted half note</u> card.

As you place it on the board on top of the <u>half note</u> you can ask, "Is this a good match?"

"Yes", they may answer at first. Move the card off the half note so they can compare the two.

"Wait, there's a dot on the card and no dot on this one," says Kim. The students have discovered the difference themselves.

"Is that dot important?" you can ask.

"No. Wait . . . Yes . . . Is it?"

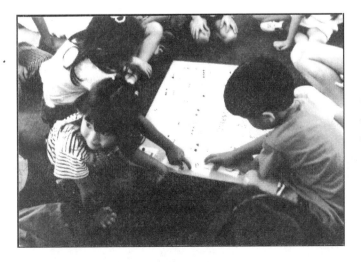

"Yes, every dot, small line or number is very important when you read rhythms," you answer. Let them help you find the correct place for the dotted half note.

Select the GOOSEBERRY card (eighth and two sixteenth notes). "Let's see where this card goes . . . ."

Place the GOOSEBERRY incorrectly on the BERRYGOOSE and let the students correct you. Now that they understand the game, they will all want to show you where the card should go. If you feel they need a little more help recognizing differences, repeat these steps with another card. If they seem "raring to go" . . . then,

"Would you like your own turns? . . . "

If you are playing with six students, pass out one card to each child. If you are playing with more than six students, pass out four cards to the four students sitting next to you around the circle. If you pass out too many cards, it may become hard to see anything on the board.

Allow the students to place their cards on the board in the correct places.

If a mistake occurs simply move the card a bit so it's not covering the incorrect note or rest. The students can compare them, and make the correct move.

Try not to interfere with their learning by talking or teaching. Smiles and quiet encouragements are appropriate.

After these four cards are on the board, pass out the four more cards to the next four students around the circle. Continue in this fashion until all the cards are passed out and the board is filled.

TO FINISH: "Wow, you did a great job. Every card is covered. Let's check our work. Can you say 'yes' if the card is correct and 'no' if it is not correct?" One at a time, move each card next to the one it's covering so the students can make a comparison. If the card is correct, the students will say "Yes" and then you can turn it over so the name *Notes & Rests* is facing up.

Checking the board this way allows all the students to study all the cards. It is also a good habit to check their work before finishing.

"Look at that! All the cards are correct! You did excellent work. Great game today!"

To clean up, just tip the board, and to everyone's delight, the cards will slide off. Let a few students straighten the cards into a pile and help you put the game away.

MATCH WITH TEAMS: This version allows two noncompeting teams to match cards without teacher involvement.

Set up the *Notes & Rests Cards* around the *Notes & Rests Board* with one color on each side.

"Are you ready for a treat today?" you can ask. "You may match your cards just like before, only this time, those who cover the note or rest first, get to leave their card there. Only one card per space. If you're looking for a note or rest and find a card already there, just pick up another card and try to get it there before anyone else does. All set?"

After you say GO, they can begin to match their cards with the notes or rests on the game board.

If you see an incorrect match, simply remove the card and place it back on the floor with the other cards of the same color.

After all the cards are covered <u>do not</u> count to see what color card was used more. That has no importance in this game.

To finish, you can check the cards one at a time as a group.

If you want, say the real names of the notes or rests as you check through the board. It gives the students a chance to hear all the real names.

"Great game. You really are getting good at matching notes and rests!"

If children grew up according to early indications, we should have nothing but geniuses.

Johann Wolfgang von Goethe

GAME 7-2: NOTE OR REST?

OBJECTIVE:
To let the students show they understand the difference between notes and rests

MATERIALS:
1) *Notes & Rests Board*
2) *Notes & Rests Cards*

IN BRIEF:
Students match cards on top of notes and rests using the backside of the cards.

REPETITIONS:
Play once or twice

AGES:
Kindergarten and early elementary

PROCEDURE:
Place the *Notes & Rests Board* in front of the students. Talk about which ones are rests and which are notes. Discuss how notes have the round note head and rests don't. Point to several examples and then allow them to do the same.

Pass out several cards to each student.

"This game is a little different from the other games you played with these cards and the board. We're going to use only the back side of the cards. I'd like you to cover all the <u>notes</u> on the board. It doesn't matter which card you use since only the back side is showing. All the cards are 'wild' cards."

After that, do the opposite. Cover up the <u>rests</u>.

GAME 7-3: FIVE NOTES - FIVE RESTS

OBJECTIVE:
To learn which notes and rests are equal and to begin learning their real names. The students make a Card Chart using *Real Rhythm Cards* and learn how to remember the difference between half and whole rests.

IN BRIEF:
Step one: Students separate sixteenth, eighth, quarter, half and whole notes and rests from the other cards.
Step two: On their own, students line up the cards from greatest to least value, then check using the *Real Rhythm Cards*.
Step three: Students hear a funny, memorable story about half and whole rests.

AGES:
Early elementary and older

MATERIALS:
1) *Notes & Rests Cards* - one set
2) *Real Rhythm Cards*:- whole, half, quarter, eighth, sixteenth (notes and rests)

REPETITIONS:
Play once in this session.

PROCEDURE:
This game is divided into three steps. You may choose to do the steps over one or more sessions or all at once.

To help the students begin to learn the names of the notes, refer to them by name as you play this game. If a student picks up a quarter note card, say aloud, "BLUE . . . quarter note." Repeat this for other cards throughout the game.

STEP ONE: "Let's find all the notes and rests that are all alone on a card." Show the students an example of a single note card and a single rest card.

"Please call out **STOP** whenever you see a note or rest card." With the students watching, as quickly as you can, toss the cards into a pile, one by one. The students will watch intently to stop you whenever they see a note or rest card and laugh when they realize how fast you're going.

"Stop! There's one! . . . Stop! . . ."

Hold on to the cards they have selected. Put the others aside since you won't need them anymore for this game.

STEP TWO: Ask the students to separate the cards into two piles: one for the notes and one for the rests. Next they are going to begin their Card Chart.

Rather than being told the values of the notes and rests ("A quarter note is equal to two eighth notes. A half note is equal to . . ."), the students are going to discover this for themselves. This innovative alternative is much more fun and challenging for them.

"Would you like to put these cards in order? The longest value note will go on the bottom."

Since the students have played BLUE JELLO games they just might be able to put the cards in order. Give them time to discuss their answers and agree somewhat on what they've worked out.

Without offering any corrections or even "that's right", take out the corresponding *Real Rhythm Cards* and hand them **face down** to the students to match next to the *Notes & Rests Cards.*.

They can turn the *Real Rhythm Cards* over to see if their *Notes & Rests Cards* are in the correct order.

Help them to see how the notes fit into this order logically by talking about how they are drawn. Your dialogue may go something like this, or the students may be able to point out some of the information on their own.

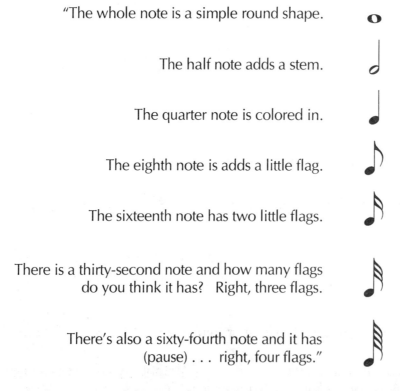

"The whole note is a simple round shape.

The half note adds a stem.

The quarter note is colored in.

The eighth note is adds a little flag.

The sixteenth note has two little flags.

There is a thirty-second note and how many flags do you think it has?   Right, three flags.

There's also a sixty-fourth note and it has (pause) . . . right, four flags."

STEP THREE: HALF REST/WHOLE REST STORY Even if the students placed the half and whole rest cards correctly, it is important to emphasize the subtle difference between the two rests. Years ago, I made up the following story and have found that students enjoy hearing it. It's a little silly, but because each child is the main character, it helps everyone remember the difference between the half and whole note rests.

Let's imagine that you are alive over 100 years ago. It's the time when Abraham Lincoln was our president. Interestingly, he is traveling through your town and because he's old buddies with your mom and dad, he writes that he wants to stop in to visit. He's very busy but says he has time to stay for lunch.

Wow. Is everyone excited! Mom and Dad are busy getting the house and lunch ready and the microwave is not working. So they ask if you can meet President Lincoln at the front door.

Knock. Knock.

You open the door and there stands President Lincoln. Wow. Is he tall, you think to yourself. And what a hat he has! But, you remember your manners and ask President Lincoln to please come in and if you can take his hat. Since he's staying only for lunch, you put his hat on the table. Here is an old time photograph of President Lincoln's hat on the table.

President Lincoln really enjoyed the meal your mom and dad prepared. You and your little brother didn't even spill your milk!

As President Lincoln was getting ready to leave, you give him his hat. "What a nice family," he says. "Next time I come through your town I'd like to stay longer. Bye. Bye."

Well, a few months later, your mom receives a fax from President Lincoln's office saying that his train is coming through your town and would it be possible to spend the week-end with your family?

Now, Mom and Dad have to get the whole house ready. You even have to clean up your room and help your little brother with his. There are lots of preparations, so once more, it's your job to greet Mr. Lincoln at the door.

"Hello, President Lincoln," you say smiling, "How nice to see you again. Please come in." He smiles and steps inside.

"May I take your hat, please?" you ask President Lincoln.

Since he is staying overnight and not just for lunch, you don't want it to get dusty. Remember all the horses and carriages going by on the street in front of your house? You put his hat under the table instead of on top of it.

"This is an old time photograph of President Lincoln's ha
under the table."

"Do you see the difference between the rests? This is lunch and this is a whole week-end. Can you tell the rests apart?"

The students will have fun with this joke of a story. Funny thing though . . . Long after I made up this story I was out shopping at a local Mall. There was a big antique show spread throughout the public areas. I began to browse around a bit. I happened to notice a small table with a shelf about 6-8 inches under the top.

"Excuse me, what is that shelf for?" I asked the antique lady standing next to the antique table.

"Oh, that table is from the mid-1800's and was used in the front entryway. That shelf under there was for hats. You know, so they wouldn't get dusty." Ah ha!

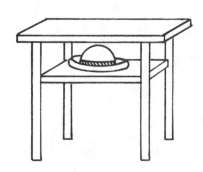

GAME 7-4: CARD CHART

OBJECTIVE:
This game lets students learn the relative values of the six basic notes and rests

IN BRIEF:
Students place *Magic Notes* and *Gold Coins* on top of the Card Chart. One *Magic Note* equals a sixteenth note or rest and four *Magic Notes* equal one *Gold Coin*. Real money is also used to help students understand the relative value of the notes.

AGES:
Mid-elementary and older

MATERIALS:
1) *Notes & Rests Cards*
2) *Real Rhythm Cards*
3) *Gold Coins*
4) *Magic Notes*
5) One dollar bill, a fifty cent piece, a quarter

REPETITIONS:
Once through in a session. May be repeated in following sessions until everyone understands it.

PROCEDURE:
Ask the students to make the Card Chart using all the cards.

It's best if the dotted notes (𝅗𝅥. 𝅘𝅥. 𝅘𝅥𝅮.)
are not used until the next game
7-5: CARD CHART COMPLETED.

"Today we're going to learn the value of these notes and rests."

Point to the sixteenth note card, "Let's say that this note is worth on *Magic Note* on top of the card. Do the same for the sixteenth rest.

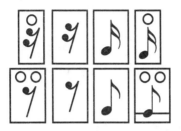

"How many *Magic Notes* would the eighth note equal?" Use the *Real Rhythm Cards* so they can compare the cards' relative lengths.

"It's worth two *Magic Notes,* isn't it? It's twice as big," the students will answer.

"Exactly right." Place two *Magic Notes,* on the eighth note card and two on the eighth note rest.

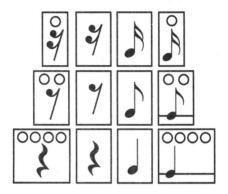

"How about the quarter note?" Let the students move the cards so they can figure out the answer.

"Four *Magic Notes!*" exclaims Andrew. They will feel confident since this is the obvious answer and they were able to figure it out.

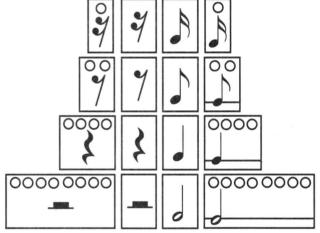

"Are you noticing that each note is worth twice as much as the note below it?"

"Yes. Yes."

"All right then, what are the half note and rests worth?"

"Easy," they'll answer. "Eight *Magic Notes!*"

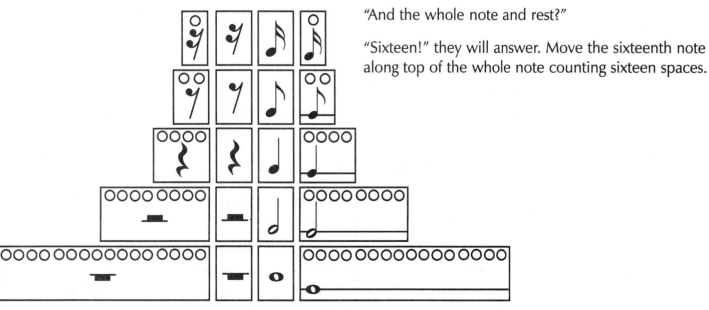

"And the whole note and rest?"

"Sixteen!" they will answer. Move the sixteenth note along top of the whole note counting sixteen spaces.

HEARING THE VALUES: "Let's clap and say the note names together. We can start with the whole note or "four". Ready, GO . . . FOUR . . OR . . OR . . OR. TOO . . OO. BLUE. JEL. HUCK." The students will laugh at the shortness of the HUCK (sixteenth note). Do this again so they can hear and see the relative value of the notes.

"Great. Let's say the rests now." Remember to whisper since you're saying rests.

"First the whole rest. Ready . . . REST . . . REST . . . REST . . . REST . . . REST . . . REST . . . REST . . . RES . . . RE " Again, the shortness of the sixteenth rest will tickle the students. This is important that they hear and feel the difference in the value of the notes.

If you have tone blocks, use them to teach the students how to play the notes at their exact value. Demonstrate by playing the note, then touching the key with your finger to stop the sound at exactly the right moment. Also play the notes and let them guess what you played. Be exact.

CONVERTING TO GOLD COINS: "That's a lot of Magic Notes. Let's say we exchange *Magic Notes* for *Gold Coins*. Four *Magic Notes* equal one *Gold Coin*." Help the students make the conversion. It will be much easier to see values now.

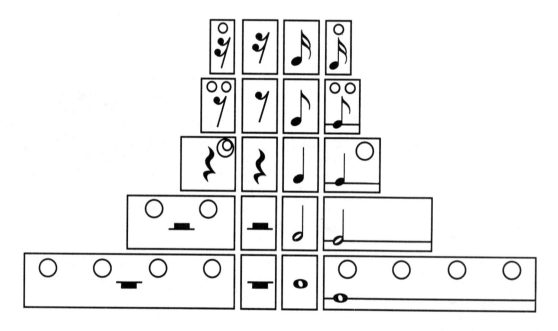

MAKING CHANGE: To check that the understanding is absolutely clear, ask them a few questions by comparing the value of these note to money. Use a dollar bill (whole note), a fifty cent piece (half note) and a quarter (quarter note) to make this lesson more memorable.

Let the students match the money to the notes.

If you have time, go right into GAME 7-6: CARD CHART MIX-UP before playing GAME 7-5: CARD CHART COMPLETED. If there's no time, play it in another session after the students have practiced laying out the Card Chart.

Children are unpredictable. You never know what incon-
sistency they're going to catch you in next.

Franklin Jones

GAME 7-5: CARD CHART COMPLETED

OBJECTIVE:
This game adds the other notes and rests to the Card Chart. It's all right to teach only some of the notes and rests in each session.

IN BRIEF:
Students use the *Real Rhythm Cards* and their understanding of the basic notes to figure out the values of note combinations.

AGES:
Elementary and older

MATERIALS:
1) *Notes & Rests Cards*
2) *Real Rhythm Cards*
3) *Magic Notes*
4) *Gold Coins*

REPETITIONS:
Repeat as many times as needed.

PROCEDURE:
Ask the students to make the Card Chart with all the cards, *Gold Coins* and *Magic Notes* that they have learned so far. Give them time to make any corrections.

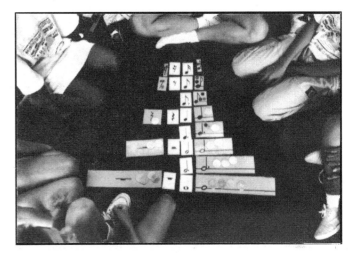

DOTTED NOTES: Lay out three *Real Rhythm Cards* and three *Notes & Rests Cards*. "Today let's add the dotted half note, the dotted quarter note, and the dotted eighth note to our Card Chart. Can you figure out how many *Gold Coins* and *Magic Notes* each of these are worth?"

To help with understanding, use the *Real Rhythm Cards*.

<u>EIGHTH NOTE CARDS:</u> The next cards to add to the Card Chart are those with eighth notes. Say the rhythms with a steady pulse to help the students hear where they fit into the Card Chart. Let them match *Magic Notes* and use the *Real Rhythm Cards* for comparison.

<u>TRIPLETS:</u> The *Real Rhythm Cards* will help the students see where these cards fit in, but I have a great story that can help them absolutely understand this concept.

Hold up the three cards in front of the students.

I use names which can be a boy's or a girl's name. Ideas are Lauren, Sandy, Chris and Pat. Or use the names of students in your class.

"Imagine that you and your best friend Sandy are invited to a birthday party.

"Your mom says she would be happy to drive both of you to the party and bring you home again. Off you go. Your mom drives, and you and Sandy sit <u>in the back seat</u> together." Point to the pair of eighth notes card.

"At the front door your mom says 'Bye, bye—remember to mind your manners, things like: Don't reach for the biggest piece of cake, don't pop all the birthday balloons.' You know, the usual stuff.

"It's a great party. You all have a lot of fun and eat lots of goodies. As you're getting ready to leave, Lauren, one of your friends needs a ride home. 'Sure, you say, I'll ask my mom.'

"Mom arrives and says, 'Sure, I can take all of you home in our car. Hop in.'

"Now, I would like you to finish this story for me. What happens to Lauren on the way home? You have two choices:

1) S/He sits in the back seat with you and Sandy, or

2) S/He runs along outside of the car holding your hand which you are sticking out the window."

The students will laugh at the second choice. "It is funny to imagine the second choice, isn't it? Well, here are the 'photographs' of this story." Point to the cards as you speak.

 "This is you and your friend riding in the back seat on the way to the party.

 "This is you and your friend riding in the back seat on the way home from the party with the new friend running outside the car holding your hand.

 "This is all three of you riding in the back seat together.

"You can see that a triplet is three eighth notes squeezed into the space of two eighth notes. Just like three friends squeezed into a back seat where two friends sat before."

<u>THE REMAINING CARDS:</u> Let the students figure out where to place these cards.

The completed Card Chart.

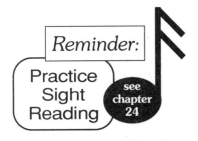

Reminder:

Practice Sight Reading

see chapter 24

GAME 7-6: CARD CHART MIX-UP

OBJECTIVE:
To have fun memorizing the note values

IN BRIEF:
The Card Chart is mixed up for students to fix. The timed version is terrific!

AGES:
Elementary and older

MATERIALS:
1) *Notes & Rests Cards*
2) *Real Rhythm Cards*
3) *Gold Coins*
4) *Magic Notes*

REPETITIONS:
Play two or three times in a session.

PROCEDURE:
Ask the students to lay out the Card Chart with all the cards, the *Gold Coins* and the *Magic Notes*.

Snap your fingers, the signal for them to close their eyes. Mix up everything. If you're confident that they know the note values, you can mix up many things. If you're not certain of their ability just yet, mix up just a few things.

Clap twice, the signal for them to open their eyes. "All right, can you fix it?"

"Oh, no! What a mess . . . Sure, this is easy . . . Oh, gosh, look at this! . . . Let's see, where can this coin go? Oh, yes." They will talk to themselves as they work. "All finished!

"Great work." Snap your fingers. This time, you may be able to make it a bit more difficult.

Clap your hands twice.

"Wow!" They will go right to work.

"Finished. Are we right?" A few things were overlooked. "Looks pretty good. I just see two things wrong."

Let them study the Card Chart until someone notices the errors and fixes them.

138

CARD CHART MIX-UP: TIMED

This game allows the students to have fun with the Card Chart, racing the clock to put it in order quickly. This is not to be a competition between students nor should it become disappointing in any way. If it isn't just loads of fun, then the students aren't quite ready for it.

It's more fun it you can move into this timed version without any explanation. Snap your fingers. Mix up the cards, notes and coins. Clap twice.

They will work together to finish.

"Did you know I was timing you while you did that?"

"Oh, no!" Someone may fall to the floor in mock shock.

"Care to know what your score is?" Smile at them.

"Tell us, please!" they will beg.

"I counted to myself the whole time you were working and I counted to . . . 52."

"Really? We can do it faster, can't we?" someone will say to the group. "May we try it again since we know we're being timed?"

"Please. Oh, please," they will beg in happy anticipation.

"Well," you can glance at your watch. "I guess we can for a few minutes."

"All right, everyone. Let's do our best."

Count to yourself in a steady, slow tempo at about one count per second.

As they're working you can tease them, "Did I tell you that for every wrong thing I find , five points are added to the total score?"

"Oh, no," they will cry out as they continue to work with excitement. Then . . . "Finished! What's our score?"

"Let me check it first . . . Hmmmm . . . Well, look at that, it's all correct. Excellent work."

"What's our score?"

"Your score is 42. Not bad. Really. That's a good score. But, would you like to try to beat it?"

"Yea! Let's do it."

Mix up the *Notes & Rests Cards, Gold Coins* and *Magic Notes* and off they will go. Each time they will improve and get a lower score. You can repeat this a few times, and even let one or two students see how fast they can do it. Ann and Meredith loved doing this.

It's great fun to be able to show how well they are able to make the Card Chart. Be certain to stop <u>before</u> they seem to tire even the slightest bit. This needs to be a high interest game.

VARIATION WITH PARENTS: The students mix up the Card Chart while the parents close their eyes. Once the chart is mixed up, the parents come and fix it.

However, it is essential that you tip off the parents before asking them to play this game with their children. <u>Ask them to make mistakes on purpose.</u>

The reason is this. If the students mix up the cards and the parents fix it easily and systematically, like adults have been trained to do, the students will be bored and not pay much attention. However, if the parents ham it up a lot and act as if this is the hardest thing they've come across since their last chemistry exam, the students will laugh with glee feeling that they have stumped their parents.

This approach also saves face for a parent that has been trying to keep up with lessons, but can't quite understand all this "rhythm math" or a dad who is enjoying a rare chance to come to class and doesn't have a clue what's going on.

To illustrate: We played this game in my own daughter's class one fall when she was seven years old. When it was time for the parents to fix the chart, I joined the other moms and stopped being the teacher for a moment. I acted as if I was as confused as the next parent . . . wondering out loud where this card or that coin went. Well, she was rolling on the floor with excitement (along with everyone else in her class, by the way) that she had fooled me. Even though she knew that I knew this stuff backwards and upside down, she unquestioningly and gleefully accepted my role as a confused player.

GAME 7-7: WAR WITH *NOTES AND RESTS CARDS*

OBJECTIVE:
To practice knowing notes and rests values

IN BRIEF:
Students play the old favorite card game "War", except *Notes & Rests Cards* are used instead of the familiar king, queen, ace, etc. This game is enjoyed by all age groups and can be played after the students have learned only the basic rhythm cards as well as throughout their study until they know all the *Notes & Rests Cards*.

AGES:
Elementary and older

MATERIALS:
Notes and Rest Cards

REPETITIONS:
Play for as much time as you have!

PROCEDURE:

"Would you like to play WAR using these *Notes & Rests Cards?*"

Divide the students into two teams. Each team will have its own stack of cards, and players will take turns drawing from the same stack during the game. Ask the teams to sit so they are facing each other. Place the cards face down between them.

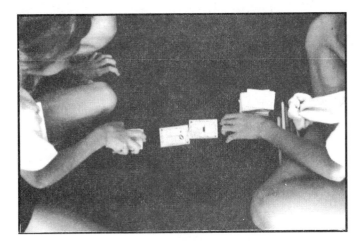

One person from each team turns over the top card and places it on the rug. Whoever has the higher value wins both cards.

The won cards are quickly pushed aside into a pile near the winning team. If the cards are the same value, then there is war! The next card is placed face down then the next one face up.

"Megan and Kevin have a double war!"

"Megan has a whole rest and Kevin has an eighth note. Who wins?"

The students will really enjoy this game and probably not need too much help from you. Tell them that it's not important to collect the most cards. This is just a game of chance. If one team's pile gets too small, you can take some from the other teams.

Someone may look at you strangely as if to say, "Hey, we won those cards."

You can answer back, "You don't need all those cards, do you?"

Allow them to enjoy the play itself and they will have fun.

OBJECTIVE:
To practice note and rest values

IN BRIEF:
Students trade in cards for the correct amount of *Gold Coins* and *Magic Notes.*

AGES:
Elementary and older

MATERIALS:
1) *Notes & Rests Cards*
2) *Gold Coins* - 54 needed (substitute if necessary)
3) *Magic Notes*

REPETITIONS:
Once through both sets of cards in a session

PROCEDURE:
Stack the *Gold Coins* and *Magic Notes* near you.

Pass out one card to each student. They are to figure out how much their card is worth and ask you for the correct amount of *Gold Coins* and/or *Magic Notes.*

"I have a whole note, so may I have four *Gold Coins*?"

"I have a sixteenth rest. Let's see — that's worth one *Magic Note.*"

Play continues with another round of cards until you have used the whole deck.

When I was younger, I could remember anything, whether it had happened or not.

Mark Twain

THIRDS ARE ONE MORE THAN SECONDS

O nce students gain a little maturity and know the letters of the regular musical alphabet, A B C D E F G, it's time to expand to thirds. Since much of our music is based on Tertian harmony (chords built by thirds), thirds are a vital part of any literate musician's vocabulary. Thirds are easy to learn since they are just a way to rearrange the alphabet.

Students who are comfortable with thirds will have a distinct advantage when learning to spell various kinds of triads and seventh chords. When thirds are automatic, it's easier to concentrate on the correct accidental(s). Analyzing the harmonic structure of music will involve just a mere reshuffling of the note letters to spell thirds.

Once thirds are learned, it's easy to move to other intervals, fourths, fifths, sixths and sevenths. This will help in remembering the notes on the staff and reading music. The staff will be friendly to a student who is comfortable moving the musical alphabet through all sizes of intervals.

Have fun with the games in this chapter. Not only will students learn thirds and other intervals, you will find their concentration and abilities growing by leaps and bounds as they master these fascinating alphabet games. Their minds will become quick, accurate and relaxed.

GAMES IN THIS CHAPTER

GAME 8-1: LEARNING THIRDS

OBJECTIVE:
To teach the concept of thirds

IN BRIEF:
Students change a set of *Alphabet Cards* from seconds, A B C D E F G to thirds, A C E G B D F.

AGES:
Early elementary and older

MATERIALS:
Alphabet Cards - 2 sets, 2 colors
Step 3: One set for each student

REPETITIONS:
Once through each step in a session. One or more steps may be repeated in later classes.

PROCEDURE:
By now the familiar *Alphabet Cards* are like old friends and have many happy associations. Students feel secure learning with them and will welcome new, intriguing games.

<u>STEP ONE</u>: Lay out one set of *Alphabet Cards*, A B C D E F G. As with all games, keep verbal explanations brief and to the point.

"Today you are going to learn about thirds. They are easy." Point to the A card.

"This is the first card." Point to the B, "And this is the second card." Point to the C. "This is the third card."

Pointing to the A and C cards as you speak, say, "If we move from the first card to the third card, this is a third. The third after A is C." Give them a moment to think about this.

Continue to point to the cards as you talk. You will know if they understand this concept if you pause, giving them a chance to say the answer before you say it. "The third above C is . . . E. Good. This third above E is . . . G."

"You are smart today! Can you study these cards and figure out what the third after G is? Remember, thirds are every other card."

"I know, it's A!"

"Close. Anyone else have an answer?"

"It's B."

"Yes. Megan is right. It is B."

Continue letting them study the cards, figuring out what the third is after and before each letter. You can also use the example that thirds are like counting by twos: 2 4 6 8 10 etc. or 1 3 5 7 9 11 etc.

<u>STEP TWO</u>: "Let's turn the seconds alphabet into a thirds alphabet." Say the letters as you move the cards.

145

Slide the A card down beneath the row of cards.

Next slide down the C.

Then the E . . . then the G . . . then B, D and F can then be moved out to the end, one card at a time.

All the cards will now be in thirds order.

"Anyone like to try this?" Eager hands will shoot up in the air, ready to take on this new challenge. Let each student have a turn in this group situation so you know that this concept of thirds is understood.

STEP THREE: Pass out a set of *Alphabet Cards* to each student. Ask them spread out around the room. At their own pace, they may move *Alphabet Cards* from seconds into thirds.

STEP FOUR: Bring everyone back into the group as you collect the cards. "Let's practice thirds another way." Snap your fingers so they will close their eyes. Lay out two sets of cards in seconds, alternating the colors. One set is turned face up, the other set face down.

Clap your hands twice for them to open their eyes. One at a time, point to a card that is turned face down, giving the students time to think of the answer. After they call out the correct letter, turn the card over.

It's fine to have a little fun with the game. Add some suspense and tease them a bit. For example:

Touch the back of the A card.

"A," they answer.

Begin to turn the card over, then stop. "Are you sure?" "Yes . . . no, it's B. No, no, it's A. It's got to be A!"

Every student will be bursting to see what the card is. Turn it over. "It's A. I knew it was!"

Continue pointing to the other cards. A random sequence is fine.

146

OBJECTIVE:
To help the students memorize thirds

IN BRIEF:
Students say the cards as the teacher tosses them down, one at a time in thirds order. This game moves at a very fast pace. A fun variation like "find the pea under the walnut shell" is played.

AGES:
Early elementary and older

MATERIALS:
Alphabet Cards - one set

REPETITIONS:
May be played for 5-10 minutes and repeated in later sessions.

PROCEDURE:
Prepare the *Alphabet Cards* by arranging them in thirds with A on the top. Hold the cards close to you throughout the game so the students can't see them. Explain that you want them to say the letter on the card as you toss it down on the rug. All letters should face the students. "Please say the cards with me."

STEP ONE: Toss down the A card and say "A" as it hits the rug.

Place the card back in your hand. This time, toss down A and then C, saying the letters out loud. "A . . . C . . . Good!"

Return A and C to your hand. Now toss down A, C and E.

Put them back in your hand. Continue to toss down cards, adding one card at a time until all seven cards have been played. It helps a lot to practice just G B D F. If anyone seems confused or tongue-tied, repeat before moving on.

STEP TWO: To keep things interesting, toss the cards face down, but continue to say the letters out loud.

Point to one card at a time, asking the students to name the letter. If you point to the cards in order, this will be easy. But it will be more fun to point to the cards out of order, only don't make it so hard that they miss.

STEP THREE: Play TOSS DOWN a few times with all seven cards. Without warning, toss the cards face down as the students say them. Turn one card face up.

Make certain everyone is watching you, then move a few cards so A isn't the first card anymore.

Point to the cards as before, one at a time, out of order, letting the students tell you the names. Turn the cards face up as they give you the answers. They will love the challenge of this game and pay close attention. Play the game so that they are able to answer correctly.

Trickier: As they become good at this, you will not need to leave a card face up. This becomes similar to that old time puzzler of "finding a small pea under three walnut shells".

Toss down all the cards face down on the rug as the students say the thirds with you. Without turning any cards over, move the A card to the end of the row, after F. Make certain the students are watching you.

Now move the C card to the end, after A. Then move the E card to the end, after C.

"Oh, no! Let's see, the A used to be there . . . I know, that's the G card at the beginning. . . . No, it's over here!" The students will talk among themselves.

If you really want to see if they are on their toes, move the E card back to the beginning.

"All right, which card is this?" Point to somewhere in the middle of the row.

"D!"

Point to the cards and let them answer. They should do fairly well. It's a lot of fun!

You can make it harder or easier, depending on the students' abilities. Reminder, make it only as hard as they can figure out, otherwise it won't be fun, interesting or appropriate for learning.

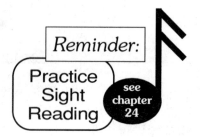

Reminder:

Practice Sight Reading

see chapter 24

GAME 8-3: EARLIER FAVORITES

OBJECTIVE:
Students practice thirds with the familiar games used to learn seconds

IN BRIEF:
Games from Chapters 1 & 2 are enjoyed as students practice thirds. Since the procedure is easy, they can focus completely on remembering thirds.

AGES:
Elementary and older

MATERIALS:
Alphabet Cards

REPETITIONS:
Your choice!

PROCEDURE:
Students will enjoy playing these familiar games again. Feel free to choose ones you like.

GAME 8-3-1. FIX THE ORDER

IN BRIEF:
Students fix a mixed-up set of *Alphabet Cards*.

GAME 8-3-2. WHAT'S MISSING?

IN BRIEF:
Students guess which alphabet card is missing.

GAME 8-3-3. SNAKE!

IN BRIEF:
Students lay out long rows of *Alphabet Cards*.

GAME 8-3-4. VARIATIONS ON SNAKE!

IN BRIEF:
Snakes start on any letter and backwards.

GAME 8-3-5. PICK A CARD

IN BRIEF:
Students randomly draw cards then lay them out in order, one card at a time.

GAME 8-3-7. ARE THESE THREE RIGHT?

IN BRIEF:
Students fix three sets of three *Alphabet Cards* each.

GAME 8-3-8: FINE
IN BRIEF:
With their own set of *Alphabet Cards*, students lay out cards as fast as possible.

GAME 8-3-6. AFTER AND BEFORE

IN BRIEF:
Students add the card after and the card before the one laid down by the teacher.

GAME 8-3-9: THIRDS SCRABBLE

IN BRIEF:
One by one, many sets of *Alphabet Cards* are laid on the floor to form short thirds sequences. Although cards may be added at any place, they must read either up or across.

GAME 8-4: WIN A TRIAD

OBJECTIVE:
To provide a new twist for practicing thirds

IN BRIEF:
Together, students build triads. Whoever places the fifth gets the root and third. The fifth becomes the root of the new triad. Colors add excitement.

AGES:
Elementary and older

MATERIALS:
Alphabet Cards - Three sets, three colors
Variation: *Alphabet Cards* - six sets, three colors

REPETITIONS:
Play for 5 - 10 minutes.

PROCEDURE:
Deal out all the cards, but keep one as the root for the first triad. Everyone might not have the same number of cards, which is all right.

The players may hold their cards as if they were playing a real card game or spread them out on the floor.

Place the extra card in the center of the rug. "This is the root of our triad." Explain that the next step is to add the third and the fifth.

You can call out the color or if a young sibling or a dad is present, s/he might enjoy playing this role.

Let's say that the root was a yellow A. The caller says "Green."
Whoever has the green C should put it down next to the yellow A.

Pink is called next. The player holding the pink E places it next to the green C.

Whoever put out the fifth, the pink E, wins the triad. S/he scoops up the root and third and puts them in with his or her other cards. The pink E is moved over to the left a bit and becomes the new root.

And so the game continues, at a fast pace, as root, third and fifth are tossed down, then grabbed up. The caller may say any of the three colors, even all of the same color. If colors are called out too quickly students will begin to think of the color first and not practice their thirds as well.

If a student uses up all his or her cards, you may take a few away from players who have the most cards. This way everyone can stay in the game.

When time is up, call out "Last round — winner take all". This round the player with the fifth collects all three cards, or the whole triad.

Compliment all the students on their good game. It's not necessary to call attention to who has the most cards, or even let the students have time to count their cards. Remember, everyone is a winner.

VARIATION: WIN A TRIAD II

This game is just like WIN A TRIAD I except it is played with six sets of cards, two of each color. This creates the added challenge of getting the right card down first. This game is excellent for older students and larger groups.

Students are quick with this game, but it may take a moment or two to look through all the cards in their hands. It helps if the colors aren't called out too quickly. Give the players a chance to look through their cards for the right third. Then call out a color and the right card will be tossed down quickly. The game is more exciting this way.

(If players begin tossing down any card in hopes of having it be the right one, simply say that wrong cards will be taken out of play.)

VARIATION: Use four cards instead of three and make 7th chords. Or play with five cards and build 9th chords. Call them by name. Build them ascending and descending.

When students become more advanced, remember this game and play it with accidentals. What fun for the mind!

Who takes the child by the hand, takes the mother by the heart.

Danish Proverb

OBJECTIVE:
To practice thirds

IN BRIEF:
The teacher shows everyone a card. Students place the third after it face down on the rug. Teacher calls out, "Show me" and everyone turns over his or her card. This game shouldn't be missed. The procedure can be applied to learning many concepts. It's a well liked game, but a bit like a test so students will be "exposed" if they play wrong cards. Play it when you're certain everyone is ready.

AGES:
Elementary and older

MATERIALS:
Alphabet Cards - one set for you and for each student

REPETITIONS:
5 - 10 sets per session

PROCEDURE:
Give each student a set of *Alphabet Cards* and keep one for yourself. Take out one of your cards and place it face up on the rug. Let's say it's an A.

"All right, look through your cards and find the third after A. Place that card face down on the rug in front of you."

Wait until everyone has a card down on the rug. "Ready? Show me."

"You're right!" Continue placing a card down and calling out SHOW ME. This is fun and they feel confidence when they see all the correct answers.

SHOW ME can also be played by asking the students to put down the third before your letter.

OBJECTIVE:
To teach the other intervals

AGES:
All ages

IN BRIEF:
Students arrange *Alphabet Cards* in seconds, in a big circle. Teacher calls out a root and an interval. Students place their hands over the correct cards. The game has a clever twist similar to "Simon says".

MATERIALS:
Alphabet Cards, one set for each student

REPETITIONS:
After the circle is made, play for 5-10 intervals.

PROCEDURE:
Ask the students to stand close together touching backs. They may sit down as you give each one a set of cards. Give different colors to players who are sitting next to each other.

Ask them to lay out their cards in seconds starting with C.

If they have trouble making their circle round, let them step out of it so they can see how to fix it.

"I'm going to call out a letter . . . the root. Put your left hand on that card. Next I'll call out an interval. Move your right hand so it's over, but not touching, the correct card. When I say GO, call out the letter and slap the card.

"If you'd like, we can play this like 'Simon says'. That means if you slap your card and say the third before I say GO, you have to sit out of the circle for one round. Would you like to?"

"Sure - sounds fun!" Be sure to keep the mood lighthearted.

"Let's try a sample play. A . . ." Pause for them to put their left hands over the A card. "Third above . . . GO!"

"C!" they call out as they slap the cards.

Call out different roots and different intervals. Progressing through each interval in order, they will be able to figure out the intervals by themselves without any explanation.

Descending intervals are just as easy. Can you tell this one?

OBJECTIVE:
To practice intervals so students become better readers

IN BRIEF:
Students place the *Bingo Dots* to create intervals with notes printed on the card.

AGES:
Elementary and older

MATERIALS:
1) *Bingo Cards*
2) *Bingo Dots* - face side
3) *One Staff Board*
4) *Clefs Puzzle*
5) *Notes With Letters*
6) Advanced - *Mini Sharps and Flats*
7) *Cardboard Keyboards*
8) *Alphabet Kids*

REPETITIONS:
5-7 intervals in a session

PROCEDURE:
Let the students select one or two *Bingo Cards* and four *Bingo Dots* per card. "This is a very simple game," you can say. "I'll call out an interval and you put your *Bingo Dots* on your card so that each of your notes forms that interval. It's easy. Ready for the first interval?   Please, a second above."

Place your notes on the staff to show a sample of a second above. You should use the notes with the faces showing.

The goal of this game is for the students to figure out the intervals without pointing to the lines and spaces and counting, "One, two, three, four, five, six — a sixth," but to recognize the intervals at sight. Encourage them in this direction.

"Let's do seconds." Do ascending seconds first, then descending seconds. They can help you figure out the other intervals.

If there isn't enough space on a card for the interval you request, the student can simply put the *Bingo Dot* face up on the printed note.

Switch cards several times.

<u>Using music:</u> Invite them to get music books. They may look for intervals and copy them onto their *Bingo Cards.* This helps them feel comfortable with the music and make the transition from these games to actual music.

An important variation:
1. Ask students to write out four different intervals of their choice on their cards.

2. While the "owner" of the card points, let another student identify the intervals.

"A second up. A fifth down. A fourth down. A second up."

One at a time let students carefully carry their *Bingo Card* up to the piano and set it on the bench. "Mary, could you please play your intervals for us? First play them with your right hand as if they were all in the treble clef."

Mary identifies each interval then finds the notes on the piano and plays them. The other students gain much from watching, noticing if Mary finds the right notes.

"Now, can you pretend these are all bass clef notes, Mary? Please play them with your left hand."

After we did this game with a class of 7 - 9 year olds one of the mothers complimented me on a clever game. "They really did some important thinking, didn't they?" She was very pleased with the concept the game taught and how smoothly the students caught on.

This game will help students recognize intervals more easily and form patterns for playing them.

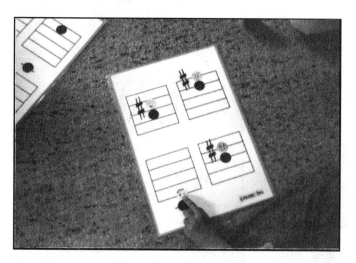

<u>Using accidentals:</u> When students understand how to spell the various intervals you can be more specific in your requests. Such as, a major third up.

<u>For pianists:</u> To illustrate the concept, place two *Alphabet Kids* on a *Cardboard Keyboard* to represent the intervals on the *Bingo Cards.*

Reminder:
Practice Sight Reading
see chapter 24

NOTES ON THE STAFF
DICTATION PART 2

At this point, students are comfortable hearing patterns and writing them with their *Number Slates*. They can also move *Magic Notes* around on the staff in various patterns.

Now they are ready to write short patterns on their own. We use grand staff *Dictation Slates* and brightly colored, movable *Magic Notes* rather than printed staff paper. It can be time consuming to repeatedly erase and rewrite, not to say how stupid you begin to feel. Sometimes in college dictation class I would have to erase so many times that I almost rubbed a hole in the paper clear through to my desk! **Music Mind Game's** magnetic *Magic Notes* can correct instantly and there is no reminder of a past mistake . . . a real aid to boosting self-esteem.

The *Melodic Bingo Cards* are versatile and fun. Two levels of difficulty allow students a chance to challenge their musical minds and succeed as their ears become more discriminating.

Playing dictation games will quiet a class that may be too excited. It's a calming experience to listen to a short melodic pattern and move *Magic Notes* around on a *Dictation Slate*. Without much interaction between students, everyone stays quiet and respectful of each other's space.

Note: One suggestion about passing out the materials. I like to toss the *Dictation Slates* on the floor so they slide. It's fun for the students to reach for the one they want. However, if you want to quiet a class down, walk around the circle holding the *Dictation Slates* for each student to take. Moving calmly and making pleasant eye contact with each student will help quiet everyone.

A fun way to pass out the *Magic Notes* is to stick the magnetic *Magic Wand* in the container, then drop the *Magic Notes* into the students' open hands. Many *Magic Notes* will spill and roll all over. They laugh and occupy themselves picking up their *Magic Notes* as you continue to pass around the circle. Try it!

I heard once that in some (perhaps imagined!) country, it is not considered improper for students to look on someone else's paper during an exam. The reasoning was this: if allowed to look, the student may be able to learn the answer. If not allowed to look, understanding may be forever elusive.

I thought this made sense . . . certainly from the student's point of view . . . so I set up dictation games in a similar way. Everyone sits on the floor, in full view of each other. Although they are encouraged to do their own work, they are free to glance around at each other's *Dictation Slates* for reassurance.

"If you think your answer is correct, even though everyone else's may be different, then keep your answer," I tell them. "I remember several times when only one student had the correct answer. It takes courage, but always believe in yourself."

The games in Chapter 5: I CAN HEAR IT - DICTATION PART 1 used middle C since it is a comfortable singing range for most voices. When using the *Dictation Slates* and *Melodic Bingo Cards*, use G, a fifth above middle C. These five notes contain no sharps or flats and don't require any ledger lines, thus making the process easier.

Most of the dictation games in this chapter continue to deal with pitch only. GAME 9-7: MORE NUMBERS combines melody and rhythm.

The games in Chapter 16: EXPANDING EARS - DICTATION PART 3 are a continuation of the games in this chapter and involve slightly more advanced ideas. They're fun and not difficult if preceded by these games.

Do feel free to adapt and use these dictation games to suit your students. Try to include dictation exercises in your classes on a regular basis. Each week is best.

GAMES IN THIS CHAPTER

GAME 9-1: STAFF DICTATION

OBJECTIVE:
To introduce melodic dictation

IN BRIEF:
Students work together using the *One Staff Board* and *Magic Notes*.

AGES:
Kindergarten, elementary and middle school

MATERIALS:
1) Piano
2) *One Staff Board*
3) *Clefs Puzzle*
4) *Notes With Letters* (blank side)
5) *Ledger Line Sheets*

REPETITIONS:
Pattern may weave in and out for 5-10 repetitions.

PROCEDURE:
Place the *One Staff Board* in front of the students and let them place the clefs correctly. Place the *Notes With Letters* (blank side) and *Ledger Line Sheets* nearby.

You may choose to let the students work together writing patterns or take turns around the circle. If turns are taken, make certain your melodies suit the ability of each student, so as not to put anyone on the spot.

Write this on the staff and play it for them.

"I'm going to play that again but with one change. Listen for the change, then we'll write it. David, would you like the first turn?"

"Great, David. Please don't take the notes off yet. I'm going to play this new pattern with another change."

"David, what good ears you have today!"

Repeat until you feel they understand the concept.

GAME 9-2: DICTATION SLATES

OBJECTIVE:
To let students write dictation patterns on the staff, using individual *Dictation Slates*

IN BRIEF:
Students use a *Cardboard Keyboard* to play along with stepwise patterns being played on the piano. They write the patterns on individual *Dictation Slates* using *Magic Notes*.

AGES:
Kindergarten and early elementary

REPETITIONS:
5-8 patterns in one session. May be played for years using increasingly difficult patterns.

MATERIALS:
1) Piano
2) *Dictation Slates*
3) *Magic Notes*
4) *Cardboard Keyboards*
5) *Grand Staff Board*
6) *Clefs Puzzle*
7) *Notes With Letters* - blank
8) *Number Slates* - Young students will benefit from first writing the pattern on *Number Slates* and then on *Dictation Slates*.

PROCEDURE:
Let each student choose a *Dictation Slate*. Pass out *Magic Notes* . Let them place the clefs correctly on the *Grand Staff Board*.

161

Let each student select a *Cardboard Keyboard*.

Seat yourself at the piano with the students sitting around you on the floor. Ask them to move until you can easily see everyone's *Slate*.

It's important that these patterns be **played two times** before the students try to write them. It's not unusual for someone to try to write as you play or to begin to write after hearing a pattern played just once. Two playings makes the memory more accurate.

The *Cardboard Keyboards* help students visualize and feel how the notes are moving. If you don't have keyboards, students can use their right hands to play on the rug as you play the dictation pattern on the piano.

"G is for free," you can tell them. This means that the starting note is G. They can prepare their staffs by putting a *Magic Note* on the second line G.

"Two playings. Everyone ready? As I play the pattern, make a tape recording in your mind that you can silently play back to yourself to help you write it."

Play a pattern such as 1 2 3 4 5 5 5. Play it again.

They will begin to write.

Allow them to work on their own. Remain quiet. After a few moments, play the pattern again. They should follow along comparing what they have written to what you play. Some students will make corrections while others sit back confidently. If anyone is still working, play the pattern again.

"Let's check it. Follow along with your finger." Play the pattern for them.

"Great. You all got it. Very good! Clear your *Slates*. Remember, G's for free. Are you ready?" Play a new pattern such as 1 2 3 3 4 5.

Continue this same procedure for several more patterns. Make certain everyone can write the patterns you play.

This game can be repeated in many sessions for <u>several years</u>, depending on the age of your students. Here are sample patterns.

When stepwise movement becomes easy, it's time to introduce skips — the next game.

OBJECTIVE:
To introduce skips in dictation patterns

IN BRIEF:
Students write out the pattern 1 2 3 4 5 4 3 2 1 on their *Dictation Slates*. As the teacher plays the pattern, a note is left out. The students hear the "space" and put a finger on the missing note.

AGES:
Elementary

MATERIALS:
1) Piano
2) *Dictation Slates*
3) *Magic Notes*

REPETITIONS:
3-4 patterns

PROCEDURE:
After doing a few regular, step-wise dictation patterns, play this for the students to write on their *Dictation Slates*.

"This game is called PUT YOUR FINGER ON IT. I'm going to play this pattern except I'll leave out a note. Follow along as I play and put your finger on the note I skip. I will play the pattern just once. This should be easy for you. It sounds as if there's a big hole where the missing note was." Play several patterns for them. This should be easy.

Without warning, leave out two notes. If they can do it, they are ready for the next game, which you can do in the same session.

Every child is an artist. The problem is how to remain an artist once he grows up.

Pablo Picasso

164

GAME 9-4: TAKE AWAY

OBJECTIVE:
To practice many skips.

IN BRIEF:
This game is so popular, you should use it to close every dictation session. Students write 1 2 3 4 5 4 3 2 1 on their *Dictation Slates*. The pattern is played with one note missing. Students remove the note from their *Slates*. The pattern is played again, leaving out an additional note which the students remove. On each playing one more note is missing until none are left. The trick is for the students to remove their notes in the same order as the examples they hear.

AGES:
All ages

MATERIALS:
1) Piano
2) *Dictation Slates*
3) *Magic Notes*

REPETITIONS:
Do the whole sequence just once.

PROCEDURE:
Play the following pattern and ask the students to write it on their *Dictation Slates*.

"This game is similar to PUT YOUR FINGER ON IT except that I'm going to continue taking away notes. Rather than putting your finger on the *Magic Notes*, just take them away. I will play each pattern only once. See if you can end up with the same note as I do. Everyone understand?"

The students must concentrate during the whole sequence. Play each pattern only once. Even if someone asks you to play a pattern again . . . don't. They can try to catch up.

While you play, watch a good student's *Dictation Slate* to help you keep track of the notes you are omitting.

It's important that the students are successful at following the sequence of notes you play.

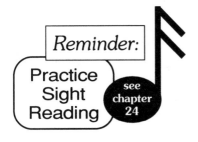

Reminder:
Practice Sight Reading
see chapter 24

A sample round could be like this:

1.

2.

3.

4.

5.

6.

7.

8.

9.

When you don't play anything, they will look up at you. You can smile and make a motion that it's all over and they will take off their last note. "Good game!" If some students didn't get all the notes, that's all right. In later sessions, they will improve.

VARIATION: As students become proficient taking away notes, use the pattern 1 2 3 4 5 4 3 2 1 2 3 4 5:

GAME 9-5: HEAR ANY THIRDS?

OBJECTIVE:
To develop students' ability to recognize thirds and triad patterns

IN BRIEF:
Dictation patterns consist of patterns with skips of thirds and/or triads.

AGES:
Elementary

MATERIALS:
1) Piano
2) *Dictation Slates*
3) *Magic Notes*
4) *Cardboard Keyboards*

REPETITIONS:
3 - 5 patterns per session

PROCEDURE:
This game is a natural transition after the previous game, TAKE AWAY.

As students become more proficient in taking dictation, they will naturally begin to group the notes into patterns. Although it may not be exactly like this, when they hear 1 2 3 4 5 4 they should think "up 5 then back down one note". Or when they hear 1 2 3 3 3 2 1 1 1 they should think "up to 3, played three times, back down and 1 three times."

This game helps them to hear thirds or triad patterns alone or mixed into stepwise patterns.

Sample patterns:

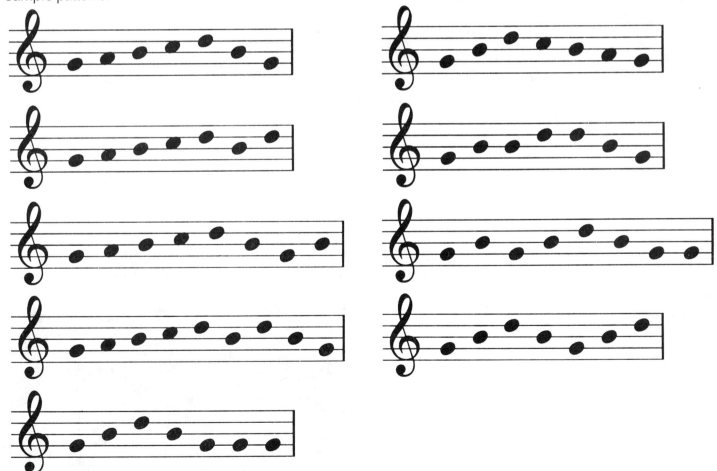

167

GAME 9-6: WRITE MINE

OBJECTIVE:
This game gives students a chance to play melodic patterns for each other.

IN BRIEF:
Students assume the role of the teacher and play dictation patterns for each other.

AGES:
Elementary

MATERIALS:
1) Piano or students' instruments
2) *Dictation Slates*
3) *Magic Notes*

REPETITIONS:
4-5 students each get one turn

PROCEDURE:
Let students take turns playing patterns for each other.

"Who would like to be the teacher today?" I've found that they usually make the patterns too hard and/or play them too fast. Remind them that they must be able to remember it and play it several times.

One summer I was assigned to teach a class of 11 flute students at a workshop in Utah. On the first day of class they opened their cases and begin putting their flutes together.

"I'd love to hear you play, but I don't think I can teach you anything about playing the flute. I've been asked to help you become better readers."

Because of a mix-up, we held class in the hallway, and there wasn't a piano for dictation.

So I invited students to take turns playing patterns. It was most successful and truly opened up the concept of reading music for them. I enjoyed hearing the lovely flute tones, and they were so pleased to be able to teach me a little about how to play the flute.

So, if it's available to you, involve other instruments in the study of dictation.

GAME 9-7: MORE NUMBERS

OBJECTIVE:
To add high 6 7 8 and low 7 6 5 to the five note patterns and to introduce descending patterns that begin on a note other than G

IN BRIEF:
Students write patterns that may dip below tonic or above dominant. Descending five note patterns may begin on the dominant. *Mini Sharps and Flats* are used for accidentals.

AGES:
Elementary and older

MATERIALS:
1) Piano
2) *Dictation Slates*
3) *Magic Notes*
3) *Mini Sharps and Flats*

REPETITIONS:
5-6 per session

PROCEDURE:
As the students' abilities grow you can give them more challenges.

Often I play a dictation pattern on a level similar to one played the last time we had class. Then I ask, "Do you want the next pattern to be trickier or easier?"

"Trickier!" they smile. Then I make it just a bit harder, usually a little longer or a different twist to the notes.

"How about the next one?" I ask.

"Trickier!" I start the pattern like all the others, but make it incredibly difficult until they look up at me with fake panic on their faces.

"Just kidding," and I have a good laugh with them.

"All right, here's the real thing."

Without warning I begin on a note other than G, often D and play a descending passage: D C B A G G A. They will take the challenge and run with it.

It's important to play patterns that use the bass clef as well so their ears become accustomed to the low sounds, too.

Patterns that dip below G are excellent. It's fine to use F natural to awaken their ears to a modal sound.

Or I may play G A B A G F# G. If I play the F# I will have the mini sharps available. They feel advanced if they are adding accidentals to their dictation patterns.

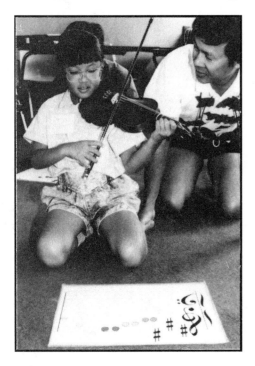

Violinists are comfortable in A major, so use patterns in this key.

Use patterns that expand into other key signatures or even contain patterns outside the major/minor modality. Be flexible and spontaneous — let the students' abilities guide you.

> If there is anything we wish to change in the child, we should first examine it and see whether it is not something that could be better changed in ourselves.
>
> *C. G. Jung*

OBJECTIVE:
This game helps train students to see patterns of notes as "melodic words"

IN BRIEF:
Students hear melodic patterns and find them on their *Melodic Bingo Cards.*

AGES:
Elementary and older

MATERIALS:
1) Piano or other instrument
2) *Melodic Bingo Cards* - side 1
3) *Magic Notes*

REPETITIONS:
Until each student has several bingos

PROCEDURE:
Let the students each choose a *Melodic Bingo Card* and pass out the *Magic Notes.*

"This game is simple. I'm going to play patterns for you to find on your cards. Everyone ready?" Play each pattern twice unless someone asks for it again.

As you progress through the game, watch the cards and play patterns so that all students find about the same number on their cards. It's possible to "fix" the game so that each student remains confident and enjoys finding patterns.

They may call out "bingo" when they have three patterns in a row in any direction. Continue playing until everyone has had several bingos. If you have time, continue until BLACK OUT, when all the spaces on the cards are filled.

GAME 9-9: I'VE HEARD THIS BEFORE

OBJECTIVE:

Combining melodic and rhythmic dictation, students write out short patterns from pieces they know.

IN BRIEF:

Students write melodies on their *Dictation Slates* and rhythms with the *Real Rhythm Cards*. Patterns are checked with the music.

AGES:

Elementary and older

MATERIALS:

1) Piano or student's instrument
2) *Dictation Slates*
3) *Magic Notes*
3) *Mini Sharps and Flats*
4) *Real Rhythm Cards*
5) *Blues* from *Blue Jello Rhythm Puzzle* (for bar lines)
6) Music books

REPETITIONS:

Several in a class session

PROCEDURE:

Pass out the *Dictation Slates*, *Magic Notes* and the *Mini Sharps and Flats*. If the class is small (six or so), just set the *Real Rhythm Cards* nearby. If the class is larger, have some do melody and some do rhythm. .

Choose a familiar phrase of music from a piece at the students' level of dictation. It can be from the beginning, middle or end of the piece. Give them the starting note.

If the whole class is writing the melody and the rhythm, let them write the melody on the *Slates* first, then move over to write the rhythm. They should choose the time signature and use the *Blues* as bar lines.

Since this is a new experience, they may need more time or a few extra playings.

If half the class did melodic dictation and the other half did rhythmic dictation, let them switch and check each other's work before checking their work in the music book.

Over the years these phrases can get as advanced as the students are able to handle.

This class chose an easy piece. Can you guess it? The answer is at the end of this chapter.

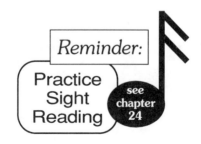

Reminder:
Practice Sight Reading
see chapter 24

OBJECTIVE:
To help students identify melodic patterns with simple rhythms. This game helps beginning readers.

IN BRIEF:
A few cards from several songs are spread out on the rug for the students to identify.

AGES:
Middle elementary

MATERIALS:
1) Piano
2) *Song Puzzle Cards*

REPETITIONS:
Until all the cards are played once

PROCEDURE:
Select several cards from each of the *Song Puzzle Cards* songs so there are 15 to 20 cards spread out on the floor, face up in the middle of the circle of students.

"Today we're going to play a game called CHICKEN SOUP.

"All right. Can you all sit like Lisa is . . . with your legs crossed and your hands on your knees? I'm going to play one of these cards. If you recognize which card it is, take your hands off your knees and quietly close them together and put them in your lap.

"I want you to do this instead of wildly raising your hands and screaming Me! me! I know which card it is! Pleeeeease!'"

This will bring a laugh and make the point if you imitate a frantic student who is dying to yell out the answer. And, by the way, once they begin playing this game, they will be very tempted to do just what I described.

"Here's the first measure. I will play it just once. Listen to the melody and the rhythm. As you know, both are important and can give you a clue to which card I played."

Play one card exactly as it's written. Use a steady tempo and play it in the correct octave. One tip: Don't look at the card you are playing (the students will notice). Instead, glance over all the cards, select one and keep glancing before you begin to play. The cards will be upside down to you . . . which makes it a little tricky.

As you play the students will scan the cards. Some will recognize it and close their hands happily. Remind everyone to stay quiet. If necessary, play the measure again.

Rather than calling on just one student, give everyone whose hands are closed a chance to say which card I played.

"Yes, that's the card! Joseph, would you turn it over please?"

"Everyone, hands on your knees please, here's the next card."

The first time this game was played many years ago, I was cooking chicken soup for dinner. The aroma spread throughout the house and was most tempting. In the middle of the game Vanessa said, "Ymmmmmmm, those yellow cards are the chicken."

"Yes," added Elizabeth, "the orange cards are the carrots."

"The green cards could be the parsley, Mrs. Yurko," smiled Vicki.

"What about the blue cards?" I thought I had them.

"Oh, silly. That's the pot!" they answered quickly.

We finished up the game and headed off to our suppers.

The next week they asked to play CHICKEN SOUP again.

"Chicken soup?" I asked, bewildered. "What's that?"

"You remember. The game with the chicken, carrot cards and the blue pot! Pleeeease . . . can we play it again?"

More than ten years later I played CHICKEN SOUP with a new group of students. As I tossed out the measure cards I explained why this game was called CHICKEN SOUP. They also thought the yellow cards were the chicken, the orange were the carrots and the green were the parsley. But their idea was to call the blue cards . . . blue noodles.

"We have BLUE JELLO - - why not have blue noodles?"

The piece in GAME 9-9: I'VE HEARD THIS BEFORE is *LIGHTLY ROW.*

GRAND STAFF NEIGHBORS

I n this chapter the students learn where A B D E F and G are found on the grand staff and the piano. These games are to be introduced after all or most of Chapter 6: GRAND STAFF C'S is mastered.

After playing the games in Chapters 1, 2 and 3, students know the musical alphabet and the basics of the staff, so they will find this chapter logical.

Once students can immediately identify the five C's on the grand staff, the remaining notes will be easier to learn. It will take less time to learn where the D's are. Learning B's will be even quicker. Since the students understand the relationship of notes on the staff, the other note names will fall into place. Interesting games will help students practice these notes.

Silly jingles are not needed to learn the notes.

Also, don't let your students count up the staff from a note they know to find out the name of a note they don't know. Master every note so they can instantly name it.

The last games in this chapter deal with helping violin and cello students relate notes on the staff to their instruments. If you teach another instrument, these charts can give you ideas.

PART TWO

10

175

GAMES
IN THIS
CHAPTER

GAME 10-1: A SECOND UP FROM C

OBJECTIVE:
To learn where D is on the grand staff and piano

IN BRIEF:
Using C as the reference, students learn that D is a second above.

AGES:
Early elementary

REPETITIONS:
Until you locate all the D's

MATERIALS:
1) *Grand Staff Board*
2) *Clefs Puzzle*
3) *Notes With Letters*
4) *Alphabet Cards* - one set
5) *Ledger Line Sheets*
6) Piano
7) *Alphabet Kids*
8) *Mini Notes*
9) *Dictation Slates*

PROCEDURE:
Spend a few minutes playing a game or two with the *Alphabet Cards* to refresh the students' memories that the second after C is D.

Place the *Grand Staff Board* in front of the students. Let them put the clefs, the five C's and the *Ledger Lines Sheets* on the staff.

"Great. Anyone have an idea where the note D is found on the staff?" They will enjoy the challenge of figuring out where all the D's are. Give them guidance only if they need it.

"Great. You found them all. Let's play PASS OUT." Pass out the *Notes* around the circle for students to put on the staff (GAME 6-2). Also mix up the *Notes* for them to fix.

KEYBOARD: Let them place the C and D *Alphabet Kids* on the piano.

Lay out notes on the staff in a particular order for them to take turns finding on the piano.

DICTATION SLATES: Let them practice placing C and D notes on their *Dictation Slates* using the *Mini Notes*.

Every person needs recognition. It is expressed cogently by the child who says, "Mother, let's play darts. I'll throw the darts and you say 'wonderful.'"

M. Dale Baugham

GAME 10-2: *GRAND STAFF CARDS* C'S AND D'S

OBJECTIVE:
To find C's and D's using the *Grand Staff Cards*

IN BRIEF:
Students look through *Grand Staff Cards* for all the C's and D's, placing them in order, then find them on the piano.

AGES:
Elementary and older

MATERIALS:
1) *Grand Staff Cards*
2) *Alphabet Kids*
3) Piano

REPETITIONS:
One time per session

PROCEDURE:
Pass out the *Grand Staff Cards*. Ask the students to spread out so they have room to play. "Can you find all the C's and the D's? Take your time and line them up neatly in front of you."

As they find their cards, help line them up so the C's and D's are arranged next to each other. There should be spaces for the notes they haven't learned yet. As students finish you can check their cards, tossing back any that are incorrect.

In later sessions, ask them to find only the D's.

KEYBOARD: Ask the students to line up at the piano. Arrange them so they can see the keyboard as they wait for their turns. Line up the *Alphabet Kids* on the music stand.

They take turns taking a *Grand Staff Card*, choosing the correct *Alphabet Kid* and finding it on the piano.

"Can you put this *Alphabet Kid* on the key that matches your staff card?"

GAME 10-3: PASS AROUND

OBJECTIVE:
To practice identifying C and D notes quickly

IN BRIEF:
Using the *Grand Staff Cards* like playing cards, each student is dealt one card per round. They quickly decide if it is a C or D. A system of counting unites the players.

AGES:
Elementary and older

MATERIALS:
1) *Grand Staff Cards* - one set
2) *Gold Coins*

REPETITIONS:
Several rounds per session

PROCEDURE:
Ask the students to sit near you on the floor. Shuffle the cards so the bass and treble clef cards are all mixed up.

"Let's find all the C and D cards. I'll pass the cards to you. Please put the C's in a pile here and the D's in a pile here. Any other notes go in a pile here. Ready? You'll each get one card."

Give them a moment to study their cards. They will put them in one of the piles.

Pass out one card each around the circle again. Give them a moment to think. Quick students will put their cards down fast.

Repeat until all the cards are in one of the piles.

Now it's time to figure up the score. Scoring is meant to be encouraging and motivational. "Let's see what our score is. Any cards in the wrong pile are worth a *Gold Coin*."

Go through the piles, checking the cards together. If you find a card in the wrong pile, hold it up for the students to identify. Put a *Gold Coin* in a pile for each incorrect card.

"Three points. Not too bad. Want to try again to see if you can get a lower score? Great. Use your minds well." Play another round as before.

"Let's check the cards and get our score. One card is in the wrong pile. One point. You all did better!" Put a *Gold Coin* in another pile next to the pile of three. Don't just add them in, but let the students see that they improved.

"One more time, please . . ." they may ask.

"Here we go again. Good luck." After this third round, check the cards together.

"No mistakes. No points. What a score! Great game today."

GAME 10-4: LET'S LEARN B

OBJECTIVE:
To learn B on the grand staff and piano

IN BRIEF:
Students locate all the B's on the staff and piano, relating them to the C's and D's they already know.

AGES:
Elementary

REPETITIONS:
Until you locate all the B's

MATERIALS:
1) *Grand Staff Board*
2) *Clefs Puzzle*
3) *Notes With Letters*
4) *Ledger Line Sheets*
5) *Alphabet Cards*
6) *Dictation Slates*
7) *Alphabet Kids*
8) *Mini Notes*
9) Piano

PROCEDURE:
Seat the students on the rug with the *Grand Staff Board* between the students and you. Let them place the clefs correctly.

Play a game or two with the *Alphabet Cards* to refresh their memories that the alphabet pattern is B C D.

Let them place the five C's and D's correctly. Point to a line or space one note below a C and ask, "Anyone have an idea what the name of this note is?" Your facial expression can be questioning and encouraging at the same time.

"I know. It's B." The students easily discovered the answer themselves.

"How right you are. Let's put the B's on."

Practice this several times.

Let them practice placing their *Mini Notes* on their *Dictation Slates*. They will enjoy dropping them and quickly arranging them. Or let them work in teams, mixing each other's up.

Before moving on to the next game in this chapter, play previous games until students are comfortable finding C, D and B.

181

GAME 10-5: I'D LIKE TO SELL A . . .

OBJECTIVE:
To practice naming C, D and B on the grand staff

IN BRIEF:
Each note is worth a different amount of *Magic Notes*. To identify the card passed to them, students sell the card to the teacher for the correct amount of *Magic Notes*.

AGES:
Elementary

MATERIALS:
1) *Grand Staff Cards* - one set
2) *Alphabet Cards* - one set
3) *Magic Notes*
4) *Gold Coins*

REPETITIONS:
Play once or twice in a session

PROCEDURE:
Explain that you are going to pass each of them a *Grand Staff Card* and they can sell their cards to you for *Magic Notes*.

Make a reference chart by laying out the *Alphabet Cards* and *Magic Notes* as you talk. "C's are worth one *Magic Note*. D's are worth two *Magic Notes* and B's are worth three *Magic Notes*."

"If you want to sell your card, tell me how many *Magic Notes* you should get. If your card isn't a B, C or D, just hand it back."

"However, if you can tell me the name of any new cards we haven't studied, A, E, F or G, since I think you're so clever, I'll give you a *Gold Coin*."

"Wow!" exclaims Heather. "Real gold. Can we keep it?"

"I bet you'd like that, wouldn't you, Heather? But, if you took all my gold, we'd have nothing to play with next time."

"Shucks," laments Heather.

"Everyone ready? Here are your cards." Pass out one card to each student. They will look at their card and identify the note.

"Please, give me two *Magic Notes*." Nathan hands me a D card and I give him two *Magic Notes*.

"I would like three *Magic Notes*, please." Maria gives me a B card.

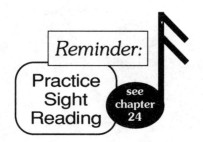

182

"May I have a *Gold Coin*, please? This is an E!" says an excited Beth. She's right, too.

And so the game continues until all the cards are used up.

NOTE: Play a variety of games until you are confident that the students can quickly and easily name B, C and D notes. Then you can introduce A, E, F and G in the same manner. Improvise new games of your own.

Here are students playing I'D LIKE TO SELL A . . . with all the notes.

GAME 10-6: ROW OF CARDS

OBJECTIVE:
To practice naming notes they are learning

IN BRIEF:
Students identify five cards using the *Bingo Dots.*

AGES:
Elementary

MATERIALS:
1) *Grand Staff Cards*
2) *Bingo Dots*

REPETITIONS:
Once through all the *Grand Staff Cards*

PROCEDURE:
Pass out a set of *Grand Staff Cards* to each student. Ask them to shuffle their cards then lay five of them in a row.

Using *Bingo Dots*, they place the correct note on each card. Watch for errors and without comment, simply remove the incorrect note.

Once all are correct, ask them to remove the *Bingo Dots*, set these five cards aside and line up five new ones. Repeat with enthusiasm until all the cards are used up.

GAME 10-7: FIND THIS NOTE

OBJECTIVE:
To match staff notes to the piano

IN BRIEF:
Taking turns, students match correct piano keys to their cards. Two "wild notes" add suspense and fun to the game.

AGES:
Elementary

MATERIALS:
1) *Grand Staff Cards* - one set
2) *Bingo Dots*
3) *Alphabet Kids*
4) Piano

REPETITIONS:
Once through the set of *Grand Staff Cards*

PROCEDURE:
Hold all the *Bingo Dots* in your hand and keep shaking them to thoroughly mix them up as if you're a lottery drum. Let two students pick one note each. These two notes are the "wild notes" and are placed at the middle of the piano on the music stand. The remaining *Bingo Dots* are put in a pile to one side of the piano.

Shuffle the cards. Standing in front of the piano, hold the cards so the first student can take the top card. S/he is to take the correct *Alphabet Kid* and place it on the correct key in the proper octave, then play the note.

If the student finds the note correctly, s/he is complimented and moves to the side. However, if the note was one the "wild notes", s/he takes a *Bingo Dot* from the pile. Or, if the student didn't find the note correctly, s/he takes a *Bingo Dot* from the pile. A student can receive only one *Bingo Dot* per turn.

When students first play the game, you can offer free assistance if there is any confusion. But soon, any assistance requires the student to take a *Bingo Dot* from the pile.

Students take turns selecting the top card, identifying it and playing the note. They will screech and laugh if they happen to draw a "wild note". Soon they will realize it's desirable to collect a small number of *Bingo Dots*, but because of the "wild notes", mistakes aren't so obvious and the game has this added fun.

This is a great game!

GAME 10-8: NATURAL HALF STEPS BC AND EF

OBJECTIVE:
To learn that BC and EF are natural half steps with no black note between them. This is especially useful for string players.

IN BRIEF:
Alphabet Kids BC and EF are placed on the keyboard.

AGES:
Open

MATERIALS:
1) *Alphabet Kids*
2) Piano

REPETITIONS:
Once is usually enough.

PROCEDURE:
Let the students practice placing the *Alphabet Kids* B, C, E and F on the keyboard in natural half step patterns.

You can play GAME 1-4: FIX THE ORDER, GAME 6-2: PASS OUT or GAME 2-3: FINE to help them remember.

GAME 10-9: *ALPHABET CARD* FINGERBOARD

OBJECTIVE:
To help students studying a string instrument to relate the staff to their instruments

IN BRIEF:
Students lay out *Alphabet Cards* into a fingerboard pattern using the BC and EF natural half steps. Different color cards represent the different strings. *Orange Symbol Card* finger numbers help relate the *Alphabet Cards* to finger patterns.

AGES:
Open

MATERIALS:
1) Four sets of different color *Alphabet Cards*
2) *Orange Symbol Cards* - finger numbers
3) Each student's violin or cello
4) *One Staff Board*
5) *Clefs Puzzle*
6) *Alphabet Kids*

REPITITIONS:
Open

PROCEDURE:
Ideally your string students have become familiar with the names of the keys on the piano and the names of the notes on the grand staff. Naturally they need to know the names of the notes on the fingerboard and how they relate to the staff. It's easy enough to just teach the student using the actual instrument, but it's also fun to use this game as a learning step. When I show this game at teachers' workshops the string teachers always smile and nod approvingly.

To represent the four open strings, let the students help you lay out four colors of *Alphabet Cards*.

The cards for each string will be a different color. For example: G A B C could be green. D E F G could be yellow. A B C D could be purple and E F G A B could be blue.

VIOLIN

Since duplicating the open string notes could be confusing, they can be left out of this initial presentation. Do include the finger numbers from the *Orange Symbol Cards* along one side of the fingerboard.

VIOLA

Let the students get their instruments and practice matching notes from this floor fingerboard. You can play a variety of games based on previous games.

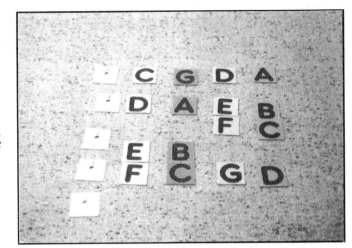

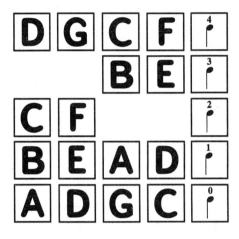

CELLO

IDEA - Snap your fingers (they close their eyes). Place an *Alphabet Kid* on one *Alphabet Card*. Clap twice (they open their eyes). Simultaneously, students are to find the note on their instruments and pluck it.

IDEA - Let a student toss on the *Toss Note* onto the *One Staff Board*. Another student is to place an *Alphabet Kid* on the correct *Alphabet Card* and then all can find it on their instruments.

IDEA - Snap your fingers. Mix up the *Alphabet Card* fingerboard. Clap twice. Moving one card at a time, students fix the cards.

IDEA - Using the *One Staff Board*, a student places the *Toss Note* on any note. Another student turns that *Alphabet Card* face down. Play continues until all fingerboard cards are turned face down.

A torn jacket is soon mended; but hard words bruise the heart of a child.

Henry Wadsworth Longfellow

GAME 10-10: MATCHING STAFF TO INSTRUMENTS

OBJECTIVE:
To practice finding notes on the students' instruments
- piano or other instruments

IN BRIEF:
1. String students relate open strings from the staff to their instruments.
2. Students work in pairs. One student places a *Magic Note* on the *Dictation Slate* for the other student to find on his/her instrument. Play continues until the whole slate is filled.

AGES:
Open

MATERIALS:
1) *One Staff Board*
2) *Clefs Puzzle*
3) *Notes With Letters*
4) *Dictation Slates*
5) *Magic Notes*
6) Students' instruments

REPETITIONS:
Open

PROCEDURE:
STEP 1: Help students decide the position of the open strings. Indicate the string they are to find using a blank note.

VIOLIN

CELLO

STEP 2: This game may also be played as a group.

Divide the students into pairs, giving each pair a *Dictation Slate* and a handful of *Magic Notes*. They all need their instruments.

One student from each pair places a *Magic Note* on the staff for the other student to find and play quietly. This can be repeated four more times. The *Magic Notes* should remain on the staff throughout the game.

Then the two students switch roles with the opposite student placing five new *Magic Notes* for the other to find. Pairs play independent of each other, and the game is over when the staff is full.

SIGNS AND SYMBOLS

I have a 10-year-old student who had studied piano in another program for four years. Francis was a good student who could read music but needed attention to his hand position and tone quality. So for 6-10 months we played by ear to improve his listening skills and to free him to watch his hands.

One week his theory class was all set to play MUSOPOLY. We were ready except for studying all the *Orange Symbol Cards*. Everyone had been reading for several years, so we decided to play the game.

"You may already know some of the cards or be able to figure them out. We can learn the others as we go along."

The game was progressing with good spirits and with lots of money being earned. On Francis' turn he drew this card.

He smiled and began, "Ahhh, I know what this . . . uh . . . is. How do I explain it? . . . . . Uhhh . . ."

"Just say whatever words you can, Francis," I encouraged him.

"Is it one of those . . . you know . . . is it a triplet?"

He wasn't sure of his answer.

I tried to help him. "Francis, there is only one note on the card. Doesn't a triplet have three notes?"

"Oh, yeah . . . well, is it? . . ." I'd encountered this before with this card, so I wasn't surprised.

Alyssa's dad was keeping one eye on the game and one eye on some papers from work. Phil was a scientist who had been sitting in on his three

PART
TWO

11

189

daughters' lessons for several years. Phil asked the kind of questions that made his daughters' eyes roll in an "Oh, Dad" way. Today I gave him a chance to shine.

"Francis, please show the card to Alyssa's dad. Maybe he knows it."

Phil smiled confidently and impressed us all with a quick answer. "You play the note with the third finger." The class smiled and applauded Phil.

Francis laughed at himself and said "Oh, yeah . . I knew that."

But, he really didn't. He had studied piano four years and didn't know what a number over a note meant. I'm sure he had read music and used the finger numbers, but it wasn't the sort of conscious awareness that indicates real understanding. Before you say, "Wow . . . my students know that," let me tell you another story.

This one is about me. It was the beginning of my freshman year in college. I had studied piano for 14 years, violin for 9 years, had sung in choirs since I was in kindergarten and was taking a placement test for music theory along with 150 other freshman.

There was a multiple choice question of a very basic nature.

1. Circle the correct answer.

I paused to think. The first one looked correct, but it sounded right to say "F sharp", not "sharp F". I sat there wondering which answer to circle. I'd read music all my life in many situations, but I still don't know if I made the right choice. The test has long since been thrown away.

That experience made a strong impression on me. I want my students to know and to talk about what the symbols mean. They must be able to recognize and demonstrate them as they learn.

So, we study them. Not only in music, but with many entertaining games.

Note: In the **Music Mind Games** materials, there are several blank *Orange Symbol Cards* to use for any symbols you may need in addition to the ones included in the set.

GAMES IN THIS CHAPTER

GAME 11-1: DYNAMICS

OBJECTIVE:
To learn pp, p, mp, mf, f, ff

IN BRIEF:
Step 1: Pronouncing the names
Step 2: Acting out a body position for each symbol
Step 3: Matching *Orange Symbol Cards* to names and placing them in order from soft to loud

AGES:
Open

MATERIALS:
Orange Symbol Cards

REPETITIONS:
Once through each step in one or more sessions

PROCEDURE:

STEP ONE: SAYING If students haven't had much exposure to these words, say each word and let them say them back to you, over and over until you feel certain they can pronounce them well.

Pronunciation guide:

pp	=	pianissimo	pee a niss' a moe
p	=	piano	pee a' no (just like the instrument)
mp	=	mezzo piano	met' zo pee a' no
mf	=	mezzo forte	met' zo for' tay
f	=	forte	for' tay
ff	=	fortissimo	for tiss' i moe

STEP TWO: ACTING OUT EACH WORD Ask the students to watch you, copy you in actions and copy you in words. The words are to be said in the volume which matches their meaning. Pianissimo will be whispered and the others a little louder until fortissimo is laughingly yelled as loudly as possible.

Tell the students: "I'd like you all to copy my body as well as my voice. Are you ready?"

1. First curl your body into a ball on the rug and motion for them to join you. They may giggle since it's most unlikely that a teacher has ever curled up in a ball on the floor in front of them. Since they are curled up and won't be able to see you, say "Ready, GO," so together you can whisper, "Pianissimo".

Sit up on your legs, hands in your lap and softly say, "Piano".

Smile and return to the curled up "pianissimo" position.

2. Whisper "Ready, GO . . . pianissimo . . . ". Sit up on your legs and softly say, " . . . piano . . .". Then move up onto your knees, hands at your side and speak, " . . . mezzo piano."

Everyone is smiling at each other now. Return to the pianissimo position.

4. Repeat the first four positions with the matching words, " . . . pianissimo . . . piano . . . mezzo piano . . . mezzo forte . . ." then still standing, hold your arms high in the air and say loudly, " . . . forte! "

Smile and return to the pianissimo position.

3. Repeat the first three positions with the matching words, " . . . pianissimo . . . piano . . . mezzo piano . . . " then stand up with your arms at your side and speak a little louder, " . . . mezzo forte."

Some laughter is beginning to bubble over but you again return to the pianissimo position.

5. This time you will lead the students through the complete six dynamic levels. "Pianissimo . . . piano . . . mezzo piano . . . mezzo forte . . . forte . . . then jump up (wildly, if it's your temperament) with your arms in the air and yell "FORTISSIMO!"

Immediately call out "Backwards!" and lead them back down, body and words, from fortissimo to the quiet sound of pianissimo. If you don't, you will leave your students in a state of uncontrollable excitement and you'll have a class full of crazies on your hands! However, if you finish with pianissimo, their bodies curled in a safe, quiet position, they will be happy and in fine control of themselves.

Soon they will uncurl and look up at you, smiling. "Fun, huh?"

STEP THREE: SEEING THE SYMBOLS Pick up the stack of *Orange Symbol Cards* and gather the students into a circle around you.

"I want you to stop me if you see any cards with a 'p' or an 'f'or 'mp', 'mf' or any of those combinations." One at a time, but as quickly as you can, toss the *Orange Symbol Cards* face up on top of each other into a pile.

Stop and remove the cards only when they say "STOP". Everyone will watch intently for the cards and try to be the first to say "STOP". This will be a lot of fun for them, they will pay very close attention, and they get a chance to see the *Orange Symbol Cards* they will be learning. Even if someone says "STOP" for the wrong card, follow their instructions. You are under their command. Someone in the class will correct you, telling you to put that card back in the pile.

After you have gone through all the *Orange Symbol Cards* and separated out the six dynamic signs, put the pile aside. Spread out the six chosen cards, out of order on the rug in front of the students.

"Do you think these are right?" Give them time to discuss among themselves how the cards should be arranged.

A class of my students (ages 7-10) were having a wonderful time playing this game. They had laughed themselves silly when we did the body motions from STEP TWO during the previous week's class. Now they were trying to arrange the cards and were not able to agree on which was softer, "piano or mezzo piano". All the students played piano well and one girl also took violin lessons. She insisted that the cards should go in this order.

To tell you the truth, I thought this was the correct order until I was in college . . . or maybe even out of college. At any rate, it's embarrassing to admit this confusion, but it's true. I knew that mezzo forte was softer than forte so I assumed that mezzo piano must be softer than piano. The fact was that I had only seen these symbols scattered here and there in the music—never in a complete sequence.

It wasn't until I made up this game to teach my students that I came face to face with my uncertainty. I checked in the **Harvard Dictionary of Music** and found the correct list.

Since the other students could use the practice (and the fun) we did the full sequence of body motions from STEP TWO again to reteach the dynamics order.

Then they were all happy to lay out the cards correctly and say them through in order.

"I didn't know you could speak Italian," you can smile at the students.

"Italian?"

"Yes, these words, 'pianissimo, piano, mezzo piano, mezzo forte, forte and fortissimo' are all Italian. You see, several hundred years ago there were many important composers writing great music. Many of them lived in Italy and used their language to tell other musicians how to play their music. If they wanted someone to play a section of their music softly, they simply wrote 'piano' in the music. The idea caught on and in no time, composers in many countries were using these Italian words for loud and soft."

"Do we have to use Italian?" asks someone.

"No, when you compose, you can use English if you want. I've seen music with the dynamics written in French or German. It's just that Italian is so common now, it's understood by all musicians. As we learn more of these *Orange Symbol Cards*, you'll learn more Italian.

"It's getting off the subject a bit, but did you notice that the Italian word for soft is the same name as that instrument over there?"

They will realize the connection. "Right. Piano and piano."

"The full name of the piano is the 'pianoforte', invented by an Italian named Cristofori in 1709. It was named this because his invention was the first keyboard instrument that could be played with a full range of dynamics merely by how it was touched by the performer. So in a manner of speaking, if you take piano lessons, you are saying you take 'soft' lessons."

"Hey, that's pretty funny. Soft lessons!"

GAME: DYNAMIC MIX-UP

Lay out the six cards, out of order.

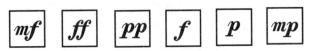

"I'd like you to fix the cards. Each of you will take one turn around the circle. When it's your turn, you may move only one card. If you think this card should go here . . . [place the ff on top of the mp] . . . then just put it on top. Someone else's turn could be to move the mp if they think it should be moved."

Playing this way holds everyone's interest and enables you to see if the students are indeed remembering the order.

Once the cards are corrected, let the learning process continue. Instead of saying, "They are all right," let the next student say it instead. S/he may even move a card, incorrectly. Then the next person will have to move it back. Eventually the group will be able to reach an agreement.

GAME: PICK A CARD   Hold the cards in your hands and let the students take turns picking, naming and placing them on the rug in the correct order.

A child's spirit is like a child, you can never catch it by running after it; you must stand still, and, for love, it will soon itself come back.

Arthur Miller

GAME 11-2: DYNAMICS YOU CAN HEAR

OBJECTIVE:
To develop an aural memory for the dynamic levels

IN BRIEF:
Students act out the dynamics while listening to each other (or you) play a solo or while listening to a recording.

AGES:
Elementary

MATERIALS:
Instrument or tape player

REPETITIONS:
Several pieces

PROCEDURE:
You may choose to play a solo for them or use a recording. If your students are good performers, let them take turns.

"Today we're going to listen to Bartok's **Romanian Dances**. Listen carefully to the dynamics you hear. To show me that you're hearing them, I want you to act out the dynamic levels with your body. If the music is really soft, then curl up in a ball for pianissimo. If it gets really loud, jump up and down for fortissimo. Ready?"

The idea for this game happened spontaneously one day after I had introduced a group of students to dynamic levels for the first time. They were a particularly happy, uninhibited group of three second grade girls and two fifth grade boys. With these five, class was always joyful and spirited.

They had laughed and fallen all over each other playing GAME 16-4: INTERVAL CIRCLE DICTATION, assumed the role of veteran card sharks as they practiced their notes with GAME 18-2: GO FISH and thoroughly enjoyed themselves learning all the preceding games in this chapter in about 15 minutes.

Our hour class time was nearly over so it was time for solos. We decided the order of performance by drawing several *Notes & Rests Cards*. Whoever drew the smallest total value of cards, had to wait the shortest time so went first. They compared cards and sat themselves in order.

Halfway through the first performance, I noticed two of the girls bouncing up and down holding hands and laughing silently. As I watched, I noticed that they were mimicking the dynamics they were hearing. Great idea!

"Josh, it's your turn to play, isn't it? Everyone else, act out the dynamics you hear. Stand up — it'll be fun."

Josh played with more dynamics than I'd ever heard. And so did all the other performers. And what fun the others had listening and moving around. I know that dynamics actually came alive for them that day.

GAME 11-3: CRESCENDO AND DECRESCENDO

OBJECTIVE:
To learn the meaning of crescendo, decrescendo and diminuendo

IN BRIEF:
Students act out the words verbally and physically.

AGES:
Open

MATERIALS:
Orange Symbol Cards

REPETITIONS:
A few times in a session

PROCEDURE:
Set out the cards in front of the students.

"Crescendo means to get louder <u>gradually</u> and decrescendo means to get softer <u>gradually</u>. Diminuendo also means to get softer <u>gradually</u>. Anyone have any idea which card is which?"

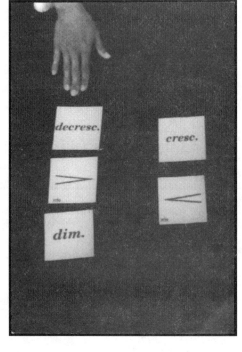

Give them time to discuss the answer among themselves. Guide them if necessary. Someone may notice that the cards look like the math symbols for "greater than" and "less than". You can ask them to imagine that sound is contained inside the lines. With a little space, there is not much sound. But as the space gradually gets bigger, so does the sound. And the opposite is true for the decrescendo.

"Let's do crescendo together. Can you copy me?"

Sit cross-legged in front of your students, and bend over so your head is in your lap and your hands are folded across your head. Gradually bring yourself upright until your hands are high over your head. At the same time, say "crescendo" slowly, starting with a small voice and gradually getting louder. They will love the chance to yell loudly in class.

Do the motion backwards for decrescendo and diminuendo, saying the words to mimic the arm movements.

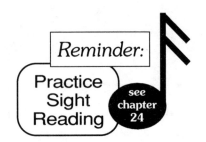

Reminder:
Practice Sight Reading
see chapter 24

GAME 11-4: FOLLOW THAT SIGN

OBJECTIVE:
To learn da capo, fine, repeat signs, dal segno, coda, first and second endings

IN BRIEF:
Using music books, students learn how familiar songs are written.

AGES:
Elementary and older

MATERIALS:
1) *Orange Symbol Cards*
2) Music
3) One *Alphabet Kid*

REPETITIONS:
Game can be done in one session

PROCEDURE:
Set out the *Orange Symbol Cards* in front of the students.

"These are all signs and symbols that tell you what part of the music to play again." I have a way of explaining the value of these signs in a little scenario that may or may not be exactly factual, but it does get the idea across to everyone.

"Years before there were printing presses and photocopying machines, scribes had to copy music, note for note, by hand. It took a lot of time, paper and ink to do the job right. Then someone in about the 12th or 13th century thought of putting dots or a few letters to tell the performers to play part of the music again. It saved those scribes thousands of hours. Clever, wasn't it? These signs are simple to learn.

"Can anyone think of a song or a piece of music where the exact same music is played more than once? It has to be an exact repetition."

"I play a Bach minuet. I think the first half of the song plays twice and so does the second half," volunteers Laurie.

"Let's look at the music together." Ask them to look through the music and tell you if they spot any of the signs found on the cards.

"I see the repeat signs right here," calls out Laurie.

"I see them, too," calls out Jesse.

Holding the *Alphabet Kid* in your hand, trace through the music, singing if possible and obeying the repeat signs so the students can understand what they mean.

Hand them a music book that contains a piece with a D.C. and Fine. Let them flip through the pages until they find it.

"There must be something on this page. Hmmmm. Wait. Here's the D.C. and here's the Fine. Look! I found them," calls out Maria.

"Where? . . . Oh, yes, there they are," says Meredith.

You can explain that fine means "the end or the finish". That will be an easy one for them to remember since they've played GAME 2-3: FINE many times.

"Da capo means to go back to the beginning of the piece. Capo means 'head'. What do you put on your head that sounds like capo?" you can ask.

"Oh, I know. A cap!" answers Joseph.

Sing through the song and let the *Alphabet Kid* guide the students through the music.

Repeat the same type of exercise with D.S., coda and first and second endings, using music and the *Alphabet Kid*.

GAME 11-5: SING THEM FASTER OR SLOWER

OBJECTIVE:
To learn signs: rit., rall., a tempo, riten., accel.

MATERIALS:
Orange Symbol Cards

IN BRIEF:
After learning what signs mean, students follow them when singing.

REPETITIONS:
Until they know what the signs mean

AGES:
Open

PROCEDURE:
The signs may be presented in whatever order you would like. Learn only as many as the students can easily understand and remember.

Place the cards between you and the students.

"If you think you know what these cards mean, speak up." It's interesting to learn what they are already thinking. Once you get the definitions narrowed down, be certain those for rit., rall. and accel. include the word <u>gradually</u>.

"Ritardando and rallentando mean to slow down <u>gradually</u>. If you are riding in your car with your mom or dad,

200

is it better if they slow down gradually as they come to a traffic light or SLAM ON THE BRAKES?" The students will laugh and probably bounce around as they act out different ways to slow down a car.

"Now, with a ritardando at the end of a piece, you just slow down gradually and stop, but if you have a ritardando in the middle of the song, you need a signal to resume your original tempo. That sign is 'a tempo'.

"Which card looks very much like "ritardando"? They will point to "riten." "That's ritenuto and it means you don't slow down gradually. You slow down <u>immediately</u>!"

Review the definitions. "All right. Let's sing Twinkle together." Leave the five cards face up on the rug in front of the students. As you sing "Twinkle, Twinkle, Little Star" (or any song you like), point to 'ritardando' or 'rallentando'. They will smile and sing gradually slower, then grin at each other as they pick up the tempo when you point to the 'a tempo' card.

The 'riten.' card will calm things down quickly. Then they may lose all control when you point to the 'accel.' card, so be ready with 'a tempo' to settle them back down.

This is very effective learning because they are seeing the card and physically reacting to what it says. If you point to the cards at unexpected times in the singing, it will not only be funnier but make a greater impression.

It's fun to place other *Orange Symbol Cards* out and create a crazy version of Twinkle. Please refer to other games in this chapter on how to teach these various symbols.

staccato		Students sing all the notes is a short, clipped, staccato style
fermata		Students keep singing that pitch until you stop pointing to the card. It's funny to point to the card for such a long time that the students pretend to pass out from lack of air.
D.C.	D.C.	Students immediately return to the beginning of the song and continue singing.
Fine	fine	When the card is pointed to shortly after the D.C. card, students stop singing.
accent		Students sing the notes with accents.
trill		Students (try to!) sing the notes with a trill.
double bar		At the end of the song, the students know that the song is finished. Or point to the card in the middle of the song to end it abruptly.

<	crescendo	Students gradually sing louder until the card is no longer pointed to.
>	decrescendo	Students gradually sing softer until the card is no longer pointed to.
accel.	accelerando	Students begin to gradually sing faster.
poco	poco	May be used in combination with some of the above cards: rit., crescendo, decrescendo, accelerando.

GAME 11-6: SHARP, FLAT AND NATURAL

OBJECTIVE:
To learn the meaning of sharp, flat and natural

IN BRIEF:
Students act out the meanings of sharp, flat and natural. Using *Cardboard Keyboards* and notes, they match notes to a staff.

AGES:
Open

REPETITIONS:
Several times in a session

MATERIALS:
1) *Orange Symbol Cards*
2) *Cardboard Keyboards*
3) *Magic Notes*
4) *One or Grand Staff Board*
5) *Clefs Puzzle*
6) *Magic Notes*
7) *Staff Sharps and Flats*
8) Piano or other instruments

PROCEDURE:
Place the three cards in front of the students. Someone may already know the definitions and want to share them with the class.

"If you accidentally sat on something sharp, like a pin, what would you do?"

♯ "Wow! We would jump up. A sharp means up," they will answer and probably jump up and down.

"What happens to a car when the tire goes flat?"

♭ "It goes down," they answer. "A flat means down."

"And natural? What does that mean?" You can give them something to think about.

♮ "Well, that means to be normal. Natural is like . . . real, not made up or changed. It's better to eat natural foods, right?"

202

"Right. A natural is just the normal note. Could you please stand up, very naturally." Hold up the natural card.

Hold up the flat card. "When I hold up the flat card, you may bend your knees a little."

Hold up the sharp card. "When I hold up the sharp card, you should stand on your toes."

"Ready? Here we go." Hold up the cards in random order. They will laugh as they bounce back and forth from one position to the other and enjoy learning the difference in the symbols.

Hand out a *Cardboard Keyboard* and *Magic Notes* to each student. Ask them to place notes on their *Cardboard Keyboards* to match the accidentals on your staff.

Ask for different sharps and flats. Include notes such as C flat, E sharp, B sharp and F flat so they understand where these notes are located.

Give the students practice finding sharps and flats on the piano keyboard. If they are learning an instrument other than piano, now would be an ideal time to discuss sharps and flats.

GAME 11-7: LEARNING THE OTHERS

OBJECTIVE:
To learn the other musical symbols

MATERIALS:
Orange Symbol Cards

IN BRIEF:
Symbols, signs and words are best learned as they are being experienced musically, otherwise students merely memorize intangible definitions. Introduce these cards at appropriate times over several years. Definitions are included in alphabetical order for ease of reference.

AGES:
Open

REPETITIONS:
Whatever is needed!

PROCEDURE:
There are five games after this one that students play in order to help them learn and remember the meanings of the various cards. Introduce a few new cards when needed and then play one of these five games.

The cards are grouped accordingly:

Number of symbol cards

1.	Symbols from games 11-1 through 11-6	27
2.	Easier symbols	27
3.	Notes and rests	14
4.	Piano symbols	8
5.	String & percussion symbols	8
6.	Time signatures	8
7.	Key signatures	14
8.	Intervals	8
9.	More advanced symbols	22
10.	Words	25

Blank cards have been included in the *Music Mind Game Materials* in case you have additional symbols you wish to add.

1. Symbols from games 11-1 through 11-6

pp   pianissimo = very soft

p   piano = soft

mp   mezzo piano = medium soft

mf   mezzo forte = medium loud

f   forte = loud

ff   fortissimo = very loud

cresc.
crescendo = gradually get louder

decresc.
decrescendo = gradually get softer

dim.   diminuendo = gradually get softer

♯●   sharp = play the note a half step up

♭●   flat = play the note a half step down

♮●   natural = the note is neither sharp or flat

rit.   ritardando = slow down gradually

riten.   ritenuto = slow down immediately

204

rall.	rallentando = slow down gradually	*D.S.*	Dal segno = repeat from the sign
accel.	accelerando = become faster gradually	𝄋	the sign = begin here after D.S.
a tempo	a tempo = resume the original speed	⊕	a sign = skip from the first sign to the second
𝄆 𝄇	repeat signs = play the music between the signs two times	***coda***	coda = an ending or concluding section
D.C.	Da capo = return to the beginning and play until fine	⌐1 ⌐2	first and second endings = play the first ending, then take the repeat. The second time play only the second ending.
Fine	Fine = the end		

---

2. Easier symbols

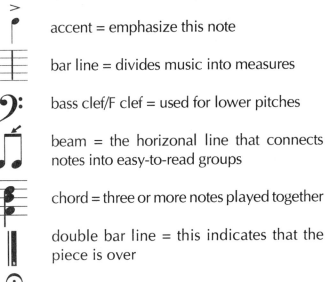

accent = emphasize this note	
bar line = divides music into measures	
bass clef/F clef = used for lower pitches	
beam = the horizonal line that connects notes into easy-to-read groups	
chord = three or more notes played together	
double bar line = this indicates that the piece is over	
fermata = hold this note longer than its value	
finger number = play the notes with the appropriate finger	
grand staff = two staves, usually the treble and bass clefs	
ledger line = notes above or below the staff	
measure = the space between two bar lines	

8va	ottava = play the notes one octave higher (𝄞) or one octave lower (𝄢) than written
	phrase = play all the notes under the curved line legato
	slur = play the 2-3 notes under the curved line legato
sf	sforzando = a sudden, strong accent
(♯)♪	sharp = a reminder to play the accidental
	staccato = make this note short
	staff = lines upon which music is written
	tie = the notes are played as one
𝄞	treble clef/G clef = used for higher pitches
	triad = a three note chord arranged in thirds
tr~	trill = two notes alternating very quickly
	triplet = three notes evenly occupy the space of two of the same value

3. Notes and Rests

♬ (64th)	= sixty-fourth note	𝄿	= sixty-fourth rest
♬ (32nd)	= thirty-second note	𝄾	= thirty-second rest
♪ (16th)	= sixteenth note	𝄿	= sixteenth rest
♪	= eighth note	𝄾	= eighth note
♩	= quarter note	𝄽	= quarter rest
𝅗𝅥	= half note	▬	= half rest
𝅝	= whole note	▬	= whole rest

---

4. Piano symbols

L.H. = left hand = play with the left hand

└─────┘ = pedal markings = pedal on and off

𝄐 = pedal sign = pedal on

✳ = pedal sign = pedal off

R.H. = right hand = play with the right hand

$\overset{\frown}{\underset{4\ 5}{}}$ = silent finger change = the note is played with one finger then silently changed to another

tre corda = tre corda = three strings — soft pedal off

U.C. = una corda = one string — use the soft pedal

---

5. Strings and percussion symbols

arco = arco = play with the bow

⊓ = down bow = use a down bow

○ = open string = use the open string

pizz. = pizzicato = pluck the string

solo = solo = one performer

tutti = tutti = everyone together

∨ = up bow = use an up bow

✕ = without pitch

---

6. Time signatures

Found at the beginning of the music, they indicate how the beats are divided into measures. Emphasize the sound as related to pulse as well as what the measures look like.

$\frac{2}{4}$ = a strong pulse every two beats. Two beats per measure. The ♩ gets one count.

$\frac{3}{4}$ = a strong pulse every three beats. Three beats per measure. The ♩ gets one count.

$\frac{4}{4}$ or 𝄴 = common time - a strong pulse every four beats. 4 beats per measure. The ♩ gets one count.

$\frac{5}{4}$ = a strong pulse every five beats. Five beats per measure. The ♩ gets one count.

$\frac{2}{2}$ or 𝄵 = a strong pulse every two beats. Two beats per measure. The 𝅗𝅥 gets one count - cut time.

$\frac{3}{8}$ = a strong pulse every three beats. Three beats per measure. The ♪ gets one count.

$\frac{6}{8}$ = a strong pulse, then weak pulse every three beats. Six beats per measure. The ♪ gets one count.

$\frac{9}{8}$ = a strong pulse, then two weak pulses every three beats. Nine beats per measure. The ♪ gets one count.

7. Key signatures

Indicates the sharps or flats in the music. Appears at the beginning of each line of music

C major
and   =
a minor

G major
and   =
e minor

D major
and   =
b minor

A major
and   =
f# minor

E major
and   =
c# minor

B major
and   =
g# minor

F# major   =

F major
and   =
d minor

B♭ major
and   =
g minor

E♭ major
and   =
c minor

A♭ major
and   =
f minor

D♭ major
and   =
b♭ minor

G♭ major
and   =
e♭ minor

C# major   =

8. Intervals

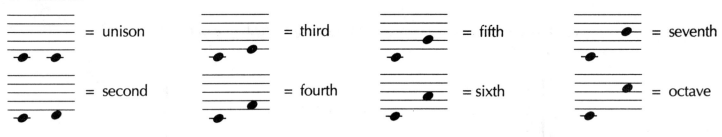

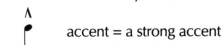

= unison

= second

= third

= fourth

= fifth

= sixth

= seventh

= octave

---

9. More advanced symbols

Λ
♪   accent = a strong accent

𝄡   alto clef - C clef = the middle line is middle C

♪♪   appogiatura = the smaller note is played on the beat - no other ornament is allowed to embellish the main note

'   breath = a slight break in the music

𝄢 𝄞   clef change = the left hand moves from the bass clef to the treble

♭♭♪   double flat = lower the pitch two half steps down

𝄪♪   double sharp = raise the pitch two half steps up

15ma   quindicessima = 15 notes higher or lower than the printed note

   glissando = a continuous sliding of the pitch

♪♪   grace note = the smaller note is played before the beat or at the grace of the notes around it

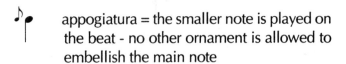   inverted mordent = embellishment

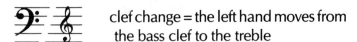

   key change = the piece is changing from one key to another

mm = 96   metronome marking = indicates the composer's choice for the tempo

   mordent = embellishment

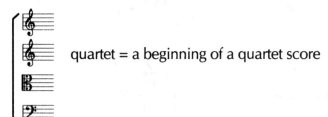   quartet = a beginning of a quartet score

♪   roll = the chord is rolled

♪   staccatissimo = a very short staccato

S.P.   subito piano = suddenly piano

♪   tenuto = play the note exactly for it's full value

♪   a turn = embellishment

f–p   on the repeat, the dynamic level changes from forte to piano

𝄆∕∕   the notes are to be played exactly again and again

10. Words

ad lib.	= ad libitum = freedom for the performer		**molto**	= very
			moto	= motion
agitato	= agitated and excited		**mosso**	= moved, agitated
alla breve	= $\frac{2}{2}$ or cut time		**non troppo**	= not too
allargando	= slowing down, usually with a crescendo at climax		**più**	= more
animato	= with animation and spirit		**poco**	= little
assai	= much, very		**rubato**	= freely - a little slowing or speeding up as the performer interprets the music
con brio	= with vigor and spirit			
dolce	= sweetly		**sans**	= without
legato	= play smoothly, connect the notes		**sempre**	= always
leggiero	= with lightness		**senza**	= without
loco	= return to the original octave		**simile**	= continue in the same style
marcato	= marked, accented		**sotto voce**	= in a soft voice
meno	= less		**subito**	= suddenly

Give a little love to a child, and you get a great deal back.

John Ruskin

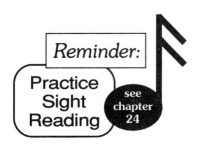

Reminder:

Practice Sight Reading

see chapter 24

GAME 11-8: WHAT CAN YOU FIND?

OBJECTIVE:
To give the students a chance to find musical symbols in their music. After this game, music will seem more friendly.

IN BRIEF:
With the *Orange Symbol Cards* spread out on the rug for reference, students look through music books, finding as many symbols as possible.

MATERIALS:
1) *Orange Symbol Cards*
2) Music books
3) *Magic Notes*

AGES:
Open

REPETITIONS:
Open

PROCEDURE:
Spread out the *Orange Symbol Cards* on the floor. Toss in a few new ones if you want. Ask the students to get their music books and look for symbols. They can put a *Magic Note* on the *Orange Symbol Card.*

Whenever a student finds one, the others check it out so they also benefit. If appropriate, discuss the symbol as it relates to the music. Try to find as many cards as possible. Some symbols will be more popular than others!

210

GAME 11-9: PASS AROUND AND ACT OUT

OBJECTIVE:
To let students enjoy becoming more familiar with symbols and their meanings

IN BRIEF:
With students sitting in a large circle, cards are passed around and accompanied by a funny, yet appropriate motion and/or verbal definition. The motion should maintain its authenticity around the circle.

MATERIALS:
Orange Symbol Cards

AGES:
Open

REPETITIONS:
Use about 15 *Orange Symbol Cards* per session

PROCEDURE:
Seat yourself and the students in a circle on the rug. "I'm going to pass cards one at a time to Scott along with a motion describing the card. Scott will pass it to Kent and so on around to all of you. The trick is to keep the motion as authentic as possible so Stacey, sitting here to my right, gets the same message that Scott got. Are you ready?"

Make your motions deliberate, yet fun. Here are some examples, and perhaps you will enjoy creating some of your own. The only rule is that the definition/motion must be musical. For example you can't say "Washington _____" for Da capo.

Some motions involve singing absurd songs and using the words. An example would be making up a simple melody to: "I went to the park one day and I saw a huge sforzando swinging on the swings." Of course, your voice would get suddenly loud in the song.

Here are suggestions for you in alphabetical order:

accel.   = sing "Oh, my. This song is having an accelerando!" and gradually get faster

   = kindly but firmly knock the person on his or her shoulder and deliberately say "accent"

animato   = sing "animato, animato . . ." and move in an animated, spirited way

   = demonstrate with fingers and voice using the word "appogiatura"

a tempo   = sing, "first in my song comes a graceful ritardando, then it's time for a tempo". Get slower, then resume your original speed

= using a finger, draw a bar down the person's full body saying "you are a bar line"

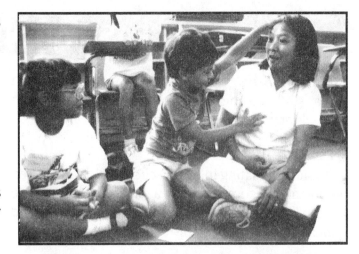

 = Ask the student to stand up. Sing "This is a bass clef - F clef" in a low voice and draw the clef on their legs.

= demonstrate an up or down bow with an imaginary string instrument

Cresc. = sing, "I am making a wonderful crescendo," gradually getting louder and doing the body motion for crescendo

D.C. = sing a short tune, " . . . la la . . . I'm going to
Fine do a da capo now," and repeat it as you point to your head - then end before you sing the whole tune again and say, "fine"

= do the motion for decrescendo and use your voice to say the word and speak gradually softer

dolce = smile and say "dolce" with syrupy sweetness

 = same for diminuendo

▌▌ = draw a double bar on the person's body and say "double bar line"

pp p mp mf f ff = all dynamic markings: assume the position learned in 11-1: DYNAMICS and also say the appropriate word in the proper volume

Here is fortissimo being passed around the circle. They really got into this one, didn't they?

= in the space in front of the person's face, trace a half circle shape and drawing your voice out, say "ferrmaa". Then touch his/her nose as you say "ta!" to make the dot. →

 = all finger numbers can be demonstrated

 = hum a pitch then sink down a little with your body as you sing a half step lower and sing "flat"

 = sing a song using the words "grace note" and include grace notes in the tune

 = all intervals can be sung or demonstrated on an imaginary violin or *Cardboard Keyboard*

L.H. = wave your left hand and fingers at the person

 = hold your hand in a horizontal position with the fingers out to represent the five lines of a staff. With your pointer finger from the other hand, draw an imaginary ledger line above or belowyour hand staff

 = draw five horizonal lines across the person's body. Then add two bar lines saying, "you are a measure"

mm=96 = hold one arm in front of your body with your elbow anchored to your waist - move your arm back and forth like a metronome at different tempos and say, "which tempo would you like?"

 = demonstrate an open string on your imaginary violin and say, "look, Ma, no fingers"

 = pretend to play the piano and put down the pedal with your right foot then take it off saying, "pedal on, pedal off, pedal on, pedal off . . ."

= sing a lovely phrase and how you're making it so nice and legato - move your hand in a giant arc at the same time

pizz. = play pizzicato on your imaginary cello and say "pizzicato" using short syllables

rall. = sing a song using the word "rallentando" as you gradually slow down - lean your body over slowly until you fall over →

 = using both your hands, draw two lines on the outside of the person's body - use three fingers in each hand, holding fingers 3 & 4 close together to represent the double lines - finger 2 will be the single line. Say "repeat" as you draw the lines, add the dots and say "signs"

R.H. = wave your right hand in the air

rit. = same as for rall. except say "ritardando"

riten. = sing a song, then suddenly slow down - use the word "ritenuto" in your song

 = demonstrate a long roll on either your imaginary piano or violin and say "roll" in ascending pitches as if you were a roll

sf = sing a song using the word "sforzando" when you suddenly get louder

 = hum a pitch then stretch yourself up a bit as you move up a half step and sing "sharp"

 = sing about how fun slurs are, making your voice do a succession of two note slurs

 = play a series of staccato notes on the person's head and say "staccato" in a short clipped style →

 = draw horizonal lines on the person's body and say staff

S.P. = sing a song and suddenly get soft as you use the words "subito piano" - when you get soft, pull your arms in and crouch over

 = sing in the meter and saying, "this is a song about 6 . . 8 . . and . . ."

 = draw a treble clef in front of the person on the upper part of the body and say "This is a treble clef" or trace the clef

tr = demonstrate with your fingers and voice

U.C. = play an imaginary piano, push down the pedal with your left foot and sing softly

215

GAME 11-10: I SEE

OBJECTIVE:
To practice identifying and defining signs and symbols

IN BRIEF:
Students sit in a circle around *Orange Symbol Cards* which are defined and/or acted out.

MATERIALS:
1) *Orange Symbol Cards*
2) Music Dictionary

AGES:
Open

REPETITIONS:
Use 15 - 20 *Orange Symbol Cards* per session.

PROCEDURE:
Ask the students to join you in a circle on the rug and help you arrange the *Orange Symbol Cards*.

Before beginning, ask the students to point out any cards they may have forgotten and need definitions for. Discuss these cards.

To play the game, definitions are given and the card is identified. Either you or the students can give the definitions. Easiest: You define the cards. Turns are taken around the circle. If a student doesn't know the card or misses, the turn passes to the next person until it's answered. You should try to select a card the student will probably know.

More challenging: Students take turns around the circle defining a card. Anyone is free to find the card and turn it over.

Use a music dictionary and this book as needed. If you are playing with a lot of cards, it isn't necessary to play until all the cards are turned over.

GAME 11-11: ORANGE PAIRS

OBJECTIVE:
To have fun defining and identifying symbols

IN BRIEF:
This game is like a T.V. game show. Working in pairs, students define symbols for each other to guess.

MATERIALS:
Orange Symbol Cards

AGES:
Open

REPETITIONS:
About 5 - 6 rounds

PROCEDURE:
Divide the students into pairs or small groups and ask them to sit facing each other. Give one student in each pair four cards. Be careful the other student doesn't see the cards.

"One at a time, define the cards for your partner. You may do anything musically that defines the card. Try to give good clues. Once your partner names the card, give it to him or her so s/he can see it. If anyone needs help, just call me over."

Here's a photo of Stephen describing "coda" to Ann. Behind them, Meredith and Henrietta jump up to describe "fortissimo". What fun!

Can you guess the symbols being described in these two photos? The answer is at the end of this chapter.

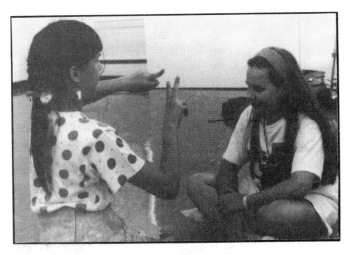

When two students finish their cards, they can exchange them with you for four new cards. The opposite person then gives the clues. The students will enjoy this game since everyone is active throughout the game.

217

GAME 11-12: ORANGE HUNT

OBJECTIVE:
To practice the signs and symbols

IN BRIEF:
Many *Orange Symbol Cards* are "hidden" around the teaching room. Just like looking for Easter eggs, students hunt for *Orange Symbol Cards*. They may pick only the ones they know. Later they sit in a circle and name the cards they found.

MATERIALS:
Orange Symbol Cards

AGES:
Open

REPETITIONS:
Once in a session using as many cards as you want

PROCEDURE:
Before class, hide *Orange Symbol Cards* all around the room. Don't make the hiding places too hard, though, or like finding old Easter eggs in July, you may not get your full deck of cards back when the game's over!

Explain that the students may pick up any *Orange Symbol Card* they like, as long as they know what it means. If they find one they don't know, they should leave it for someone else.

After the hunt is over, sit in a circle and let students in turn, quickly go through their piles, naming each card. This way all students benefit from each other's finds and may remember any cards they have forgotten.

Answer to GAME 11-11: ORANGE PAIRS
1. The difference between ➤ and ♪
2. 𝄢

Reminder:
Practice Sight Reading
see chapter 24

TEMPOS

Can you imagine music with only one tempo? Consider a Bach minuet, Chopin nocturne, a Mendelssohn Scherzo and all of Stevie Wonder's hits in the same tempo. Inconceivable.

The thought is impossible since the mood of music is so dependent on what tempo is used. A tender love song just can't rip along at a brisk, march-like speed any more than John Philip Sousa's "Stars and Stripes" can be enjoyed at a sweet, calm tempo.

Students encounter tempo markings at the beginning of pieces. Or they hear a piece played in a particular tempo and try to match it themselves. But by doing this, will they really learn if Andantino or Andante is faster? They have to play many pieces in these two tempos in order to make a judgement.

Anyway, what exactly is the tempo for Andante?

When I was in graduate school the Dean of our music department, Dr. Thompson substituted in our musical history evolution class one day. I'm glad he did since what he told us was memorable. He ask us to think about tempos in a new light. First we talked about the meaning of Allegro.

Someone said that it meant fast and lively. He agreed. "Now," he asked us, "Think about what fast and lively meant to a composer like Beethoven. What was the fastest thing he could imagine?"

"Probably a runaway horse," one of us answered.

"Exactly," said Dr. Thompson. "What is the fastest thing you can think of?"

The answers came quickly. "A race car. A plane. The SST, supersonic transport. A rocket ship. The Space Shuttle." It was exciting to think how fast these new creations went compared to the "slow" runaway horse.

"So, perhaps Beethoven's Allegro wasn't the same Allegro in the minds of our present day composers. I'm not saying it's one way or the other. I want you to think about this comparison, how it affect composers and their music and ultimately how musicians decide to perform that music."

This thesis gives us freedom of thought. In other words, please don't simply bring out a metronome and expect students to think there is only a slim margin of choice when using particular tempo markings.

And as they become familiar with tempos, substitute statements like, "That was good, but try it a little faster," with "That was a good allegretto tempo. I think you're ready for allegro. Want to try it?"

PART TWO

12

219

GAMES IN THIS CHAPTER

GAME 12-1: LEARNING TEMPOS

OBJECTIVE:
To teach the 11 basic tempos

IN BRIEF:
Students pronounce tempos and learn the order

MATERIALS:
Yellow Tempo Cards

AGES:
Elementary and older

REPETITIONS:
The steps may be done in one or more sessions.

PROCEDURE:

STEP 1: Practice saying the words without the cards. Pronunciation will be easy and quick.

"I've got some new words for you today. Can you repeat them after me? Allegro."

"Allegro," respond the students.

"Largo," you say.

"Largo," they respond.

Continue with all the words, out of sequence, repeating some of the new ones like adagio and vivace many times.

"I have all those words on cards." Show the cards out of sequence, saying the words together. Repeat each word several times.

STEP 2: LEARNING THE ORDER

I have discovered a sequence for quick learning and reliable retention. Rather than memorizing from slowest to fastest, establish the middle tempo, then work in from the slow end and fast end simultaneously.

Lay out the cards out of order. "Let's put the Yellow Tempo Cards in order. Anyone know what might be the middle tempo?" Move your hand above the cards. "When I'm above the card you think is the middle tempo, call out stop." Move in a suspenseful way, one card after another until you're finally over "Moderato".
"STOP!"
Lay the moderato card out in the middle of the rug.

> *moderato*

"Which one do you think is the very slowest?" Move your hand over the cards. Hopefully when you're over "Largo", someone will say "STOP!" Place the largo card far to the left of the moderato so there is space for the other cards.

> *largo*   *moderato*

"What about the fastest tempo?" you can ask. Move your hand over the cards until you hear "STOP!"
"Right, it's Prestissimo", you answer.

221

"In Italian, 'issimo' means very. Like in fortissimo or pianissimo," you can explain. Lay out the prestissimo card far to the right of the moderato card.

| largo | | moderato | | prestissimo |

"What do you think is a slow tempo but a bit faster than largo?" Move your hand over the cards. "STOP!" "Right, it's lento"

"It surely is. The words are alike, aren't they."

| largo | lento | | moderato | | prestissimo |

"So what could be a very fast tempo, but a little less than prestissimo?" Move your hand over the cards. "STOP! Presto!"

| largo | lento | | moderato | | presto | prestissimo |

"We have six left. Which ones are fast and which ones are slow?"

After several guesses someone will say, "Adagio".

| largo | lento | adagio | | moderato | | presto | prestissimo |

"How about the tempo just a little less than presto?"

"Adagio is a new sounding word. Is the other different one, vivace, the answer?"

"Yes, now only four are left. I'll give you some clues. There are two main words left and two words that are similar to them."

"Oh, I get it. Allegro and allegretto are alike. And andante and andantino are alike."

"How smart you are! So, how should we arrange these cards?" Let them discuss this among themselves and reach a consensus.

"Congratulations. You've done it!"

If there is time you can move right into the next game.

GAME 12-2: TEMPO SAY IT LIKE IT IS

OBJECTIVE:
To help tempo definitions come to life

IN BRIEF:
After lining up the *Yellow Tempo Cards* in order, students 1) sing the first four notes of Twinkle in the appropriate tempo for each card, 2) say the words in order, in tempo.

MATERIALS:
Yellow Tempo Cards

AGES:
Open

REPETITIONS:
Once

PROCEDURE:
Mix the *Yellow Tempo Cards* up on the floor and without your help, let the students line them up in order. If they finish and a card or two are switched simply tell them, "It's great except for two cards."

"What? Where?" and they will jump back to work and figure it out.

"I knew those cards weren't supposed to be that way," Sally smiles and says, after the cards are all in order.

"Looks good. All right, I would like to sing the beginning of *Twinkle* in each of these tempos." Point to the largo card and say, "Largo". Then sing in a extremely slow tempo. The looks on their faces will be most interesting, but continue without a pause.

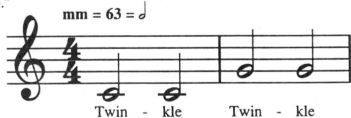

"Lento."

Move through each tempo one by one, gradually increasing your tempo until prestissimo. Everyone will burst into laughter as they sing prestissimo as incredibly fast as possible.

"Great job. All right, now, let's say the words in the correct speed." Point to each card in turn.

"Lllllllaaaaaaarrrrrgggggggoooooooo."

"Lllllleeeeeennnnnttttttooooo."

"Aaadddaaagggiiiooo."

"Aannddaannttee." And so on until you come to prestissimo which you say in a microsecond.

Again, laughter and more laughter. But, they are certainly understanding the concept of relative tempo.

GAME 12-3: TEMPO MIX UP

OBJECTIVE:
To practice tempos

MATERIALS:
Yellow Tempo Cards

IN BRIEF:
Students fix *Yellow Tempo Cards* after they're mixed up.

AGES:
Open

TEMPO BODY ORDER:
Students draw *Yellow Tempo Cards* and arrange themselves in order.

REPETITIONS:
Once or twice. Body Order - once. Repeat in later classes.

PROCEDURE:
Once the *Yellow Tempo Cards* are laid out in order, snap your fingers so the students will close their eyes. Mix up the cards. "Oh, no. It sounds as if the cards are getting all mixed up," they may say.

Clap twice so they will open their eyes. "You're right. The cards are all mixed up. Can you fix them?" Working together, the students will easily rearrange the cards.

An intriguing way to fix the cards: Tell the students that they can move only one card at a time, even if they have to put one card on top of another. Explain that there are eleven spaces and they are to arrange the cards within those spaces. They play by taking turns around the circle, either playing (moving one card) or saying "Pass' (not taking a turn). Let them know it's okay to pass -either they don't know what to do - or they think all the cards are right. I usually communicate this without words - with a smile when someone opts to pass.

After everything is fixed, rather than saying, "That's right," just keep going around the circle until everyone has said pass. This can allow the game to stretch out a bit if someone doesn't quite remember the order and wants to keep switching a card after it's correct.

Watch as the students correct the cards this way, they will continuously look at the cards. It's amazing. By looking at the cards - they will learn and remember the order quicker and easier. Try it with other games!

Children bored and asleep will not be affected by a well-intentioned teacher. They need to be awakened to their potential, and they will save themselves.

Dr. Haim G. Ginott

GAME 12-4: BODY ORDER

OBJECTIVE:
To practice tempos

IN BRIEF:
Students draw *Yellow Tempo Cards* and arrange themselves in order.

MATERIALS:
Yellow Tempo Cards

AGES:
Open

REPETITIONS:
Once. Repeat in later classes.

PROCEDURE:
Let everyone draw a tempo card. Ask them to look at each other's cards and get in order. This takes cooperation and brings out lots of smiles.

When they're all in order, ask them to hold their cards across their stomachs. "I'd like each of you to say the name of your tempo. And please say it <u>in tempo</u>. We'll start with you, Josh, since you have the slowest tempo." I guarantee everyone will be smiling by the time you finish this little exercise.

If you're adventurous try this: Have the students sit out of order. Moving down the row, each student sings one measure of "Twinkle" but in the tempo of his/her card. It will be wild!

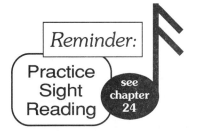

Reminder:
Practice Sight Reading
see chapter 24

225

GAME 12-5: GUESS MY TEMPO

OBJECTIVE:
To practice identifying tempos when hearing them in performance

IN BRIEF:
Students take turns playing short pieces or parts of longer pieces for each other to name the tempo. They can check the music book to compare their choices.

MATERIALS:
1) *Yellow Tempo Cards*
2) Music books
3) Students' instruments

AGES:
Elementary and older

REPITITIONS:
Several pieces

PROCEDURE:
Toss the *Yellow Tempo Cards* on the rug for the students to arrange in order.

"I'd like each of you to think of a piece you'd like to play for us. After you play, we'll each guess which tempo you chose. If your piece is long, you may just play part of it. To be more interesting, you may use any tempo you want. Anyone want the first turn? Great — Francis, you're on. What would you like to play for us?"

"Ummm. I'll play **The Wild Rider** by Robert Schumann," says Francis. He plays well and uses a very slow tempo.

The students smile since they know the piece was intended to be played quickly. "All right, everyone, what tempo did I use?" asks Francis. He calls on each student in turn who gives him an answer.

"You're right. I played Adagio. And the horse could barely creep along at that tempo."

Give everyone a turn. This game will help them be aware of tempos as they listen and as they play.

Youth lasts much longer than young people think.

Comtess Diane

226

REAL RHYTHMS

This chapter is called REAL RHYTHMS because the cards used with these games show the real value of notes and rests so clearly that students can learn exactly what their relationships are.

Although printed music usually shows the value of notes and rests, the horizonal space allotted each of them isn't always exactly the value of sound it represents. The performer must have a steady sense of beat and keep an accurate pulse even when a measure with one whole note is written in the same amount of space that four sixteenth notes occupied in a previous measure.

If there is a music teacher reading this who has never had a student ignore rhythm in favor of playing the right note, please stand up.

I suspect that most of you are still sitting down. I know I am.

Let's look back into history for a possible explanation. It was in the middle ages that theorists developed the sophisticated system of writing notes that not only represented pitch but rhythmic duration as well. Before that there had evolved a system of writing notes, but rhythms were improvised or guided by a teacher who knew so and so, who had met so and so several years ago, who knew how the rhythm was supposed to be performed.

Having a note show not only pitch, but rhythmic duration was an amazing development in the history of musical notation. It had taken many centuries of thought by brilliant minds. When pitch and rhythm finally came together . . . it was indeed an event in the music world.

So, if students occasionally favor notes over rhythm, go easy on them. Their minds are still getting used to the idea of putting two concepts together within the same notational marking.

Besides spending hours practicing music reading, are there steps to speed up this process of the evolving centuries and help students become great readers right now?

First, continue what was developed in the other chapters. Keep rhythm separate from melody. Let it stand on its own so the student's mind can deal with one learning step at a time.

Second, make the information exact so there's no room for misunderstanding.

Third, sneak a little melody into these games, even though the eye is not aware of anything extra. This moves the student towards the goal of putting melody and rhythm back together.

Fourth, read without playing. During group class, I often ask the students to follow along in the music while their classmates are performing solos.

They will lie on the floor and move their fingers over the music with great concentration, seemingly fascinated by the whole process. Ask them to listen for something specific and they are even more engrossed. Will they be following pitch? rhythm? the dynamics? the symbols? YES, all of it.

But, rhythm will do the most to keep them on track. It is a vital element in the composition of music. Without comprehension of how rhythms sound, music will continue to remain a mystery of curious looking shapes.

THE MATERIALS   All the notes are the exact size of their value in relationship to each other. Four quarter notes are the exact length of one whole note card. And the five kinds of rests are the exact match to their respective notes.

These cards eliminate a lot of confusion.

The games in this chapter should be played simultaneously with those in Chapter 7: NOTES AND RESTS - PART 1. The success of both chapters depends on the multi track understanding of all these games. They are in different chapters only for the sake of organization.

This chapter should follow Chapter 4: BLUE JELLO - INTRODUCING RHYTHM. An understanding of those games will be a helpful prelude to playing these games.

GAMES IN THIS CHAPTER

GAME 13-1: INTRODUCING *REAL RHYTHMS*

OBJECTIVE:
To relate BLUE JELLO to real rhythms

IN BRIEF:
Students discover relative values of notes and rests

AGES:
Kindergarten and older

MATERIALS:
1) *Real Rhythm Cards*
2) *Rhythm Bingo Cards*
3) *Gold Coins*
4) *Magic Notes* and *Magic Wands*

REPETITIONS:
Once or twice

PROCEDURE:
Use notes and rests from various patterns on the *Rhythm Bingo Cards* to help students match *Real Rhythm Cards*.

It's particularly fun to learn about eighth notes. First we find the notes on the *Rhythm Bingo Card* and *Real Rhythm Cards*. Then we stand up and become eighth notes by turning our feet (note heads) to the side and sticking out one arm (flag).

Then I help two students form a JELLO.

Here are four students forming a JELLO JELLO.

Three eighth notes can also be taught now. We like to make a Card Chart like in Chapter 7: NOTES AND RESTS - PART 1.

GAME 13-2: CLAPPING MEASURES

OBJECTIVE:
This game helps students discover how rhythms form measures using *Real Rhythm Cards*.

IN BRIEF:
Students write out rhythms using notes, rests and bar lines and discover $\frac{4}{4}$ time.

AGES: Kindergarten, early elementary and older

MATERIALS:
1) *Real Rhythm Cards*
2) BLUE bar lines from the *Blue Jello Rhythm Puzzle*

REPETITIONS: 3 or 4 patterns in a session

PROCEDURE:
"Let's make a rhythm SNAKE using these cards." Let the students write out a long SNAKE. →

"I had trouble keeping track of where I was since it was so long. How about if we divide it every four beats? We can use the BLUES as bar lines." Add or take away a few cards to make the measures even.

"We can use two BLUES to make a double bar line." This is an ideal time to discuss the $\frac{4}{4}$ time signature card. Use the side with the 4 and the quarter note.

← Place the card at the beginning of the rhythm.

"Let's clap our rhythm. Ready, go." Use a steady tempo and give the first beat of each measure a little extra pulse. "Didn't the bar lines make it easier to read?"

While they close their eyes, mix up the BLUE bar lines, add a few more, or take some away.

231

GAME 13-3: BECOME A BEAT

OBJECTIVE:
This is a terrific game of rhythmic dictation with a fun twist. The concept of ties may also be practiced with this game.

IN BRIEF:
Four students, sitting in a row, are each one beat of a measure. You clap one measure, and they select the appropriate card for their beat.

AGES:
Early elementary and older

MATERIALS:
Real Rhythm Cards

REPETITIONS:
6 - 8 patterns per session

PROCEDURE:
The first time you play this game, set two piles of cards in front of the students: quarter notes (BLUES) and pairs of eighth notes (JELLOS).

Explain that each student is one beat of the rhythm. Use four students per pattern, or it might get too complicated for you and for them.

Look each student in the eye and say, "Alyssa, you are beat 1. Meredith, you are beat 2. Francis, you are beat 3. Josh, you are beat 4."

Clap a rhythm for them. Look at the students as you clap their particular beat and direct your clapping right at them as you move around the circle, your right to left.

Clap the rhythm again if they request it. They each put out their correct card. Alyssa goes first, Meredith second, Francis third and Josh fourth. They may help each other if needed.

"Right! Let's clap it together."

Once this gets easy, add more kinds of quarter note value cards.

It's a good idea to change the students' seating. Whoever was the fourth beat moves so s/he is sitting first and everyone slides over one place. Clap a few rhythms for them.

"Okay, change places again." If you have a group, let them take turns around the circle.

ADVANCED PLAY: This game can be played in many different sessions with all combinations of notes. If you use a note that occupies more than one beat, the student on that beat will just "sit out" that round and not put out a card.

Using dotted rhythms is an excellent idea and fun.

This is an ideal time to introduce the concept of a tie. Clap a rhythm with a quarter note tied to another quarter note. They will understand if you make the tie card available and not the half note.

MORE ADVANCED: **BECOME A MEASURE** Students write out measures.

As the students bodies get bigger, so can the length of rhythmic dictation patterns. Give each student a bar line and a number slate.

To make it easier for you to remember the pattern accurately, write it on a number slate. Clap it twice for them. They can write their measure on their slates if it helps. Then they select the correct cards and write their measure.

OBJECTIVE:
To help the students become rhythmically literate by writing out the rhythms to familiar songs

IN BRIEF:
Singing and clapping, students write the rhythmic pattern to familiar songs.

AGES:
Elementary - adult

MATERIALS:
1) *Real Rhythm Cards*
2) BLUE bar lines from the *Blue Jello Rhythm Puzzle*

REPETITIONS:
Several songs in a session

PROCEDURE:

STEP ONE: Singing Depending on the ages and abilities of the students, this may be done a class or two before Step two or in the same session .

Select a song that is familiar to all the students. The easiest meter to choose is common time, $\frac{4}{4}$. Before trying this with the students, try singing it yourself to make certain your choice of songs is easy enough. Begin with a simple song. A good example is **Lightly Row**. Ask them to clap with you and sing "BLUE or JELLO" at the appropriate time.

The students will not be reading the rhythm, but with your help and concentration they will begin to feel where the beats are. If you watch them, you will know if they understand this or not.

Choose several more songs to try. They will also become each others' teachers, learning together.

STEP TWO: Writing Refresh everyone's memory and practice singing the song again. Set the *Real Rhythm Cards* and the BLUE bar lines in front of the students. Help them select the meter.

"One way to figure it out is to count along with the music. I will sing **Lightly Row** while you count. Let's try $\frac{3}{4}$ first. Just count 1 2 3 1 2 3 over and over while I sing. If it matches, we know the meter."

Sing and let them count. Soon they will realize that counting "1 2 3 1 2 3" just doesn't match at all. Do the same thing with $\frac{6}{8}$ time. It won't match either.

"Maybe it's $\frac{4}{4}$. Ready? Go." Sing and let them count. Their faces will show how well the 1 2 3 4 counting matches **Lightly Row.**

Set out the *Meter Card* and let the students take turns writing out **Lightly Row** measure by measure using the *Real Rhythm Cards* and the BLUE bar lines. They can correct each other as they go along.

"Wait, Bita. That measure has five beats in it," notices Josh.

"Oh, yes. So it does," smiles Bita.

Older students can write out more challenging songs. This group of piano students wrote out half of a piece they all knew. Try to guess it if you can. The answer is at the end of this chapter.

We sing it to check the rhythm. →

GAME 13-5: WHAT SONG IS THIS?

OBJECTIVE:
To develop the students' ability to look at rhythmic patterns and "hear" the song they represent

IN BRIEF:
Students guess a song written out with the *Real Rhythm Cards*.

AGES:
Elementary - high school

MATERIALS:
1) *Real Rhythm Cards*
2) BLUE bar lines from the *Blue Jello Rhythm Puzzle*

REPETITIONS:
2 - 3 songs per session

PROCEDURE:
This game is loads of fun when students can guess the songs you write out with the *Real Rhythm Cards*, but it's a real dud if they can't. Be certain to prepare them for the success they deserve by playing previous games and choosing appropriate level songs.

Using the *Real Rhythm Cards* and BLUE bar lines, begin writing out the first song. They will chatter among themselves. Just smile and keep writing.

"What's that?" "Is this a new game?" "Hey, what's going on here?" "I know — I bet we have to clap it."

Shake your head. "Not clap it?" "Oh . . . we have to guess what song it is . . .!"

Nod your head and finish writing. It is not necessary to write the whole song. Eight measures or so will be enough.

"Okay. This is a song you all know. It is in your mind. Here's a hint on how to figure it out. Start at the beginning and sing the rhythm to yourself. It may help if you lightly tap the rhythm on your cheek. This way you won't bother each other."

"Imagine that your mind is a tape recorder with the volume turned clear down. When you recognize the song, the volume will come on."

"I'm going to step over here, just outside the doorway. When you think you know the name of the song, tip toe over here and whisper it in my ear.

Sometimes a student won't remember the title, but if s/he can sing the beginning, that counts as the correct answer.

The students will study the rhythm carefully and pop up excitedly to tell you the answer. After confirming an answer with you, s/he will return to the circle.

236

"Did you guess it?" the others will ask. "All right!"

Some students may be totally perplexed, and you will have to help them out. "Let's all clap it together. Careful now. If you gave me an answer, please don't sing along."

This will help some students guess it.

Before letting the game drag on too long, ask everyone to clap it and invite those who know the song to sing along. Can you guess the song in this photo? The answer is at the end of this chapter.

"Oh, I knew it!"

"Right." It's best if there is time to write another song so anyone who didn't guess the song will be able to guess the new one.

GUESS MY SONG (gives students practice writing songs)

Assign students to write out the rhythm of the song on a piece of paper for class the next week. Encourage them to do their own work without looking at the music. This way you will know if they are becoming rhythmically literate.

In class the following week, you can check their papers and ask for a volunteer to write out his or her song with the *Real Rhythm Cards*. Play the game as described above.

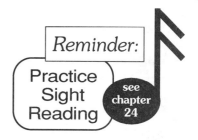

Reminder:
Practice Sight Reading
see chapter 24

OBJECTIVE:
To help students develop the ability to recognize meters by listening and writing

IN BRIEF:
By clapping or using live or recorded music, students identify meters they hear. Then they write the rhythms in these meters.

AGES:
Later elementary, middle school, high school

MATERIALS:
1) *Real Rhythm Cards*
2) BLUE bar lines from the *Blue Jello Rhythm Puzzle*
3) *Number Slates*
4) Instruments or recorded music

REPETITIONS:
Open

PROCEDURE:
In keeping with the spirit of discovery, students will enjoy the challenge of guessing new meters.

Set out all the *Meter Cards* found in the *Real Rhythm Cards* in front of the students. Either clap or play music for them. First let them establish where the beat falls (they can tap along with the music) and where the strong pulses are. Ask them to write the meter they think they hear on their *Number Slates*. If it will be less confusing, tell them what kind of note gets a count.

Discuss their answers and help them hear why they were right or wrong.

Using the *Real Rhythm Cards* and BLUE bar lines, write out several measures in the meter(s) they heard.

$\frac{6}{8}$

$\frac{3}{4}$

238

GAME 13-7: *REAL RHYTHM SNAKES*

OBJECTIVE:
To practice writing long rhythmic patterns

IN BRIEF:
Long rhythm patterns are written out, one above the other, and clapped simultaneously.

AGES:
Elementary and older

MATERIALS:
1) *Real Rhythm Cards*
2) BLUE bar lines from the *Blue Jello Rhythm Puzzle*

REPETITIONS:
One per class session

PROCEDURE:
Lay out the *Real Rhythm Cards* and ask the students to write measures in a particular time signature. They should put in BLUE bar lines and *Tie Cards* from the *Real Rhythm Cards.*

Ask them to clap the rhythm after it's written.

They can also write out one rhythm above another.

After practicing clapping both rhythms, divide the students into two groups and let them clap the rhythms simultaneously.

If you're feeling ambitious, let them write as many levels of rhythm SNAKES as you have cards. It will be fun clapping, that's for certain.

"Wow! Look at that. We've written the first five bars of a duet," calls out Meredith.

239

Answer to piece written in GAME 13-4: WRITE A SONG

Clementi Sonatina Op. 36 No. 1 (Allegro)

1 Sonatina

Allegro   M. Clementi Op. 36, No.1

Answer to piece written in GAME 13-5: WHAT SONG IS THIS?

Minuet in G major by J.S. Bach

8 Minuet 2

Con moto   J.S. Bach

I already know what a child needs. I know it by heart. He needs to be accepted, respected, liked, and trusted; encouraged, supported, activated, and amused; able to explore, experiment, and achieve. Darn it! He needs too much. All I lack is Solomon's wisdom, Freud's insight, Einstein's knowledge, and Florence Nightingale's dedication.

An anonymous teacher

MUSOPOLY

According to many fans of *Musopoly*, this is the best music game around. Made up in the late 1970's, its popularity was instant and remains timeless.

The game contains thrills and challenges and like the other games in **Music Mind Games**, it's cooperative, not competitive. The name is pronounced: Mu (as in music) zop' o lee and means "many musicians having fun together".

It's an amazing game. You'll find it marvelous for allowing students to cover all aspects of music theory in a short time period. They listen to each other's answers, clap each other's rhythm patterns and help each other with the *Rhythm Money*. Laughter and learning combine in a unique way.

During the game, players win *Rhythm Money* and *Gold Coins* for naming notes on the grand staff and finding them on the piano (or other instruments), for defining musical symbols and tempos, clapping rhythms, performing solos, taking dictation and answering questions about music and their instruments.

THE OBJECT of the game is not to win the most money. Instead, teammates combine their *Rhythm Money* at the end of the game and add up measures of a chosen time signature. Although they enjoy building their own earnings, players work for a common goal and are kind, helping each other learn. With *Musopoly*, everyone is a winner.

AS A CELEBRATION: Designed not so much to teach, but to reinforce basic music reading skills, *Musopoly* is best introduced after students have played some of the games in Chapters 1 through 12. If students can roll the *Large Dice*, draw cards and answer them with confidence, their self-esteem flourishes. On the other hand, if the game points out uncertainties, it won't be much fun. Teachers should introduce *Musopoly* at the right time so the game is viewed as fun, easy and exciting. Then the memory becomes as quick as the smile.

As with all the games in this book, *Musopoly* is easily adapted to fit various age groups and student levels. You are welcome to improvise to suit your teaching needs. Some specific suggestions are written at the end of this chapter.

There will be time in a one hour class to play the game. After the students help you set up the game, let the *Large Dice* roll and explain the game as they are playing. When they understand the game, step away and let them enjoy themselves.

PLAYERS ONLY: Unless young students are playing, the game is best played without too much teacher or parental participation. This way the students relax, relate better to each other, respond to each other's answers and have more fun. Although this game is for learning, it should be enjoyed in a playful atmosphere. Then it will be played often.

Musopoly is simple, easy to understand, and suitable for ages six through adults. Once your students know about *Musopoly*, they will beg to play it often!

GAME 14-1: *MUSOPOLY*

OBJECTIVE:
To reinforce basic music reading concepts:
1) Grand staff note names
2) Grand staff relationship to the piano
3) Rhythm
4) Notes and rests relationships
5) Musical symbols
6) Tempos
7) Dictation
8) Intervals
9) Performance

IN BRIEF:
Students roll *Large Dice* and move *Alphabet Kids* around a colorful board answering musical questions, taking dictation, clapping rhythms and performing solos. Cooperative play involves winning *Rhythm Money* and *Gold Coins*.

AGES:
Age 6 through adult

PLAYERS:
Although the game board is large, the flow of the game is best if no more than six players use one board. If there are more players, it's best to use more than one game board and have several independent games going at the same time.

If that isn't possible, divide the students into pairs or trios for up to five or six teams. Teams will move their *Alphabet Kid* and answer the questions together. They will enjoy helping each other, and the pace of the game keeps moving.

REPETITIONS:
An hour of play will fly by! Play often.

MATERIALS:
1) *Musopoly* game board
2) *Alphabet Kids*
3) *Gold Coins*
4) *Rhythm Money*
5) *Large Dice*
6) Cards: *Grand Staff Cards*
   Yellow Tempo Cards
   Orange Symbol Cards
   Pink Fermata Cards
7) *Real Rhythm Cards* or *Blue Jello Rhythm Puzzle*
8) Piano and/or students' instruments
9) One *Dictation Slate, Magic Notes* and *Magic Wands*

PROCEDURE:

TO SET UP THE BOARD:
Grand Staff Cards, Orange Symbol Cards, and *Pink Fermata Cards* are placed <u>face up</u> on their corresponding color squares in the middle of the game board. Players can see which cards are next and be ready with the answers in case they draw one of them.

A rhythm is written out with the *Real Rhythm Cards* or the *Blue Jello Rhythm Puzzle*.

Yellow Tempo Cards, the *Dictation Slate, Magic Notes* and *Magic Wands* are set out near the game board.

The container of *Gold Coins* is placed in the center of the game board. The *Rhythm Money* will be passed from player to player during the game.

Each player selects an *Alphabet Kid* and places it on any corner.

GENERAL RULES:

WHO ROLLS FIRST: After shuffling the deck, each player draws one *Rhythm Money*. Whoever drew the smallest value note or rest will take the first turn. Whoever has the next smallest value will go second and so on. This way, the shorter the note value, the shorter the players wait for their turns. Players can rearrange themselves around the board in the order of play and return the *Rhythm Money* to the pile.

TURNS: To be fair, all players must have the same number of turns. When it's time to finish, announce, "This is the last round." The player who was last on the first round will be the last to play.

Players move in the direction of the arrow.

Each player has one roll of the *Large Dice* on each turn unless doubles are rolled, certain *Pink Fermata Cards* are drawn, or after a polished performance when landing on PLAY.

DOUBLES: If doubles are rolled, another turn is taken. A second double in one turn is also worth an extra turn. If the third roll is also a double, the player moves backwards, does what the space asks and . . . the turn's over.

CARDS: Once cards are drawn, they should be kept face up in front of the players throughout the game. If put back under the bottom of the pile, cards cannot be learned. If kept in view, they may be easier to remember the next time.

A correct answer to any card wins one ♪ or one 𝄾 unless the card states otherwise. If a card is not answered correctly or something is not done correctly, no money is given up.

If *Musopoly* is played as a learning game, teachers may choose to let students collect *Rhythm Money* for trying to answer a card or whatever the turn requires. Gaining confidence is an important step to learning.

ANSWERS: Rather than the teacher, students check each other's answers. This keeps everyone involved with each turn and provides for more learning.

RHYTHM MONEY: Notes and rests are interchangeable. It's easier to use the *Rhythm Money* if the pile is kept in order throughout the game. Place the 16th notes and rests on top, then through the pile in order, ending with the whole notes and rests on the bottom. The *Rhythm Money* is passed from player to player during turns. Players should trade in *Rhythm Money* for equivalent higher values, trying to keep as few bills as possible. For example: Once a player has two sixteenth notes or rests, they should be traded in for an eighth note or rest. Trading continues throughout the game.

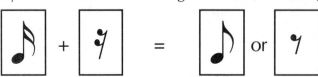

GOLD COINS : A *Gold Coin* is won for every quarter note value. (If you don't have enough *Gold Coins*, make it for every half note value.) Players keep their *Rhythm Money* as they win *Gold Coins*.

SAMPLE TURNS:
Both *Large Dice* are rolled and the *Alphabet Kid* is moved the amount shown. If players land on:

TREBLE CLEF: The top treble clef card is named and a ♪ or 𝄾 is won. If the player can also find that note on the piano, or other instrument, an extra ♪ or 𝄾 is won.

BASS CLEF: The top bass clef card is named. Follow the same rules as for the treble clef.

SHARP: The top *Orange Symbol Card* is identified and defined and a ♪ or 𝄾 is won. If the player also demonstrates it and/or finds it in a music book, another ♪ and/or 𝄾 is won.

FERMATA: The top *Pink Fermata Card* is drawn and either the question is answered or the instructions are followed to win a ♪ or 𝄾. If the card says to move ahead or back an interval, players refer to the letters above the spaces. Players must remember to count the letter they are on as one (A - C is a third, F - B is a fourth.) A ♪ or 𝄾 is won for moving the correct interval and also whatever is appropriate for the space landed on.

EIGHTH NOTES: Players clap a rhythm written with the *Real Rhythm Cards* or *B J R Puzzle*. The teacher or the other students may help, especially to tap the pulse. Everyone claps after the player has his/her turn. →

A new rhythm should be prepared so it is ready for the next player. The "composer" shouldn't make it too hard or easy since s/he could be the next player. Double money, a ♪ or 𝄾 is won for this space.

OR Sight-Reading: The player opens a music book to any page and teammates select a short excerpt. It may be clapped or played.

DICTATION: The teacher or another player plays a short melodic dictation pattern for the player to write on the *Dictation Slate* using the *Magic Notes*. The pattern is played twice before anything is written. It may be played again if needed. Double money, a ♪ or 𝄾 is won for this space.

(Please don't look closely, I'm merely an amateur with the violin.)

| tempo |

TEMPO: Four *Yellow Tempo Cards* are drawn from the pile and put in order from slowest to fastest. A small space should be left between the cards not drawn. A ♪ or a 𝄾 is won.

PLAY: The player performs a solo. The name of the piece and the composer should be announced and a bow taken before and after playing. If the player feels his or her performance was polished (congratulations) s/he wins the money and another roll of the *Large Dice*. Different pieces should be played when landing on PLAY again. This space is worth ♩ or 𝄽 .

FREE CHOICE: The player chooses anything on the game board (except the corners) to do or may even make up something appropriate. The *Alphabet Kid* stays on the Free Choice space. When landing on Free Choice again, something different should be chosen.

CORNER SHARP: The player wins a ♪ or 𝄾 for every *Orange Symbol Card* in the pile that is identified (not necessary to define them) up to 16 cards. S/he must go through the pile in order, one card at a time. Any miss and the turn is over. All cards should be returned to the pile.

ANSWER TOP CARDS: The player wins a ♪ or 𝄾 for each of the top cards from the four piles answered correctly.

CORNER TREBLE CLEF: The player wins a ♪ or 𝄾 for every treble clef card in the pile identified correctly. This turn does not include finding the note on an instrument and winning double money. S/he must go through the pile in order, one card at a time. Treble clef cards that other players are holding may also be named after the pile is finished correctly. Any miss and the turn is over. All cards should be returned to the pile or the players.

This is worth a lot of money — teammates may help figure out earnings.

CORNER BASS CLEF: Same as for treble clef.

GAME FLOW: When a player is performing, everyone should be polite and listen, thus momentarily stopping the game. At other times, it may be all right for them to continue playing *Musopoly* <u>very quietly</u>. The teacher can monitor this situation and decide what's best.

END OF PLAY: Everyone puts the *Rhythm Money* together. After choosing a time signature, the whole group divides its notes and rests into measure piles. How many measures were accumulated? Can players clap the cards? Notes may be exchanged for equivalent values if it makes it easier to clap.

CLEANUP: All players pitch in to sort the cards and put everything away. *Musopoly* is always ready for the next exciting class.

<u>YOUNGER PLAYERS:</u>

As with all the games in this book, teachers may adapt the rules in *Musopoly* to suit the needs of their students. Perhaps a group of kindergarten/first graders are eager to play *Musopoly* but they haven't played all the games up to Chapter 12. How can the rules be changed?

DURING THE GAME - The teacher may sit with the students, helping them learn how to roll the *Large Dice*, move their *Alphabet Kids*, draw cards and become familiar with the rules. If facts are forgotten, players can help each other and the money is still collected. It isn't necessary to use all the cards.

GRAND STAFF, ORANGE SYMBOL* and *PINK FERMATA CARDS - Use only the ones being studied.

YELLOW TEMPO CARDS - These can be included even if tempos haven't been studied. To create an awareness of different tempos, ask the player to sing or play a few bars of a piece and choose a fast or a slow tempo. To help everyone get used to the vocabulary of tempos, say, "Good, John, that sounded like the tempo marking of Allegretto," showing them the card. Another idea: After the student is finished, the teacher can define three tempos and let the student try to choose which tempo s/he used.

RHYTHM - Let the whole class clap the rhythm together. The student who landed on the space can pass out the *Rhythm Money* to everyone.

RHYTHM MONEY - Begin by using just the five basic notes and rests. Set out a Card Chart or *Real Rhythm Cards* so players can learn relative values.

The most important thing is that the game be encouraging, exciting, and full of stimulating information to help students grow in their understanding of musical facts as well as to reassure them of what they already know.

ADVANCED PLAY:

What about advanced students? How can *Musopoly* be more challenging?

To begin play - Students can draw more than one *Rhythm Money* and add up their beats to see who goes first, second, etc.

GRAND STAFF CARDS - 1) Students name a key signature using the note on the card as tonic. 2) Students play a scale beginning on that note - either major or one of the minor scales. More sharps or flats equal more money since one ♪ or ♪ equals each sharp or flat. 3) Students spell a seventh chord, then play it on the piano and resolve it. The green *Grand Staff Cards* can be one chord type and the blue *Grand Staff Cards* another.

ORANGE SYMBOL CARDS - After naming and defining the card, students can point out the symbol in written music, then play an excerpt from music containing an example of the symbol.

PINK FERMATA CARDS - More cards can be made and added to the pile. Questions related to music history could add a whole new dimension to the game.

YELLOW TEMPO CARDS - Students draw one card and play a short piece, or part of a piece in that tempo, then check themselves against the metronome.

RHYTHM - Students sight-read several lines of new music.

Actually, *Musopoly* can be adapted to fit any situation. Have fun coming up with some creative ideas on your own!

All children smile in the same language.

Bumpersticker

NOTES AND RESTS
PART 2

The games in this chapter allow students to expand and have fun with the knowledge they've acquired about notes and rests. Intermix these games with those in Chapter 13: REAL RHYTHMS as well as singing or playing experiences so students can apply their understanding of rhythm to actual musical sound. This will give them a more solid foundation.

When studying in Japan, I met many Japanese who had studied English but were reluctant to speak it. They had not had enough practice speaking English to feel confident. So be sure your students not only understand how the notes and rests are related, but how they sound and are played.

One of my classes began the study of dotted notes. Later that week, one of the students was reading a piece full of dotted quarter notes, which she didn't hold for their full value.

"Do you remember what we studied about dotted half notes?" I asked her. We got out the *Real Rhythm Cards* and she easily remembered how many *Gold Coins* the notes were equal to. But, she hadn't been applying any of this knowledge to her playing.

"Oh, now I get it. I think I can do it now." With only slight assistance, she played all the dotted rhythms correctly.

Although that episode was a success, I noticed that a few weeks later, she and some of the others in her class were still confusing the values of dotted notes. Again, we played various games, and I think they finally got it! This is a common pattern for learning and retaining information. Repetition is essential. That's why it's important to play a variety of games.

Continue to review some of the games in previous chapters and to practice making the Card Chart.

And don't forget the old favorite . . . WAR. I've had students beg to keep playing "just a few more rounds" even before lunch time.

GAMES IN THIS CHAPTER

GAME 15-1: EQUAL MATCH

OBJECTIVE:
To practice matching equal values of notes and rests using the *Notes & Rests Game Board*

IN BRIEF:
Students match notes and rests of equal value.

AGES:
Elementary and older

MATERIALS:
1) *Notes & Rests Game Board*
2) *Notes & Rests Cards* - both sets
3) *Real Rhythm Cards* - for reference

REPETITIONS:
A couple of repetitions per session

PROCEDURE:
Set the game board in front of the students on the floor with the cards spread on the floor around the board.

Ask the students to place cards on the board except this time they should not match the same card, but one of equal value. Thus, a quarter note can be placed on a pair of eighth notes. Or a half rest can be placed on a half note. Or a PURPLE can be placed on top of a HUCKLEBERRY.

Two or more cards can be placed together to equal a space on the game board. Those cards can be turned sideways.

251

OBJECTIVE:
To practice fitting notes and rests into measures. This fun, challenging game is the reason I made this game board. It's a favorite!

IN BRIEF:
Alternating between two teams, students place cards on the board to form measures. Eight time signatures can be studied.

AGES:
Middle elementary and older

MATERIALS:
1) *Notes & Rests Game Board*
2) *Notes & Rests Cards* - both sets
3) *Gold Coins*
4) *Alphabet Kid* - one
5) *Real Rhythm Cards* - if needed for reference

INTERMIX:
Students will do better with this game if they truly understand the Card Chart from Chapter 7 and have played games from Chapter 13: REAL RHYTHMS.

REPETITIONS:
Once in a session

PROCEDURE:
Place the game board in front of the students and divide them into two noncompeting teams. Each team lays its cards around the bottom and sides of the game board.

COMMON ($\frac{4}{4}$) TIME: Place the *Alphabet Kid* on the $\frac{4}{4}$ space to indicate that the game is being played in $\frac{4}{4}$ time.

The two teams form measures by taking turns placing cards on the board. Cards can be played in any order as long as the beats are rhythmically correct. Students call out the beats as they are used up. Play continues until the entire board is covered. You should sit at the top of the board and help keep track of the beats.

Here is the beginning of a sample game:

TEAM 1: Places its half note card on the board. "One two."

TEAM 2: Gives its half note card to the teacher to show that it has been played on the game board.

TEAM 2: Places its four sixteenth notes (HUCKLE-BERRY) card on the board. "Three."

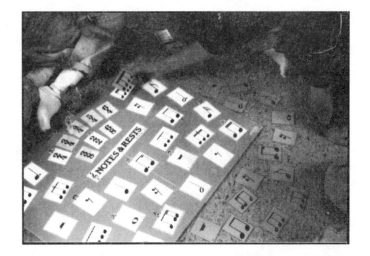

TEAM 1: Gives its four sixteenth notes card to the teacher since it's now out of play.

TEAM 1: Places its quarter note card on the board and says, "Four. Measure."

TEAM 2: Gives its quarter note card to the teacher. A *Gold Coin* is placed near the *Alphabet Kid* to show that one measure has been made.

The three cards from this measure which have been placed above the top of the game board during play are clapped.

"All right! Good clapping." Play continues with teams alternately placing cards on the game board to form another measure.

Guide them so the beats are musical as well as mathematically correct.

                    Possible to Clap   Impossible to clap!

Also help them to remember to turn over the card the other team uses on the game board.

Using ⁴₄ time, the game board will evenly complete eight measures. The students are always so pleased when they have filled up the entire board, and it works out exactly!

The students will enjoy this game very much. However, if it is tried before they are ready, it will be too much work for them.

<u>OTHER METERS</u> Below is a chart of how the game board will work using the other time signatures. In some cases cards will not be needed. Those cards can be placed, picture side up on the game board to show that they are out of play.

In other cases, there will be an uneven number of beats. If the students are told this before play, they won't come to the end and feel as if they had made an error.

The <u>whole rest</u> may be used in all meters to designate a full measure of rest. However, the <u>whole note</u> always counts for four beats.

TIME	MEASURES	OUT OF PLAY	LEFT OVER BEATS
$\frac{4}{4}$	eight	none	none
$\frac{3}{4}$	nine	o	none
$\frac{2}{4}$	eleven	♩. o	one beat
$\frac{5}{4}$	six	none	three beats or two beats if 𝄻 is played as four beats
$\frac{6}{4}$	four	none	two beats
$\frac{3}{8}$	nine	𝄻 ♬♬ ♩ ♩. o ♫	three ♩ values
$\frac{6}{8}$	six	𝄻 ♬♬ ♩ o	none
$\frac{2}{2}$	eight	none	none

254

GAME 15-3: SHORT SNAKES

OBJECTIVE:
To practice arranging notes into measures

IN BRIEF:
Students arrange the *Notes & Rests Cards* into short SNAKES of several measures.

AGES:
Middle elementary and older

MATERIALS:
1) *Notes & Rests Cards* - both sets
2) BLUE bar lines from the *Blue Jello Rhythm Puzzle*

REPETITIONS:
Two or three times per session

PROCEDURE:
Pass out the cards to small groups of students.

Ask them to write out three - five measures in whatever time signature you designate, using the BLUES as bar lines. If they need help dividing the measures, assist them. Either check the cards yourself or let them check each other's.

"Would you like to try to clap your rhythms?"

"Oh, no. I thought we might have to do something like that," smiles Maria.

It is important that you provide a pulse.

"Do you think you could clap your own rhythms <u>at the same time</u>?"

Continue to provide a pulse and maybe count out loud to help them keep their places. This is fun and enjoyable.

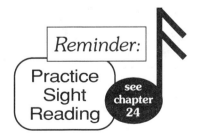

Reminder:
Practice Sight Reading
see chapter 24

OBJECTIVE:
To reinforce the relative value of notes and rests

IN BRIEF:
Two teams form *Notes & Rests* SNAKES with the cards from each SNAKE lining up vertically.

AGES:
Upper elementary and older

MATERIALS:
1) *Notes & Rests Cards* - both sets
2) *Real Rhythm Cards* - time signatures
3) BLUE bar lines from the *Blue Jello Rhythm Puzzle*

REPETITIONS:
One SNAKE per session

PROCEDURE:
Divide the students into two noncompeting teams. Decide on a time signature and place the *Notes & Rests Cards* on the rug.

The two teams are to each make a SNAKE with their cards, moving measure by measure together and lining up the notes vertically. They may take turns writing their measures and adjusting the spacing of their cards to line the notes up correctly.

The BLUES are to be bar lines.

When all the cards have been used, practice with the students so they can clap either line of cards. It may be necessary to practice measure by measure.

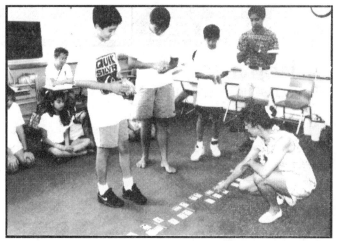

Once that is accomplished, have the teams clap their Rhythm SNAKES <u>at the same time</u> . . . together. This can be tricky so pick a sensible tempo!

Perhaps a child who is fussed over gets a feeling of destiny; he thinks he is in the world for something important and it gives him drive and confidence.

Dr. Benjamin Spock

OBJECTIVE:
To practice hearing rhythms in three different meters

IN BRIEF:
Rhythm bingo - side 2 contains more difficult rhythms and meters of $\frac{4}{4}$, $\frac{3}{4}$ and $\frac{6}{8}$.

AGES:
Upper elementary and older

MATERIALS:
1) *Rhythm Bingo Cards* - side 2
2) *Magic Notes* and *Magic Wands*

REPETITIONS:
Until everyone has several bingos

PROCEDURE:
Let each student choose a *Rhythm Bingo Card* and pass out the *Magic Notes*. Clap each rhythm twice for them to find on their cards. Repeat the rhythm if someone asks to hear it again. Watch the cards so everyone stays about even.

Tell them whether you are clapping a pattern in $\frac{3}{4}$ or $\frac{6}{8}$.

GROUP BINGO: It's a lot of fun to play this game as a group. There's more interaction among the students so they can learn from each other. Set the cards up so everyone can see.

↓

Clap each rhythm several times, even after the pattern is found. Then students look at it, hear it and even clap it. They could take over the game, clapping the patterns for each other to find.

To finish the game, choose one card as the main card. Matching the position of the spaces on the cards, not the rhythms, have them move the *Magic Notes* from the other cards to the main card. They can see how many times they got BLACK OUT (the whole card filled), and the game has a sense of completion.

OBJECTIVE:
To practice notes and rests on an advanced level, adding values on a coordinate graph. At cleanup, students practice rhythmic reading and dictation.

IN BRIEF:
Two rows of six *Notes & Rests Cards* are set out, one horizonal and one vertical. Students place *Gold Coins* and *Magic Notes* equal to the addition of two cards at the point where they meet. At cleanup, students clap the rhythm of both cards. Other students guess which cards were clapped and remove the appropriate pile of *Gold Coins* and *Magic Notes.*

AGES:
Upper elementary and older

MATERIALS:
1) *Notes & Rests Cards*
2) *Gold Coins*
3) *Magic notes* and *Magic Wands*

REPETITIONS:
Once through the game in a session

PROCEDURE:
Lay out the *Notes & Rests Cards.* Using fewer cards will produce a shorter game. Place the containers of *Gold Coins* and *Magic Notes* nearby.

"You may have done coordinate graph math charts similar to this one in school. It's really easy." Point to the cards as you explain. "Select one card from the horizontal row and one from the vertical row. Let's use the GOOSEBERRY and the quarter rest as our example. The GOOSEBERRY is worth . . . right, one *Gold Coin.* The quarter rest is worth . . . right, one *Gold Coin.* So we put two *Gold Coins* at the point where the two cards meet."

Help them figure out a few of the card combinations and make little piles of money.

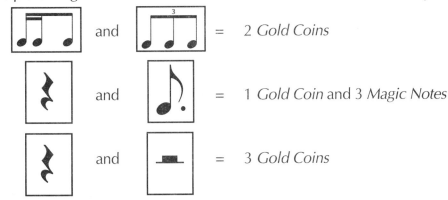

"Oh, I get it! Can we try it?" Now they are eager.

"Yes, please make your moves next to an answer already given, either vertically, horizontally or on the angle." This keeps it easy to read and lets them practice similar values one after the other.

The students will enjoy this game and should be able to do most of it on their own.

The completed chart:

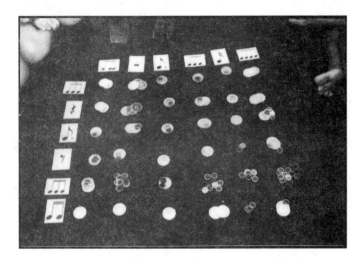

<u>CLEANUP</u>: "You made that look so easy. Good work. Now, how shall we clean this up?"

"Let's push it all into one big pile!" smiles Alison.

"Ohhhhh, not yet. I have an idea. Don't you think it would be too easy to just put the cards and *Gold Coins* away?"

"Hmmmmm." They're suspicious.

"Each of you may have a turn clapping two of the cards — one from each row," you explain.

"What?"

"The person sitting next to you has the first chance to guess which notes or rests you clapped. Whoever guesses correctly, can remove the little pile of *Gold Coins* and *Magic Notes*.

"Once an entire row or *Gold Coins* and *Magic Notes* is removed, the card is also removed. When it's all gone — we'll be finished. You may choose any pair of cards you'd like. You don't have to go in any order."

"Oh, I get it! This sounds like fun," says Mary.

For example: Mary claps -

Alison is sitting next to her so she has the first try. "Is it the three eighth notes and the eighth rest?"

"Yes," says Mary. Alison removes the two *Gold Coins.*

<u>VARIATION</u>: Cards of equal value can be placed on top of each other and thus included in the chart. When it's time for cleanup, the cards in a pile can be rotated after the top card has been used. This way more notes are used and a variety of rhythmic combinations are clapped.

260

EXPANDING EARS
DICTATION PART 3

Did your students enjoy the other games with dictation? Are they confident about hearing music and writing it down? Do you feel they are eager for more challenges?

The games in this chapter expand dictation to identifying intervals, harmonic concepts and combinations of melodic and rhythmic dictation. The *Song Puzzle Cards* are used to make song SNAKES. The interval circle introduced in Chapter 8: THIRDS ARE ONE MORE THAN SECONDS, now becomes an arena for dictation with intervals.

Even at this level it's great to end dictation sessions with the GAME 9-4: TAKE AWAY. Use minor scales or other interesting patterns.

As students' identification skills continue to be more focused and discriminating, they can move into the aural world of minor, diminished and augmented sounds using these same game ideas.

Simply put . . . keep the excitement coming.

PART
TWO

16

GAMES IN THIS CHAPTER

OBJECTIVE:
To expand the limits of five note patterns

IN BRIEF:
The last note of a dictation pattern becomes the first note of the next pattern.

AGES:
Elementary and older

MATERIALS:
1) Piano
2) *Dictation Slates*
3) *Magic Notes* and *Magic Wands*
3) *Mini Sharps and Flats* if desired.

REPETITIONS:
5-7 per class

PROCEDURE:
After passing out *Dictation Slates, Magic Notes* and *Magic Wands* to the students, play a pattern for them to write. Play it twice.

Explain that the last note of this pattern becomes the first note of the next pattern. They can clean off their *Dictation Slates* except for the "D" note. Play the next pattern for them to write.

Continue on for several rounds, weaving in and out of both clefs. You may pass out the *Mini Sharps and Flats* or not use them — depending on your preference and their ability. Without accidentals, students are writing in modal patterns. Once they have studied key signatures, you may want to include accidentals.

GAME 16-2: THREE INTERVALS

OBJECTIVE:
To introduce harmonic intervals

IN BRIEF:
Using G as the root, each student arranges six *Magic Notes* on a slate to form three major thirds. The teacher plays these intervals harmonically (at the same time), changing the top note. Variations may be included as students progress.

AGES:
Middle elementary and older

MATERIALS:
1) Piano
2) *Dictation Slates*
3) *Magic Notes* and *Magic Wands*

REPETITIONS:
5-7 per session

PROCEDURE:
Pass out the *Dictation Slates* and *Magic Notes*. Seat the students on the rug and move them until you can see everyone's *Dictation Slates*. Ask them to arrange their *Magic Notes* as shown here. Play the intervals on the piano as they are writing to let them get used to the sound.

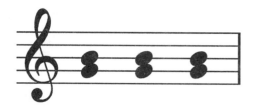

"During this game, you may move your *Magic Notes* while I play. I'll play what you wrote except I will change the top note. The lower note will stay the same. Let's try one together as an example."

Play the notes with good, clear tone at about the same tempo as a clock chimes the hour.

When seconds are played, some students will need your help to write them correctly.

In later sessions change the bottom note, use the bass clef, use intervals other than thirds or use intervals with *Mini Sharps or Flats*.

264

GAME 16-3: MAJOR OR MINOR?

OBJECTIVE:
To teach students to distinguish between the major and minor sounds. Play with older students to learn to hear the tonal differences of triads, chords, scales, etc.

IN BRIEF:
Several harmonic triads are played. Students compare the sounds and write the sequences on their *Number Slates*.

AGES:
Elementary

MATERIALS:
1) Piano
2) *Number Slates* and pencils

REPETITIONS:
6-8 chords per session.

PROCEDURE:
Let them watch your fingers as you play several examples of major and minor triads on the piano. Give them turns to play.

Ask them to write an upper case M and a lower case m on their slates. Explain that the M stands for the major and the m stands for the minor.

M m

"I'm going to play two triads for you. One will be major and the other minor. If the first triad is major, write a 1 under the upper case M. If the second triad is minor, write a 2 under the lower case m." Play both triads in the same key and with the same root note. Be careful not to play the minor triad softer than the major triad.

It's all right to play the same triad twice. If you played two major triads, their slates would look like this.

M m
1 2

Without warning, you can also play three triads.

M m
2 3 1

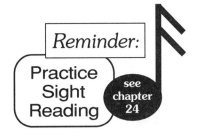

Reminder:

Practice Sight Reading

see chapter 24

GAME 16-4: INTERVAL CIRCLE DICTATION

OBJECTIVE:
To recognize intervals and name them

IN BRIEF:
Students sit inside a big circle of *Alphabet Cards*, matching the sounds of melodic intervals to the cards in front of them.

AGES:
Elementary and older

MATERIALS:
1) Piano
2) *Alphabet Cards* - one set per student

REPETITIONS:
6-8 intervals per session

PROCEDURE:
Ask the students to stand close together touching backs. They may sit down as you give each one a set of cards. Give different colors to players who are sitting next to each other.

Ask them to lay out their cards in seconds starting with C. If they have trouble making their circle round, let them step out of it so they can see how to fix it.

It is easier for students to identify melodic intervals (one note is played after the other) than harmonic intervals (two notes are played together). So you may want to save harmonic intervals until later sessions. Or you may want to give a few "bonus intervals" at the close of each session, letting anyone who wants the extra challenge, to try harmonic intervals.

To play "I'm going to start on C." Play middle C. "Please place your left hand just above your C card. I will play a second note. Move your right hand so it's over the top of the correct *Alphabet Card*." Play D.

"When I say GO, smack the D card and say "Second!"

Look to see if everyone is ready. "GO!"

SMACK. SMACK. SMACK . . . .

"That's the idea!"

In the first session, play just a few intervals, repeating some over and over. Develop their ability to recognize basic intervals, then expand from there.

Terrific game!

266

OBJECTIVE:
To develop students' ability to "hear" a melodic pattern with their eyes and to practice clapping rhythms in a steady tempo.

IN BRIEF:
Each student is dealt several measures of a song. As a team, they put the song back together. A variety of games can then be played.

AGES:
Middle elementary and older

MATERIALS:
Song Puzzle Cards

REPETITIONS:
One or more songs in a session

PROCEDURE:
Make certain they understand that the face must be in the <u>lower left-hand</u> corner. If the card is turned upside down, it will be a different measure of music. Pass out the cards.

Give them a moment to study their cards and turn them right side up. The object of the game is to write the song by putting the cards in order.

The students can keep their place in the music more easily if they sing as they write out the song. As much as possible, let them work on their own. If they make a mistake, they'll find it sooner or later. Only step in if someone does too much and doesn't let everyone else play.

"Hey, look at that. We did it!"

Once all the cards are out and they have checked their work there are a few interesting possibilities.

Ask everyone to sing the song using one of these ideas. Use others in other sessions.

1. Note names
2. Solfège (do re mi, etc)
3. Any singable syllable
4. Numbers

Before cleaning up, snap your fingers to signal them to close their eyes.

"Uh oh, what's going to happen now?"

Turn about one-third of the cards face down. It's better not to turn every other card over, nor the beginning or ending card nor more than two cards in a row.

Clap twice for them to open their eyes.

"Okay now, I want you to clap this song for me, but . . . I want you to be silent for any of the cards that are face down. Then, come back in at the exact time for the next card. I want to see if you can keep a perfectly steady tempo. It's just like turning the volume on a tape recorder clear off, then on again, then off again."

If necessary, you can clap with them or lightly tap the pulse so they learn to feel it when the music is only inside their heads. Later, let them keep pulse on their own and clap too.

GAME 16-6: *MELODIC BINGO - SIDE 2*

OBJECTIVE:
To train students to see trickier patterns of notes as "melodic words"

IN BRIEF:
Students hear melodic patterns and find them on their *Melodic Bingo Cards*.

AGES:
Elementary and older

MATERIALS:
1) Piano or other instrument
2) *Melodic Bingo Cards* - side 2
3) *Magic Notes* and *Magic Wands*

REPETITIONS:
Until each student has several bingos

PROCEDURE:
Let the students each choose a *Melodic Bingo Card*. Pass out the *Magic Notes*.

"This game is simple. I'm going to play patterns for you to find on your cards. Everyone ready?" Play each pattern twice unless someone asks for it again.

As you progress through the game, watch the cards and play patterns so each student finds about the same number on her card. It's possible to "fix" the game so that each student remains confident and enjoys finding patterns.

They call out BINGO when they have three patterns in a row in any direction. Continue playing until everyone has several bingos. If you have time, continue until BLACK OUT, when all the spaces on the cards are filled.

GROUP BINGO: It's a lot of fun to play this game as a group. There's more interaction among the students so they can learn from each other. Set out the cards so everyone can see them. They are free to find patterns on any of the cards.

Clap each rhythm several times, even after the pattern is found. Then students look at it and hear it. Or let them take turns clapping the rhythm after it's been found. They can even take over the game, clapping the patterns for each other to find.

To finish the game, choose one main card. Matching the position of the spaces on the cards, not the rhythms, have them move the *Magic Notes* from the other cards to the main card. They can see how many times they got BLACK OUT, and the game has a sense of completion.

The wildest colts make the best horses.

Plutarch

GAME 16-7: INTRODUCING HARMONIC DICTATION

OBJECTIVE:
To identify, write and play harmonic patterns

IN BRIEF:
Students learn to identify I, IV, V harmonic progressions.

PRE-GAMES:
Students must study triad inversion GAME 21-10: TEACHING INVERSIONS through GAME 21-13: INVERSION DROP before playing this game.

AGES:
Elementary and older

MATERIALS:
1) Piano
2) *Alphabet Cards*
3) *Dictation Slates*
4) *Magic Notes* and *Magic Wands*
5) Music
6) *Cardboard Keyboards*
7) *Number Slates*

REPETITIONS:
Once through game. May be repeated.

PROCEDURE:
"You are getting very good at melodic dictation. Today we are going to learn to write harmonic dictation. Melody is one note at a time. Harmony is chords . . . thirds played at the same time."

Let the students take a *Cardboard Keyboard, Dictation Slate* and *Magic Notes.* "Please write a C major triad on your *Dictation Slates.*" Play this for them and let them watch your hand.

"I'm going to play a second chord in between two C triads. Please listen and tell me which note stays the same."

Play:
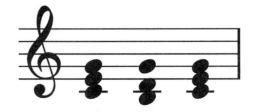

"It's G." "I think it's . . . G." "Me, too. G."

"Right you are. And how did the other two move?"

"Up?" "Down." "I think so, too. Down a second." "Down."

270

"Down a second is right. Can you please write these three chords?"

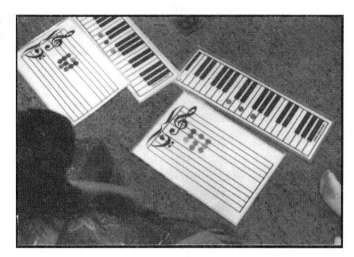

Play it for them again. Let everyone take a turn playing.

Write the chords with the *Alphabet Cards*. Remind them that BDG is a GBD triad just scrambled up. Let them discover that GBD is the fifth tone of the scale so we label it with a V card.

Repeat the same sequence with the IV chord.

Repeat both these chords using bass clef notes.

Play several familiar melodies that use I, IV and V harmonies. First let them identify the chords as you play them. Then let them tell you which chords you should play. Assign several songs for them to play at home.

People with bad consciences always fear the judgment of children.

Mary McCarthy

OBJECTIVE:
To do dictation games in minor modes

IN BRIEF:
Previous dictation games may be played in minor modes before and after minor scales (Chapter 23) are studied.

AGES:
Elementary and older

MATERIALS:
See each particular game

REPETITIONS:
Elementary and older

PROCEDURE:
Why not expand your students' listening capabilities to include the minor modes? This is possible before, after and during the study of minor scales.

Many of the games from Chapter 9: NOTES ON THE STAFF - DICTATION PART 2 and this chapter can be adapted to minor scales. Here are some ideas:

GAME 16-8-1: TAKE AWAY (Like GAME 9-4)

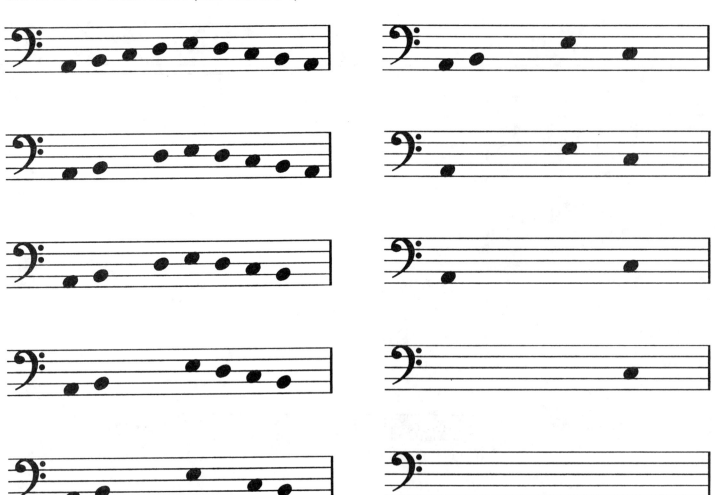

GAME 16-8-2: *MELODIC BINGO* (Like GAME 9-8)

ADDITIONAL MATERIALS:
1) *One Staff Board*
3) *Clefs Puzzle*
2) *Staff Sharps and Flats*

PROCEDURE:
Rather than using G major, the patterns can played in g minor. Ask the students to arrange the *Treble Clef* and g minor key signature on the *One Staff Board*. The students won't see the accidentals on their *Melodic Bingo Cards*. This is all right since we don't have the key signature next to each measure in printed music either.

(Just to see if you're on your toes — Can you see an error in this photo? Answer is at the end of this chapter.

GAME 16-8-3: *SONG PUZZLE* SNAKES (Like GAME 16-5)

ADDITIONAL MATERIALS:
The *Treble Clef* from the *Clefs Puzzle*

PROCEDURE:
Rather than seeing the song in F major in the bass clef, ask them to see it as d minor in the treble clef.

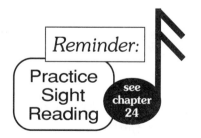

Reminder:
Practice Sight Reading
see chapter 24

273

OBJECTIVE:
To practice identifying ten triads, seventh chords or scales with the same root but in different tonalities

IN BRIEF:
Students identify five to ten triads, seventh chords or scales played in a row using *Magic Notes*. This game is played during or after study in Chapters: 19, 20, 21, 22 or 23.

AGES:
Elementary and older

MATERIALS:
1) *Magic Notes* and *Magic Wands*
2) *Song Puzzle Cards* - backside
3) *Alphabet Cards*
4) *Number Slates*
5) Piano
6) *Cardboard Keyboards*

REPETITIONS:
3 or 4 times in a session

PROCEDURE:
You can play this game with:

4 kinds of triads

6 kinds of 7th chords

4 kinds of scales

In this game students use the colors of the *Magic Notes* to represent the four basic tonalities:

Purple = major   Blue = minor   Green = diminished   Pink = augmented

Our example will be four kinds of triads. Using the *Number Slate*, write out the tonality of the ten triads you are going to play.

M m d A d M M A m M

To help them remember the four triads, the students have written each of the triads on four *Cardboard Keyboards*, matching colored *Magic Notes* and the colored borders of the *Cardboard Keyboards* to represent the tonalities. They will use these as reference during the game.

Let's give the game a fun element of chance. Ask the students to lay out ten *Alphabet Cards* face down using colors to guess the tonality of the triads you are going to play. The letters on the cards will have no significance. →

Pass out one *Song Puzzle Card* and a handful of *Magic Notes* to each student. "Okay. Listen carefully and try to put your ten *Magic Notes* in the same order as the triads I play. Use the backside of your card. I will play each triad twice."

Play the ten triads using the same note as tonic.

"Ready to hear how you did?" Read off your list, playing each triad so they can hear it identified with the correct tonality label. To keep score, they should slide their own incorrect *Magic Notes* and group's set of *Alphabet Cards* below the rows.

"Amazing! You got six right with your *Alphabet Card* guesses. Wow! How did you each do with hearing the tonality of the triads?"

Repeat several more times. Remember that they are comparing their own scores, not to each others.

As students become more proficient in this, use different notes as tonic when you play the triads.

Answer to what's wrong in this photo from GAME 16-8-2: MINOR IDEAS - MELODIC BINGO: The second flat in the treble clef is on space F rather than on space E.

CHILDREN LEARN WHAT THEY LIVE
by Dorothy Law Nolte

If a child lives with criticism, he learns to condemn.

If a child lives with hostility, he learns to fight.

If a child lives with ridicule, he learns to be shy.

If a child lives with shame, he learns to feel guilty.

If a child lives with tolerance, he learns to be patient.

If a child lives with encouragement, he learns confidence.

If a child lives with praise, he learns to appreciate.

If a child lives with fairness, he learns justice.

If a child lives with security, he learns to have faith.

If a child lives with approval, he learns to like himself.

If a child lives with acceptance and friendship, he learns
to find love in the world.

NAME ANY NOTE

The work's been done. The concept is understood. The notes are learned . . . and remembered. Well, almost.

Now it's time for interesting games to help students commit the names of the lines and spaces to memory for keeps. Some of these games are variations of earlier favorites. Others are new.

Some can be played even before all of the staff notes are learned. Simply use the cards that have been mastered, adding new ones when students are ready to learn more.

Unless you're teaching in a general music program, your students will be having regular practice reading pieces to learn new songs. They should be reading by intervals (relating notes to each other) rather than by naming notes. These games will strengthen memory and the ability to read music.

PART TWO

17

GAMES IN THIS CHAPTER

GAME 17-1: PASS OUT

OBJECTIVE:
To name notes and relate them to instruments

IN BRIEF:
Notes With Letters are passed out for students to place on the Staff Board and find on their instruments.

AGES:
Elementary and older

MATERIALS:
1) *One* or *Grand Staff Board*
2) *Notes With Letters*
3) *Ledger Line Sheets*
4) *Clefs Puzzle*
5) *Staff Sharps and Flats*

REPETITIONS:
Several rounds per session

PROCEDURE:
Lay out the *Staff Board* and let the students place the clef(s) correctly.

Pass out one note to each student. Ask them to place their notes on the staff correctly. Repeat until all the notes you want to practice are on the staff.

"Hey, I already have my note on that line, Robin!"

In this session or another one, point to different notes so students can find them on their instruments. You may use the *Staff Sharps and Flats* also.

GAME 17-2: MATCH THIS CARD

OBJECTIVE:
To practice naming notes

IN BRIEF:
Playing together, students identify their own row of notes using *Alphabet Cards*.

AGES:
Elementary and older

MATERIALS:
1) *Grand Staff Cards*
2) *Alphabet Cards* - five sets different colors

REPETITIONS:
4 - 6 rounds per session

PROCEDURE:
Toss the *Alphabet Cards* in the middle of the circle and mix them up.

Pass out all the cards and ask the students to line them up.

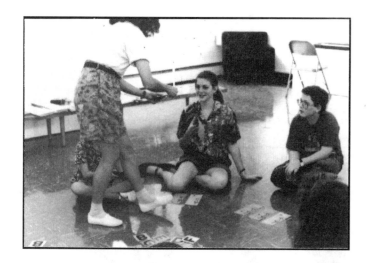

Ask the students to name each note by placing the correct *Alphabet Card* below the staff card. If they put the *Alphabet Card* above the staff card, someone may accidentally think it's one of the ones in the center and grab it away!

If you see a mistake during play, simply remove the card so the student knows to look again for the right one.

They call out FINE when they have identified all their notes. Move around the room, checking to see if their answers are correct.

"Great. Please hand me your *Grand Staff Cards* and put the *Alphabet Cards* back in the center of the circle."

Pass the *Grand Staff Cards* out again. On each round pass the cards to the player who received the last card on the last round so everyone gets a turn to receive the first card.

NOTE: This game works well even before students know all the notes on the grand staff. I played this with a class of six-and seven-year-old students who knew all their C's, D's, B's and had just learned the E's the previous week. We took a moment to review the new note E, then moved right into the game.

I passed out all the *Grand Staff Cards*, even the ones we hadn't studied yet. "You may have some new cards in your row. Please look through your cards and give me back any F's, G's and A's. Keep only the B's, C's, D's and E's."

After they studied their cards my hands began to fill with cards they "didn't" know.

"Here's an A, Mrs. Yurko," said Anita.

"This is a G and this is an F," said Wendy.

"Here's another A," said Christopher.

"Here's an F," said Blake.

I had to chuckle at how easily they were identifying notes we hadn't studied.

GAME 17-3: *GRAND STAFF CARDS PAIRS*

OBJECTIVE:
To practice naming notes

MATERIALS:
Grand Staff Cards

IN BRIEF:
Pairs of students take turns naming notes.

REPETITIONS:
Several rounds in a session

AGES:
Elementary and older

PROCEDURE:
Divide the students into pairs and give each pair four *Grand Staff Cards*. Keep the remaining cards.

One student shows the cards, one at a time, to the other. After the cards are named, they return them to you in exchange for four new cards. Now it's the other student's turn to show the cards.

All the pairs work at their own pace.

GAME 17-4: BINGO BOTH CLEFS

OBJECTIVE:
To practice naming notes

IN BRIEF:
Students locate notes on the *Bingo Cards*. The notes may be either bass or treble clef.

AGES:
Elementary and older

MATERIALS:
1) *Bingo Cards*
2) *Bingo Dots - letter side*
3) *Alphabet Cards* - two sets

REPETITIONS:
Once until each student fills a *Bingo Card*

PROCEDURE:
Hold out the *Bingo Cards* so each student can choose one. Pass out four *Bingo Dots* to each player. They should place their cards on the rug in front of them.

Turn over one *Alphabet Card*.

Student look over their cards and try to find any B, either clef, and cover it with a *Bingo Dot*.

As their minds become quick at moving around the staff, this game will be easier. If students overlook a note, it's better not to intercede. When you show the second set of Alphabet Cards, they will no doubt find all the notes. Can you spot the notes that could have been covered with the B alphabet card?

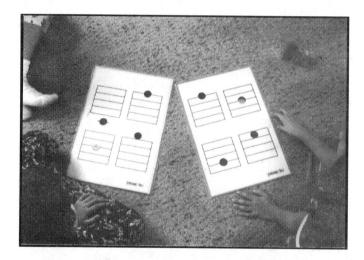

As with the other BINGO games, watch so all the cards fill up at about the same rate. Continue play until everyone's card is filled.

VARIATION: If students want a little extra challenge, let each one play two or even three cards at once.

Note: There is the right number of *Bingo Dots* for students to identify all the treble clef <u>or</u> all the bass clef if all the cards are turned in the same direction.

GAME 17-5: BINGO TOSS

OBJECTIVE:
To practice grand staff notes

IN BRIEF:
All the *Bingo Cards* are laid out in a large rectangle. Students toss a note onto the cards, naming notes and trying to fill up each card.

AGES:
Elementary and older

MATERIALS:
1) *Bingo Cards*
2) *Bingo Dots - face side*
3) A BLUE from the *Blue Jello Rhythm Puzzle*
4) *Toss Note* from the *Clefs Puzzle*

REPETITIONS:
Until all notes have been covered

PROCEDURE:
Lay out the *Bingo Cards* as shown in the photo. Putting out half the cards will make the game shorter.

"Please stand behind this stick when you toss. If it doesn't land in a staff, you may have another toss. The top four cards are the treble clef and the bottom four cards are the bass clef. After you name the note please put a *Bingo Dot* on it. Think you can aim well enough to hit all the notes?"

If students are a little unsure of their notes, let them take turns tossing, but everyone can try to name the note.

They will enjoy tossing the *Toss Note* and naming notes.

GAME 17-6: FISH

OBJECTIVE:
To practice naming notes

IN BRIEF:
With rules similar to the familiar card game, students ask each other for cards trying to get those of the same note name.

AGES:
Elementary and older

MATERIALS:
1) *Grand Staff Cards*
2) *Alphabet Cards* - one set

REPETITIONS:
One game in a class session

PROCEDURE:

Shuffle the cards as you explain the game. Then deal out four cards to each student and place the others face down in a pile in the center of the students. Tell them they may look at their cards but not to look at each other's.

Students will love playing this "real-type" card game. It's a wonderful game to encourage interaction among students as they develop cooperative play techniques.

"Today we're going to play a game called FISH. It's similar to the regular card game GO FISH with a few changes.

"Look through your cards and name each one silently. Arrange them in alphabetical order in your hand. Everyone shouldn't put A first or we may be able to tell which cards you have. If you have some that are the same, put them behind one another."

"There are six of some cards and five of others. Once you get three of the same letter, put the cards down. After that, whoever gets the other two or three may put them down.

Six cards

Five cards

The first player asks anyone for a card to match one in his or her hand.

"Bruce, do you have a D?" asks Elaine.

"No, go fish," responds Bruce who doesn't have a D card. Elaine picks up the top card from the pile and adds it to those already in her hand. If she drew a D, she would not have an extra turn, a rule not borrowed from the regular GO FISH game.

284

Dana is sitting next to Elaine and begins to use the strategy needed to collect lots of cards. He asks, "Elaine, do you have a D?"

"Yes! How did you know I had a D?" asks a surprised Elaine, handing her D card over to Dana.

"Simple," he laughs, "you just asked Bruce for a D, so you must have one in your hand. I have one too, so I asked for yours!"

Great logic and memory!

The game continues around the circle with students asking each other for the notes they need.

Once a player collects three cards of one letter name, s/he shows them to the other players, who check to make sure they're the same. Then they are placed face up on the rug.

This player, or someone else may put down the remaining two or three cards of the same letter name on later turns.

If someone puts down his or her last cards or gives up the last card to another player, s/he may draw the top card and stay in the game.

The game continues until all the cards are "fished" and in piles.

During the game students will be very animated as they plan their strategies and gain or lose cards. They will hardly realize they are practicing notes as they enjoy each other's company and the excitement of the game.

You can't be too careful what you tell a child because you never know what he'll take hold of and spend the rest of his life remembering you by.

Frederick Buechner

GAME 17-7: NOT REALLY TRIADS

OBJECTIVE:
To review thirds and practice naming notes

IN BRIEF:
In a quick paced game, students lay out *Grand Staff Cards* by intervals like GAME 8-4: WIN A TRIAD.

AGES:
Elementary and older

MATERIALS:
Grand Staff Cards

REPETITIONS:
Play for 5 - 10 minutes per session

PROCEDURE:
Ask the students to practice saying thirds while you deal out the cards. Keep the last card and place it in the middle of the circle. Players should turn all their cards right side up and arrange them in front of themselves, ready to play.

"This is a . . . right, a D. And the third after D is . . . yes, F. Look through your cards and if you have an F, any F, please put it here next to the D. Whoever is first, gets to leave it there." The card can be from any octave.

"The third after F is . . ., whoever has that card, any clef, can put it here . . . right, Caitlyn, that's an A."

Since Caitlyn put down the last card, she gets to keep the "root" D and the "third" F. "Wow! Lucky me," laughs Caitlyn.

The A card becomes the new "root" for the next triad.

Players will look through their cards and quickly slide cards into the correct place. The game doesn't need much verbal help at all, you need only to hand the "root and third" to whoever put down the "fifth" and move that "fifth" over so it becomes the new "root".

If someone gets low on cards, simply take a few from a player who has lots of cards and hand them over.

VARIATION: Use other intervals or build descending chords.

GAME 17-8: WAR WITH *GRAND STAFF CARDS*

OBJECTIVE:
To have lots of fun practicing naming notes

IN BRIEF:
Played similar to the regular WAR card game, the student who names the note first takes both cards.

AGES:
Elementary and older

MATERIALS:
Grand Staff Cards

REPETITIONS:
For approximately 10 minutes of play

PROCEDURE:
Divide the students into two teams. Give the first player of each team half the *Grand Staff Cards*. Each pile should have bass and treble clef cards. They should place the piles face down.

The instructions are easy. "Ready? After I say GO, quickly turn over your top card. Whoever names his or her note first, wins both cards. Are you ready? . . . GO."

"D!," calls out Greg. "F!" says Cleary right after him. Greg's team takes both cards.

Greg and Cleary pass the pile face down to the next players in line to take the next turn.

If there's a tie, it's time for war! A second card is placed face down, then a third card is turned face up after you say GO. Whoever names his or her card first wins all six cards. If there's another tie, then it's another war! There may be a lot of happy joking around.

<u>Variation</u>: Three teams can play using the same rules.

287

GAME 17-9: PIANO WAR WITH *GRAND STAFF CARDS*

OBJECTIVE:
To have lots of fun practicing finding notes quickly on the keyboard. May be easily adapted to other instruments.

IN BRIEF:
This game is played like GAME 17-8: **WAR WITH** *GRAND STAFF CARDS* except students race to play the correct note on the piano. The student who plays the note first takes both cards.

AGES:
Elementary and older

MATERIALS:
1) *Grand Staff Cards*
2) Two pianos - can be easily adapted to one piano

REPETITIONS:
For approximately 10 minutes of play

PROCEDURE:
Divide the students into two teams. Place half of the *Grand Staff Cards* (each pile should have bass and treble clef cards) face down on each music stand.

After you say GO, the students turn the top card over and quickly play the note. Whoever plays his note first, correct octave of course, gets both cards.

Other students in the class can identify the interval created by the two notes by sight or sound. This is a good time to talk about dissonant intervals.

If there's a tie, it's time for war! A second card is placed face down, then a third card is turned over after you say GO. Whoever plays his or her note first wins all six cards. If there's another tie, then it's another war!

It's easy to tell which clef is next because treble clef cards are blue and bass clef cards are green. Suggest that they turn the card over with the opposite hand so they can find the note easier.

If you're using one piano, separate the cards into two piles, treble clef in one and bass clef in another. One team will find treble clef cards and race with the team who uses the bass clef cards. If there's time, switch positions and play again.

GAME 17-10: SUSPENSE - NOTES

OBJECTIVE:
To play a real card game with the *Grand Staff Cards*. This has to be one of the best games in the book! Look for the rhythmic variation in Chapter 18.

IN BRIEF:
Students are dealt four cards, two of which they can look at, two which they can't until they swap them. Each note has a different value from 1 - 7 points. The goal is to get a low score.

MATERIALS:
1) *Grand Staff Cards* - one set
2) *Alphabet Cards* - one set
3) *Gold Coins* and *Magic Notes* (optional)

REPETITIONS:
One game in a session

PROCEDURE:
This game is designed for four players or four teams of several players each.

Hold the *Alphabet Cards* in your hand and let six students take turns drawing one. This randomly determines the points for each letter during the game. Lay the seven cards out in order near the players so they can see what each card is worth. The first letter drawn is worth seven points, the second six points and so on.

Deal out 16 cards in the formation shown below. The remaining cards are placed face down in a pile in the center. The top card is turned face up and placed next to the pile, becoming the first card in the discard pile.   →

The object is to finish the game with four low point cards. On each turn, the team takes the top card from the discard pile or draws from the pile. They can discard that card, or exchange it for one they have that is not as low in points.

Players see the cards closest to them, but must not turn over the two cards closest to the middle unless they are going to switch them. The cards in this position must remain face down during the entire game.

"Okay, Henry. You may take the first turn." Lucky Henry draws a C, a one pointer. He smiles at his good fortune and the other players know he got a good card.

"Ah, yes. This card can go right here." Henry takes away an "A", one of the cards that's face up and places his new card in the vacated space, face up. He discards the "A". "What a way start the game," he kids his friends.

Remember, the players know the value of the two cards closest to them so it's easy to know whether or not to exchange those cards. It's the two cards they don't know about that creates the suspense. They have to gamble on when to exchange those cards. When they decide to switch one of these unknown cards, they cannot reconsider once the card has been turned over. It will either be a good switch - "Yea! All right. Good move. Way to go!" or the next player will benefit by snatching up the card from the discard pile - "Oh, no! I just gave away a two pointer. Gosh, how could I do that!"

When the last card has been played and no one wants the top card in the discard pile, the players turn over their cards and by naming notes, figure out their scores. You can use *Gold Coins* and *Magic Notes* if you wish.

Cards should be exchanged to check each other's scores and practice naming each other's notes.

Enjoy this great game!

GAME 17-11: SHOW ME WITH NAMES

OBJECTIVE:
To practice naming notes

IN BRIEF:
Students can silently identify a *Grand Staff Card* by selecting an *Alphabet Card* and turning it face down. Teacher calls SHOW ME and cards are turned over.

AGES:
Elementary and older

MATERIALS:
1) *Grand Staff Cards* - one set
2) *Alphabet Cards* - one set per student

REPETITIONS:
5 - 15 cards per session

PROCEDURE:
This game is great fun if the students are able to get all or most of the answers correctly. It could be unfortunate if a student can't name the notes, so play this game only when students are ready.

Give each student a set of *Alphabet Cards*. Place one *Grand Staff Card* in front of you so that everyone can see it.

"Please look through your *Alphabet Cards* and find the name of this note. Try not to let anyone see your card. Put it face down on the rug in front of you."

Once everyone has a card face down, call out SHOW ME. They will turn their cards over and be very happy if they have the correct answer.

Occasionally, someone will miss. Reassure him or her in a lighthearted manner.

GAME 17-12: NAME THAT NOTE

OBJECTIVE:
To practice naming notes

IN BRIEF:
Students toss a note onto the *Grand Staff Board* and name it.

AGES:
Elementary and older

MATERIALS:
1) *Grand Staff Board*
2) *Clefs Puzzle*
3) *Ledger Line Sheets*
4) A BLUE from the *Blue Jello Rhythm Puzzle*
5) Optional - *Gold Coins*

REPETITIONS:
Give each student several turns

PROCEDURE:
Place the *Grand Staff Board* on the floor and hand the students the clefs to place on the staff. Place the BLUE a foot or so from the bottom of the board.

"Would you like to stand behind the stick, toss the note and name the line or space where it lands?"

"Yes, that'll be fun!" They will all want a turn.

Keep the students seated around the board so they can silently name the notes on each other's turns. If they are behind each other, they won't be able to see and may get into mischief.

If the students are good at naming the notes, you can add *Gold Coins* to make the game more enticing.

Two *Gold Coins* = Quick, first try answers
One *Gold Coin* = Slower, later answers

As with all games in ***Music Mind Games***, make certain the students are successful and challenged at the same time.

VARIATION: The notes can be named then played on the piano. Either the same student can name the note and find it, or the next student in line can be the one to play it on the piano. If you teach an odd number of students, this will work out so they alternately name and find notes.

291

GAME 17-13: DROP AND MOVE INTERVALS

OBJECTIVE:
To practice naming notes and intervals - very helpful for reading skills

IN BRIEF:
Five *Mini Notes* are dropped on each student's *Dictation Slate*. They receive the same number of *Magic Notes* as the interval they had to move each note, to get it to it's correct line or space.

AGES:
Elementary and older

MATERIALS:
1) *Dictation Slates*
2) *Mini Notes*
3) *Magic Notes* and *Magic Wands*

REPETITIONS:
4 - 5 rounds

PROCEDURE:
"Gather around so I can show you a new game!" Randomly select five *Mini Notes* and holding your hand about 10 inches above the *Dictation Slate*, drop them.

Working together, move each note to it's correct line or space. As you do so, name the interval you moved the note.

This is after the notes were corrected.

The D was correct	=	0 *Magic Notes*
The A moved up a third	=	3 *Magic Notes*
The C moved down a second	=	2 *Magic Notes*
The G moved up a second	=	1 *Magic Note*
The E moved down a third	=	3 *Magic Notes*

"So we win nine *Magic Notes*! Would you like to try with your own slates and notes?"

Let everyone take a *Dictation Slate* and a bag of *Mini Notes*. They can pick up five *Mini Notes* while their eyes are closed and drop them onto their slates. Like you did together, they move the notes to their correct line or space, keeping track of the interval moved. Encourage them to recognize the intervals at sight rather than counting lines and spaces. This helps with music reading skills.

Try this game with teams — it's great. →

RHYTHM
PLAYING CARDS

Board games and video games are entertaining, but playing cards, popular for centuries, remain intriguing.

Could rhythm values replace the A 2 3 4 5 6 7 8 9 10 J Q and K?

Could a sixteenth note or rest become an ace and the whole rest or whole note become the king?

Easily. This deck of *Rhythm Playing Cards* has 52 cards and many common games can be adapted to practicing note and rest values. But, there is one monumental change.

Everyone is a winner. Even with solitaire games, you always end up winning. Give me Las Vegas!

If you like fun games, you've found them here. Your students will enjoy learning and become totally involved in these games. They will be laughing, rolling around, and planning strategy to place their cards correctly or ask another student for the card they need . . . and all the while becoming more comfortable with the names and relative values of notes and rests.

You will enjoy these games and may end up playing along. There are beginning rhythm games for little children and many others that adults find challenging. Let me know if you come up with some of your own.

These cards are also known as *Rhythm Money* and are used with other games such as *Musopoly*.

PART
TWO

18

GAMES IN THIS CHAPTER

OBJECTIVE:
To match shapes of notes and rests

IN BRIEF:
Students take turns drawing cards from the pile. If they find a match from a card already drawn, everyone collects a *Magic Note*.

AGES:
Preschool, kindergarten, any age

MATERIALS:
1) *Rhythm Playing Cards* - one deck
2) *Magic Notes*

REPETITIONS:
Once in a session

PROCEDURE:
I created this game to give my preschool sons practice recognizing notes and rests. David was sitting on the sofa in my studio.

I sat down on the floor with a deck of cards and the container of *Magic Notes*. "David, I just made up a new game with these cards. Want to play?"

"No." He went right on flying his little green plane in the airspace above the sofa. He did look a little curious, but I could tell he was afraid to try since he didn't know if the game might be too hard for him.

"Come on. It's really easy and lots of fun."

"Maybe." I felt encouraged when I saw him land his plane next to the cushion. His brother, Andrew, was eager to play a new game.

"Come on, David. Me too," Andrew encouraged.

"Okay." And David slid down to join us.

I shuffled the deck and opened the note container. David cut the deck then turned over the top card, placing it above the pile.

"Okay, Andrew, you may turn over the next card. If it's the same as the first one, put it on top of it. But if it's different, put it next to the first one."
He understood this easily.

The boys took turns drawing cards. I would say the name of the note or rest as they drew cards to help them begin learning the names.

"Hey," noticed David, "This card is the same as that one. Shall I put it on top of it?" And he did.

"Since David got a match, we all get a note."

"Wow!" David and Andrew were smiling.

And so the game continued. If the card was a match, we simply put it on top of the same card. If it wasn't, a new pile was started. Each time a card was the same, everyone took a note. When David took a note he would say, "I'm getting the most. I'm winning."

And I would say, "David, in this game, everyone wins. No one tries to get more than someone else. We work together." I realized this was a new concept for him. Other games he'd played with friends at home or school were "Me games", games with only one winner. After a few explanations of this he caught on and turned into a supportive player.

They loved the game, laughing each time they found a match. They loved collecting the notes and begged to play again and again.

GAME 18-2: GO FISH

OBJECTIVE:
To help students get used to calling notes and rests by name and to practice values

IN BRIEF:
Students ask each other for notes or rests they need to make matches or runs.

AGES:
Early elementary and older

MATERIALS:
1) *Rhythm Playing Cards* - one deck
2) *Real Rhythm Cards* - one of each note and rest

REPETITIONS:
Once in a session

PROCEDURE:
This game is best played with four to six players. If your class is larger, use more decks of *Rhythm Playing Cards* and divide up the students.

LEVEL 1: Since this is a matching game, you can use all the cards.

If they have not learned how to make the Card Chart, let them lay out the notes, positioning the cards by their relative length. Practice saying the name of each note and rest. →

Keep the Card Chart out as reference during the game.

After the cards are shuffled, each player is dealt four cards. They should not show their cards to each other. Young children may not be too concerned about this. The remaining cards are put face down in a pile in the middle of the players.

1. The object of the game is to get four of the same. Notes and rests are interchangeable.
2. If players draw what they had just asked for on a "Go Fish" turn, they do not get another turn.
3. If a player runs out of cards, two cards may be drawn from the pile in order to stay in the game.
4. Points are not counted up at the end of the game since play is cooperative.

Encourage the students to decide what they are going to ask for and whom they're going to ask ahead of time. Then they will be ready for their turn. Otherwise the game will drag.

The first player, Lisa, decides to ask Brian for a half rest since she already has one. She can see that he is holding a lot of rest cards in his hand because of the color of the cards.

"Brian, do you have a half rest?"

"What does it look like?" asks Brian. Lisa points to the Card Chart.

"Yes, I do have one." Brian gives Lisa his half rest card.

Now it's Brian's turn. He asks Kathy, "Kathy, do you have a whole note?"

She doesn't. "No, GO FISH," she tells him. Brian draws the top card from the pile. "Hey, look. I got a whole note!" His turn is over.

Now it's Francis' turn. He has a quarter rest and a quarter note and wants to ask Josh for one. But he doesn't remember what to call them. He points to the quarter note on the Card Chart and asks, "What is this note called?"

"Ummmm, that's a quarter note," answers Josh.

"Oh, right. Josh, do you have a quarter note?"

"Yes, I have two!" exclaims Josh. He gives both cards to Francis, who places the four cards on the rug. →

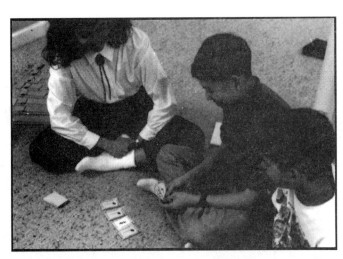

And so the game progresses until all the cards are down and placed appropriately on the rug.

<u>LEVEL 2</u>: Play is as described in Level 1 except players collect runs of four cards rather than simple matches. Instead of asking for cards by name, they ask:

"Do you have a note or rest one less than a whole note?"

"Do you have a note or rest card equal to two quarter notes?"

The first time I played this game it was a big hit. The students had played many rhythm games and by nature, were very happy.

It took only a few turns for them to understand the game. Then I couldn't believe how excited they got! They were rolling on the floor, laughing, teasing each other with rhyming names, jumping up, using louder than normal voices, completely involved in the fun they were having with the game.

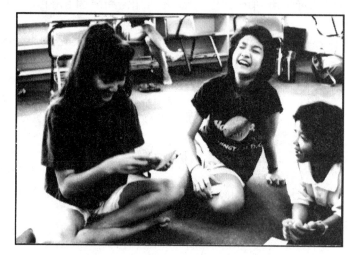

I was smiling and laughing right along with them. They felt so special whenever someone called them by name and asked for a card. Even when they had to give up two treasured cards there would be laughter. And, of course, they were feeling more secure in the names and relationships of notes and rests.

The best way to give advice to your children is to find out what they want and advise them to do it.

Harry Truman

OBJECTIVE:
To practice note and rest values

IN BRIEF:
52 cards are thrown in the air! Students pick up cards and identify their value in notes and coins.

AGES:
Elementary and older

MATERIALS:
1) *Rhythm Playing Cards* - one deck
2) *Gold Coins*
3) *Magic Notes*

REPETITIONS:
Once in a session

PROCEDURE:
"Anyone ever heard of a game "52 . . ."

"Oh no! Don't!" Hands started waving in the air.

" . . . Pick up." And up flew all the cards. →

"Wow! There are cards everywhere!"

"Each of you may pick up around 10 cards. BUT, you must do it with your eyes closed." They thought this was for fun, but it keeps them from choosing cards. I remembered when my older brother so kindly showed me good ol' 52 CARD PICK UP. As a little girl, I had to play it only once to remember it. But this version is great fun.

"Please think of the value of each note or rest and put the correct amount of money on top of each card."

"Oh, I get it." "So do I." They were quickly on task.

"Call out FINE when you're finished."

Several of the students got every value correct, but a few needed corrections. I just turned those cards face down without comment so the students would know to rethink those answers.

GAME 18-4: WAR WITH *RHYTHM PLAYING CARDS*

OBJECTIVE:
To practice note values with a classic card game

IN BRIEF:
Notes and rests are played against each other with higher values winning over lower values.

AGES:
Elementary and older

MATERIALS:
Rhythm Playing Cards - one or two decks

REPETITIONS:
Play for 5-10 minutes of class time.

PROCEDURE:
Students love this game!

Divide the students into two (or three) teams. Set two piles of cards face down in the space between the teams.

One player from each team turns the top card over and places it face up between the piles. Whoever has the larger value card, takes both cards.

A second player from each team draws the next card and places it face up. Whoever has the larger value takes both cards.

When two cards of the same value are drawn, then there is War and more cards are laid out. Whoever has the largest value of the third card, wins all six cards.

300

Sometimes there's Double War!

When a pile is used up, the cards the team won are shuffled, straightened and play continues. If one team's pile becomes a lot larger than the other's, simply move some of those cards from the larger to the smaller pile. "Hey, you took some of our cards," protests Claire with mock indignation.

"I sure did. Thank you very much," I say, smiling at Claire's team. They've gotten used to the games being noncompetitive and don't protest.

We play for several rounds until it's time to move on. What fun!

GAME 18-5: EXACT CHANGE

OBJECTIVE:
To practice adding note and rest values

IN BRIEF:
Students buy *Magic Notes* with *Rhythm Playing Cards*

AGES:
Middle elementary and older

MATERIALS:
1) *Rhythm Playing Cards* - one deck
2) *Magic Notes*
3) *Gold Coins*
4) *Real Rhythm Cards*

REPETITIONS:
Once through the deck in a session

PROCEDURE:
This game uses a different money system from the Card Chart to further challenge the students' understanding of notes and rests values.

Our example today will be the quarter note. "Each *Magic Note* costs one quarter note. In order to buy one, you must have exact change."

Deal out one card to each student

Jennifer got a	♩	half note
Maria got a	♪	sixteenth note
Gus got a	♩.	dotted quarter
Lara got a	𝄽	quarter rest

Jennifer, "I'd like to buy two notes, please."

Maria realizes she must wait to get more *Rhythm Playing Cards.*

Gus waits since he doesn't have exact change.

Lara buys one note.

Deal a second card to each student.

Jennifer got a	♩.	dotted half
Maria got a	♪.	dotted eighth
Gus got a	♪	sixteenth note
Lara got an	♪	eighth note

Jennifer buys three notes.

Maria buys one note since a dotted eighth and a sixteenth note equal a quarter note. →

Gus continues to wait.

Lara waits for more *Rhythm Playing Cards.*

And so the game continues, passing out cards and students buying notes. If they need help, use the *Real Rhythm Cards.* Once they have four *Magic Notes*, they may trade them in for a *Gold Coin.*

The game is a lot of fun and doesn't need to be competitive.

Look what we won! →

302

OBJECTIVE:

Ever wish you could always win at the most common of solitaire games? Amazingly with this version, you will win every time! Played with a group, it's loads of fun and just complicated enough to challenge everyone. Students practice relative values of notes and rests.

IN BRIEF:

Cards are laid out so students take turns adding cards in descending value in one place and ascending values in another. The double version adds speed to the thrills.

AGES:

Middle elementary and older

MATERIALS:

Rhythm Playing Cards - one or two decks

REPETITIONS:

Once per session

PROCEDURE:

Quite by accident, I discovered this version of solitaire in which it's possible to win with every game! Using my handmade *Rhythm Playing Cards*, I thought I had less than the 52 cards in a standard deck. So I set up this game with six rows rather than the regular seven. It was years later that my student Alexis counted the cards and - surprise - there were 52! Here is a sample game. Obviously, the cards will be different in every game.

Sitting with the students on the floor, lay out **six** cards.

Then one row at a time, lay out cards to form this:

The remaining cards become the reserve pile.

SAMPLE GAME

<u>First turn</u> The first player plays all possible cards as they appear in the columns. S/he does not use the reserve pile.

1. Sixteenth notes and rests are placed face up above the columns. Notes and rests must not be mixed in these piles. Piles "build up" from the sixteenth value to the whole note value. The goal of the game is to put all the cards in order in these piles.

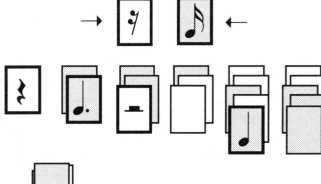

303

2. Whenever one card is moved to expose a card which is turned face down, this card is then turned face up and is available for play.

3. Columns "build down" from whatever card is turned face up. Notes and rests may mix on these columns. Dotted notes must be included.

4. If a blank space opens up, only the whole note or whole rest cards can be put in the space. Then other cards may be added in order.

5. Continue to turn cards over and play them as described in Steps 1-4. Can you see the cards that can be moved on this turn?

304

6. This sample game was great. Lucky cards kept turning up one after the other. Now we're stuck.

7. The next player takes the reserve pile. Just as in regular solitaire, this pile of cards must be kept in order. The player takes the top three cards, flips them over and sets them on the rug. The top card can be played anywhere. If it's used, then the next card can be played. If there's a choice, a card should be placed on the upper piles (where notes and rests are not mixed and cards build up from sixteenth value to whole note value). Once no more cards can be played anywhere, the player is stuck.

Students take turns, passing the reserve pile around the circle. Each plays every possible card until getting stuck. Students may help each other, but should be polite and let the player who's having the turn find the moves.

Reserve pile - once through When the players have gone through the reserve pile once, the cards are turned over and are ready for play again. They should not be shuffled.

When an upper pile is finished (containing all cards in order from sixteenth to the whole), it is turned face down to show that it's completed.

The game continues.

Eventually the game progresses until all the top piles are completed and the game is finished. Rarely, but sometimes it happens near the end of the game that we get completely stuck. Then the reserve pile can be shuffled.

The class will be very intense and have a lot of fun at the same time. Everyone will be watching for a card that can be moved here or there. Most likely it will take everyone's attention to finish the game correctly.

The game is finished when all of the top piles are completed.

"We won. We did it!"

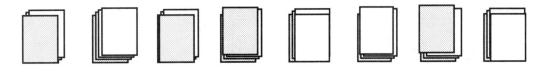

DOUBLE SOLITAIRE This version is played with two decks of cards. Players sit facing each other with the cards between them. Each team can play its set of six columns, but <u>both</u> can play on any card in the top piles which are building up from sixteenth values. Some quick actions result!

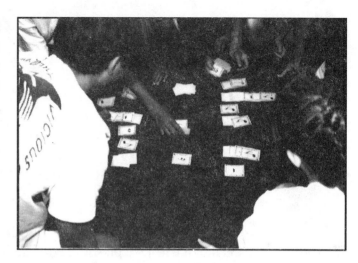

GAME 18-7: RHYTHM POKER

OBJECTIVE:
Please don't misunderstand the inclusion of this game. This is a off-the-wall way to practice notes and rests and it is competitive. It also teaches an excellent lesson in why it's not good to gamble.

IN BRIEF:
Students play a mild version of poker using *Rhythm Playing Cards* instead of playing cards.

AGES:
Later elementary and older

MATERIALS:
1) *Rhythm Playing Cards* - one deck
2) Money of some kind - *Gold Coins* or *Magic Notes*

REPETITIONS:
One round in a session

PROCEDURE:
Rhythm poker is different from regular poker in what makes a winning hand.

Straights and runs always win over 2, 3, 4, or 5 of a kind because even though disguised, this is still a game for learning, and it takes more ability to put together a straight or a run than just matching notes or rests.

Higher values always win over lower values, e.g. a run of half, dotted half and whole wins over a dotted eighth, a quarter, and a dotted quarter. And 3 of a kind half notes wins over 3 of a kind eighth notes. Here's the winning order:

1. Five card run

2. Full house (all five cards used in any combination)

3. 4 card run

4. 3 card run

5. 5, 4, 3 or 2 of a kind

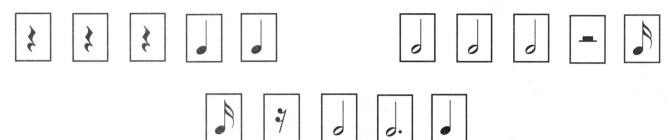

HOW TO PLAY

Pass out a handful of coins to every player.

Players are each dealt five cards. They arrange their cards to get the best values needed to win the hand. Notes and rests are interchangeable.

The player to the left of the dealer (the teacher) decides the amount of the ante. Let's say it is two coins. Everyone throws in two coins to the center of the circle.

The players then trade in any or all cards that won't help them get a winning hand. The player to the dealer's left goes first.

"Hit me two," clowns Kevin, as if this were a real poker game. He tosses two cards face down into the center. The dealer gives Kevin two new cards.

"I'll take one," says Caroline. She tosses her card in the center on top of Kevin's two cards. She is dealt a new card.

"Oh, I don't know what to do? Uh . . . give me four, please," requests Joyce quietly.

And so on around the circle.

Players do not have to trade in cards if they like the ones they were dealt.

On the second round any player can fold (give up). Cards are tossed down and the player is out until the next round.

If a player stays in the game, s/he must match the ante and can ask for new cards.

If his/her hand is a good one, s/he can raise the ante by adding a coin or two to the pile. Anyone who wants to stay in the game must match the ante.

After a few rounds of this, it's time for players to show their cards.

Whoever has the best hand wins all the money.

If there's time, another hand can be played. If anyone needs more money, pass out more *Gold Coins.* You can move to another part of the circle so two different students are now sitting next to you.

Since this is a competitive game, the ending may not be as much fun as the other games. I find this an excellent opportunity to talk about games of chance and gambling.

"How do you feel about winning, Kevin?"

"Absolutely terrific!"

"How do you all feel about Kevin winning?" I ask the others.

"Uh, well . . . "

We talk about how you don't have much choice in a chance game like this and if it were real money you were gambling with, how awful you'd feel to lose.

"We don't want to ever gamble!" they conclude.

You can do anything with children if you only play with them.

Otto von Bismarck

GAME 18-8: SUSPENSE - RHYTHM

OBJECTIVE:
To practice note and rest values - great game!

IN BRIEF:
Students are dealt four cards, two of which they can see, two which they can't until they swap them. The goal is to finish with small value cards. Large values can win in a game another day.

AGES:
Middle elementary and older

MATERIALS:
1) *Rhythm Playing Cards* - one deck
2) *Magic Notes*

REPETITIONS:
Once in a session

PROCEDURE:
Remember GAME 17-10: SUSPENSE - NOTES with the *Grand Staff Cards*? This rhythm version may be even more fun!

Deal out 16 cards in the formation shown. The remaining cards are placed face down in a main pile in the center. The top card is turned face up and placed next to the pile, becoming the first card in the discard pile.

"Look! We got a sixteenth note on the deal! Great!"

"Right. But we also have a whole note. Got to get rid of that one."

On each turn, the team takes the top card from the discard pile or draws from the main pile. They can discard that card, or exchange it for one they have that is not as low in points.

Remember, players know the value of the two cards closest to them so it's easy to know whether to exchange those cards. It's the two cards they don't know about that creates the suspense. The players have to gamble on when to exchange those cards. If they decide to switch one of these unknown cards, they cannot reconsider once the card has been turned over. It will either be a good switch. "Yea! All right. Good move. Way to go!" laughs Zak.

Or they will give away a good card. "Oh, no! I just gave away a sixteenth note. Gosh, how could I do that!" The next team will benefit by snatching up the card from the discard pile.

When the last card has been played and no one wants the top card in the discard pile, they turn over their cards. *Magic Notes* may be useful in figuring their scores.

GAME 18-9: MEREDITH'S TOWER

OBJECTIVE:
To practice values of notes and rests of one quarter note or less. Very popular game.

IN BRIEF:
Ten cards are arranged face down in a tower shape and exchanged until each one is one beat or less. *Magic Notes* determine the number of beats. To finish, cards are grouped into beats.

AGES:
Middle elementary and older

MATERIALS:
1) *Rhythm Playing Cards* - two decks
2) *Magic Notes*

REPETITIONS:
Several times in a session

PROCEDURE:
This is the only game in this chapter specifically for reinforcing beat subdivision.

One hot July evening my children and I sought relief in my cool lower level studio. I was creating games so the rug was strewn with cards, *Magic Notes* and all the rest of the **Music Mind Games** materials. While my young sons slid on the cards as if they were patches of ice, Meredith joined me to see what my new GAME 18-10: MEASURES, was like. "Good game, Mommy," she smiled. "May I try to make one up?"

"Sure," I said encouragingly. The result was this terrific game. I helped round it out somewhat, and she was delighted that I wanted to use it in this book.

Lay the cards face down in what Meredith thought looked like a tower. The extra cards are kept face down in a pile.

One at a time, starting in the lower left hand corner, the tower cards are turned over and left face up or replaced by the top one from the pile, if it is a lower value.

After one round, if any cards in the tower are more than a beat, they are replaced by ones from the pile in the same way.

Magic Notes are placed on top of the cards in matching values. One *Magic Note* equals a sixteenth value.

These notes are placed in piles of four to show how many beats the tower produced. Then the cards are grouped in rows to equal one beat. The number of beats should match the piles of *Magic Notes*.

Two or more noncompeting teams play simultaneously, each with its own deck of cards. It is also possible to play with half a deck that has been divided evenly.

OBJECTIVE:
To practice putting notes into measure groups

AGES:
Middle elementary and older

IN BRIEF:
Cards are played one at a time in an attempt to make a measure in a designated time signature. Once a measure is completed, it is removed. The goal is to finish with the fewest cards left over.

MATERIALS:
1) *Rhythm Playing Cards* - one deck
2) *Gold Coins* and *Magic Notes*

REPETITIONS:
Once in a session

PROCEDURE:
This game is mathematical in nature and not one of speed. The sample game is in $\frac{4}{4}$ time.

The pile is turned face down. The top card is turned over.

Cards are turned over one at a time and placed to the right of the first card if the row doesn't exceed four beats.

If the next card drawn has too many beats, a new row is started.

Here the game continues.

The next card is an eighth rest so it is moved to the top row to complete a measure. That row is removed and the game continues.

The game is scored with *Magic Notes* and *Gold Coins.*

Whatever man learns, the beginning will be slow until the "bud of ability" takes hold. The procedure requires time, but gradually a high ability will develop. It is therefore a matter of patience and repetition. Watching splendid training, we can well understand that ability breeds ability.

Shinichi Suzuki

GAME 18-11: SPEED

OBJECTIVE:
To become very quick at knowing note values

IN BRIEF:
A terrific game! Students race to use up a pile of cards. Cards are discarded according to value.

AGES:
Upper elementary and older

MATERIALS:
Rhythm Playing Cards - one deck

REPETITIONS:
One or two games per session

PROCEDURE:
This game works with two students or two groups.

Set up cards as shown in the photo. There are five cards face down in the piles on either side of the two cards in the middle, and each team has a reserve pile of 15 cards.

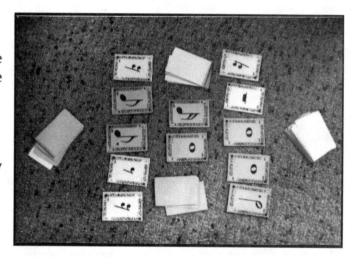

Turns are not taken – each team works fast and furiously at the same time. The goal is to be the first team to use up their five cards plus the 15 in the reserve pile by discarding into either center pile.

1. Cards are placed on the top cards in the center piles in either the next lowest or highest in value.
2. Notes and rests are interchangeable.
3. The piles go up or down in value at any time in the game.
4. Sixteenth values may be placed on whole values, since they are the next value sequentially. Whole values may also be placed on sixteenths for the same reason.

Below is a sample pile which has been spread out.

When players discard one of their five cards they immediately replace it with a card from their reserve pile. →

When both players are stuck, two new cards from the piles of five are placed on the center piles. If these piles are used up before the game is over, the cards from the center piles are shuffled, turned face down and play continues.

314

OBJECTIVE:
To practice comparing values of notes and rests

IN BRIEF:
One or more cards are placed on either side of two *Jellos*. After deciding the value of the notes and/or rests, students form greater than, less than or equal signs.

AGES:
Upper elementary and older

MATERIALS:
1) *Rhythm Money* - one deck
2) Two *Jellos* from the *Blue Jello Rhythm Puzzle*
3) May also be played with *Notes and Rests Cards*

REPETITIONS:
Until everyone has several turns

PROCEDURE:
Turn the deck of cards face down. Turn over the top two cards and place them on either side of the *Jellos*.

"I've got two cards with two *Jellos* between them. After studying the cards, you can either make the *Jellos* look like greater than, less than or equal signs. Norma, you look as if you can do this one."

"I do," smiles Norma.

"Exactly right. Good."

"May I be next?" asks Peter.

"Hope he gets a hard one," says Norma, smiling.

"Fine with me," Peter responds. Turn over the next two cards.

"How about that?" asks Peter proudly.

It's also fun to lay out more than one card on either side of the *Jellos*. Here are some samples:

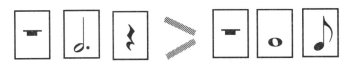

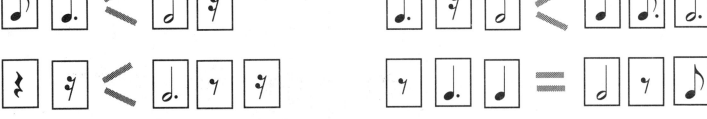

You can ask the students to tell you how many beats each side to the Cards adds up to and what the difference is if they aren't equal. Note: one of these examples is incorrect. Can you find it? The answer is on the next page.

"This side is worth two more beats than the other," says Wendy.

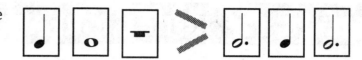

As students become more advanced, ask them to add missing cards to a partially completed equation.

Sample:

Possible answer:

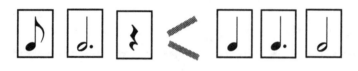

Answer:

Parents should spare no effort in guiding children to become noble human beings.

Shinichi Suzuki

SHARPS AND SCALES
KEYS - EASY

an it be true? Easy to learn key signatures? Fun to learn scales?
Simple to remember them?

Yes. Yes. Yes. Yes.

I used to look at a key signature, usually say the correct alphabet letter, but
I didn't have a clue to what I was talking about.

In fact, it wasn't until I developed these games and played them with my
students, long after I was out of graduate school, that I really learned my key
signatures and understood how they worked. Thus I became better at
reading in the different keys and better at playing scales.

Music Mind Games teaches scales by ear and by logic. When students are
ready to learn about scales, their ears are accustomed to the major scale
sound. Using cards and a few simple rules, students discover the necessary
accidentals on their own. Scales and key signatures are arranged on
Dictation Slates and *Cardboard Keyboards* and played on instruments.

The games are paced so the steps are covered in a timetable set up for
maximum memory efficiency. Since the sequence is easy to master, the
rules are clear, the instructions minimal and the games intriguing. Students
actually like learning scales and key signatures.

And so will teachers . . .

GAMES IN THIS CHAPTER

OBJECTIVE:
To introduce, but not memorize, how major scales C, G, D, A, E, and B are formed

IN BRIEF:
By listening, students learn that each scale is formed by adding one new sharp on the seventh degree. Students write out scales on the *Dictation Slate* and *Cardboard Keyboard* and each key signature on the *Dictation Slate*.

AGES:
Older elementary, middle school and high school

MATERIALS:
1) Piano
2) *Alphabet Cards* - two sets, two colors
3) One *Blank Card* - same color as one set of *Alphabet Cards*
4) Six *Pink Sharp/Flat Cards*
5) One *Alphabet Kid*
6) Two *Dictation Slates*
7) *Magic Notes* and *Magic Wands*
8) *Mini Sharps*
9) One *Cardboard Keyboard*

REPETITIONS:
Once through each scale in this session. Although there is a lot of material, it moves quickly and smoothly.

PROCEDURE:
Divide the students into three groups. Give them these materials:

Group 1: *Cardboard Keyboard* and eight *Magic Notes* to write each scale

Group 2: *Dictation Slate*, *Magic Notes* and *Mini Sharps* to write each scale

Group 3: *Dictation Slate* and *Mini Sharps* to write each key signature

Ask each team to rotate to a new place for each scale. This way they get practice at each skill.

STEP ONE: C MAJOR Lay out the cards for a C major scale. "A scale is made up of eight tones. Pretend this *Blank Card* at the end of the scale is C."

"Here's a C scale." Play:

"There are no sharps or flats in the C scale."

STEP TWO: G MAJOR "To find the scale with one sharp, we move up a fifth to . . . yes G. Sally, can you arrange the cards so they form a G scale, please?"

"I'm going to play a scale beginning on G. Please listen, watch the cards, and tell me which note needs the sharp." Play:

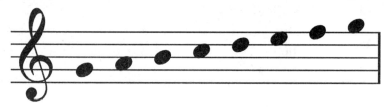

"The F needs the sharp!" they exclaim.

"That's exactly right."

Play the scale again, using F sharp. Place the *Pink Sharp Card* above the F card on the *Alphabet Card* scale. Let the groups write out their scales and key signatures.

Keep track of the sharps on the rug above the *Alphabet Card* scale.

STEP THREE: D MAJOR "Ready to learn the next scale?

"Great — what interval do we move up to? . . ." Pause for their answer. "Yes, up a fifth to . . . right, D is the next scale. Ryan, could you arrange the cards to read a D scale, please?"

As he arranges the cards you can ask some questions to help them begin to learn this process of scales.

"How many sharps will the D scale have?

"Two?" they ask.

"Will one of the sharps be F or will it be two new sharps?"

"F will be one of the sharps." They are catching on!

"So, let's leave the F sharp on our *Alphabet Card* scale."

Play a D scale using only the F sharp.

"I know the new sharp! It's C. I could hear it." Play the corrected scale with two sharps and add the sharp to the *Alphabet Card* scale. Give them time to fix their scales and key signatures. Add C to the row of *Pink Sharp Cards* above the *Alphabet Card* scale.

"What degree of the scale is C in this scale?" you can ask.

They will count the cards. "It's the seventh degree."

"Do you think the new sharp in the next scale will also be on the seventh degree?" Watch them as they are thinking.

"Yeah, it'll be the seventh." "Maybe it will be." "I don't know." "I think it'll will be the seventh."

STEP FOUR: A MAJOR "I think you are hearing and understanding these scales really well. Let's move up a . . . " pause for their answer " . . . right, a fifth to find the new scale on A. Henry, will you move the *Alphabet Cards* please?"

"Before I play this scale, let's make a bet that the new sharp will be on the seventh degree and put this *Alphabet Kid* on G."

Play the A scale with F sharp and C sharp.

"It <u>is</u> G. We got it!" They can put the *Pink Sharp Card* on G in the *Alphabet Card* scale, add G to the row of *Pink Sharp Cards* and arrange their scales and key signatures. →

STEP FIVE: E MAJOR Let them move the cards to get ready for the next scale. They can place their bet for the new sharp and put the *Alphabet Kid* on D.

Play an E scale without the D sharp.

"I hear it — we need the new sharp on D."

"Right again." Play the scale correctly.

They will go to work adding the sharp to the *Alphabet Card* scale, adding D to the row of *Pink Sharp Cards* and writing their scales and key signatures.

STEP FIVE: B MAJOR "We'll do one more scale today. Can you move the *Alphabet Cards*, please? Remember, up a fifth to B. Right. Care to place a bet for the new sharp? Okay — all set . . . ears ready?" Play the B scale without the A sharp.

"We're right again. The new sharp is A!" Play the corrected scale and let them do their writing. Look! We did it!

This is the last sharp scale I suggest you study in this introductory session. Later, students can go on to learn F sharp and C sharp major scales. These scales are not often found in the music which students this age study, and it will be enough to remember the first six scales and their key signatures.

322

OBJECTIVE:
To memorize the order of sharps used in major scales and key signatures. Surely this game is more useful and enlightening than memorizing "fat cats go down and eat breakfast".

IN BRIEF:
Through imitation, students tap and clap out a simple routine while saying "F C G D A". If they ever forget the order of sharps, this body language routine will help them remember.

AGES:
Upper elementary and older

MATERIALS:
None

REPETITIONS:
Once through all the steps in one session. The last step may be repeated in later classes.

PROCEDURE:
This game is to be taught nonverbally, played like "follow the leader". First you will show them what to do and then without missing a beat, they will do all of it again with you.

This game is fun and really helps with memorizing this important sequence of letters. Whenever students practice scales or write out key signatures during later games in this chapter, they will rely on "F C G D A".

Since using rhythm and body motions to match the letters helps students to remember them, I have saved this concept until now. This is the only game that uses rhythmic body motions.

The first pulse for each movement should be stronger than the other three throughout all the steps. mm=160=♩

STEP ONE: Floor Hit the floor four times with your hands.

Then do it together.

♩ ♩ ♩ ♩
x x x x
floor

Knees Repeat step one and add slapping your knees four times.

Then do it together.

♩ ♩ ♩ ♩ | ♩ ♩ ♩ ♩
x x x x | x x x x
floor   **knees**

323

<u>Hands</u> Repeat steps one and two, then add clapping your hands four times.

Then do it together.

floor   knees   clap

<u>Shoulders</u> Repeat steps one, two and three and add touching shoulders four times.

Then do it together.

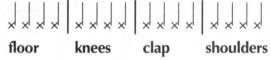

floor   knees   clap   shoulders

<u>Head</u> Repeat steps one, two, three, four and add tapping the top of your head.

Then do it together.

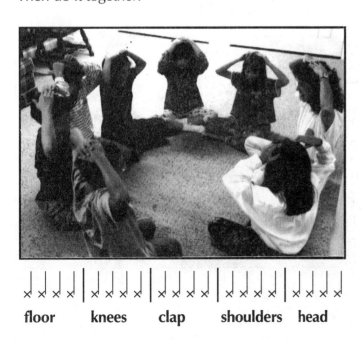

floor   knees   clap   shoulders   head

Reminder:

Practice Sight Reading   see chapter 24

324

STEP TWO: All the motions saying the letters. Repeat steps one to five exactly as before. The only change will be to say the correct letter (the order of the sharps) on the first beat.

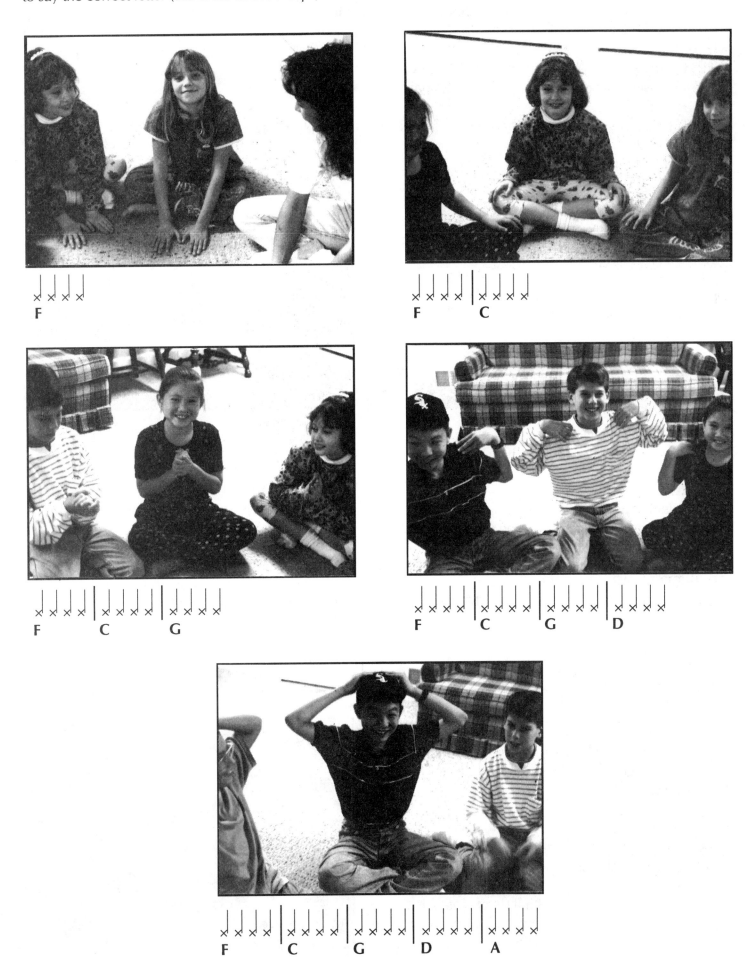

325

STEP THREE: FCGDA and motions. You will do each motion with **two** counts instead of four, saying the letter on the first beat. After you finish, the students should do the whole sequence with you.

F   C   G   D   A

STEP FOUR: F C G D A on one beat. Say F C G D A and do the motions but use only one beat. Pause for the students to copy you. This may suddenly confuse them and make everyone laugh.

F   C   G   D   A

STEP FIVE: Just say F C G D A. The last step is to leave out the motions and just say F C G D A.

Pause for the students to say it.

THAT'S THE GAME!

If students forget the order of the sharps, just ask them to do Step Four. A few times through the body movements will help them think of the letters, and the memory will be clear again.

Optional: If you choose to include "E" and "B" in these body movements, please do so. "E" can be a clap above the head and "B" can be hands reaching up high.

GAME 19-3: WRITE A SCALE - SHARPS

OBJECTIVE:
To give students practice writing sharp scales

IN BRIEF:
Each student writes out the sharp major scales using *Alphabet Cards*, *Dictation Slates*, and *Cardboard Keyboards*. They do this together as a class.

REPETITIONS:
Once through each major sharp scale. This game can be played over and over in different sessions.

AGES:
Upper elementary and older

MATERIALS:
1) *Alphabet Cards* - one set per student
2) *Blank Cards* - one per student
3) *Alphabet Kids* - one per student
4) *Pink Sharp/Flat Cards* - five per student
5) *Cardboard Keyboards* - one per student
6) *Magic Notes* and *Magic Wands*
7) *Mini Sharps*
8) *Dictation Slates* - one per student
9) Piano

PROCEDURE:
Ask the students to repeat STEP 4 of GAME 19-2: F C G D A, going through the sequence several times until they remember it easily.

Give students a moment to take their materials. The color of the *Blank Card* should match the color of the *Alphabet Card*. If your class is large, cooperative teams of two or three students can work together with a set of materials. They may move out of the circle and find an open spot big enough to work in but still remain close.

In this game, students move their cards, writing out all the sharp scales they learned in GAME 19-1: SHARP MAJOR SCALES. The game is designed for students to use their own set of materials with the class moving through the steps together.

To insure success in writing out each scale correctly, please follow these steps <u>exactly</u>.

1. Write out the scale with the *Alphabet Cards* and *Blank Card*.

2. Place the *Alphabet Kid* on the seventh degree.

3. Add the *Pink Sharp Cards,* in order (F C G D A), stopping when they place the sharp on the seventh degree, the one with the *Alphabet Kid.*

4. Write the scale on the *Dictation Slate* using the *Magic Notes* and the *Mini Sharps.*

5. Write the scale on the *Cardboard Keyboard* and ask them to "play along" with you as you play it on the piano. If some of the students know how to play any of these scales, you can let them take turns playing.

C MAJOR

6. Remove the *Pink Sharp Card* and the *Alphabet Kid.*

7. Move up a fifth to find the new scale.

Write the scales in order.

G MAJOR

D MAJOR

A MAJOR

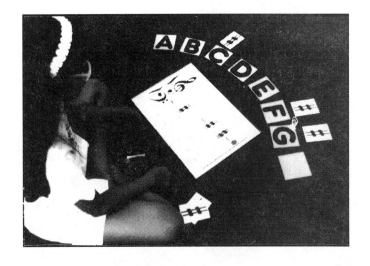

E MAJOR

B MAJOR

A GAME OF GUESSING THE NUMBER OF SHARPS - (for another day)

Students write out scales after first placing a guess as to how many sharps the scale has.

"Let's do B major. Think about how many sharps are in the B scale and hide that many *Magic Notes* under your *Blank Card*." Give them a moment to think. "Don't worry if you can't remember. This is just a guess. One day you'll be able to remember easily." Let them write the scale.

"Look under your *Blank Cards*. Did any of you happen to bet five sharps?"

I firmly believe that any child can become superior, and my confidence has never been betrayed. I test the children to find out how much they have so far acquired of the ability that is being inculcated in them. In order to do this I play games with them.

Shinichi Suzuki

GAME 19-4: FIX THE SHARPS

OBJECTIVE:
To practice naming key signatures

IN BRIEF:
As a group, students match the correct number of *Pink Sharp Cards* to *Alphabet Cards* representing key signatures.

AGES:
Upper elementary and older

MATERIALS:
1) *Alphabet Cards* - many sets
2) *Blank Card* - one pink
3) *Pink Sharp/Flat Cards*

REPETITIONS:
Several times in a session

PROCEDURE:

Give each student a set of *Alphabet Cards* and play a few rounds of GAME 2-3: FINE, using the order of sharp major scales - C G D A E B.

Using one set of *Alphabet Cards* and the *Pink Sharp Cards*, ask the students to help you match the number of sharps in a scale to the correct *Alphabet Card*.

Snap your fingers for them to close their eyes. Mix up the *Alphabet Cards* and the *Pink Sharp Cards*. Clap your hands twice for them to open their eyes.

"If you think a *Pink Sharp Card* is in the wrong place, you may move it. Each of you can move only one card on your turn." The students take turns moving cards until they are correct. If a sharp is moved incorrectly, someone will see and fix it.

GAME 19-5: FIX THE SHARP KEY SIGNATURES

OBJECTIVE:
To practice writing key signatures

IN BRIEF:
Using the *One* or *Grand Staff Board*, students fix mixed-up key signatures.

AGES:
Upper elementary and older

MATERIALS:
1) *One* or *Grand Staff Board*
2) *Clefs Puzzle*
3) *Staff Sharps*
4) *Alphabet Cards* - one set

REPETITIONS:
Once or twice for each key signature

PROCEDURE:
Review F C G D A a few times.

Place the *Staff Board* in front of the students and let them place the clef(s) correctly. Snap your fingers so they will close their eyes. Set out an *Alphabet Card* to identify the key signature and arrange the *Staff Sharps* incorrectly on the staff.

Clap twice for them to open their eyes. With fake innocence you can say, "I can't seem to write this key signature correctly. Can anyone help me?"

Write more key signatures for them to correct.

Allow children to be happy their own way; for what better way will they ever find?

Dr. Samuel Johnson

OBJECTIVE:
To practice identifying key signatures

IN BRIEF:
Using *Alphabet Cards*, students identify six key signatures written on six *Dictation Slates*.

AGES:
Upper elementary and older

MATERIALS:
1) Six *Dictation Slates*
2) *Mini Sharps*
3) *Alphabet Cards* - one set per student

REPETITIONS:
Two or three rounds per session

PROCEDURE:
Pass out a set of *Alphabet Cards* to each student. Write one key signature on each *Dictation Slate*.

As quickly as possible students are to identify the key signatures by lining up their *Alphabet Cards* in the same order as the key signatures. They can call out FINE when they finish.

Can you spot an error in this photo? The answer is at the end of this chapter.

GAME 19-7: SHARP KEY SIGNATURE TURNS

OBJECTIVE:
Working together, the students practice writing key signatures by playing an intriguing game

IN BRIEF:
Using the *One* or *Grand Staff Board*, students take turns writing key signatures or turning cards.

AGES:
Upper elementary and older

MATERIALS:
1) *One* or *Grand Staff Board*
2) *Clefs Puzzle*
3) *Staff Sharps*
4) *Alphabet Cards* - one set without F

REPETITIONS:
Once or twice through the *Alphabet Cards*

PROCEDURE:
Ask the students to sit around the *Staff Board* with you. Hand them the *Clefs* to place correctly. Review F C G D A briefly.

To refresh their memories, quickly review the key signatures as a group. Spread the *Alphabet Cards* out on the *Staff Board*, picking up the *Alphabet Cards* after they answer you. "Key signature with no sharps or flats?"

"C."

"One sharp?"

"G."

"Two sharps?"

"D."

Continue until all the cards are picked up.

Place the *Alphabet Cards* face down near the *Staff Board*. "All right! Here's how the game works. Each of you has one turn as we go around the circle, either adding or removing Staff Sharps or turning cards over. I'll help you get the idea, then you can play on your own." Turn over the first card.

"D major is our first key signature. Rebecca, you make the first move and put on the first sharp."

Jessica adds the second sharp.

332

Elizabeth turns over the next card.

Jonathan adds a third sharp.

Alexis turns over a card.

Rebecca removes a sharp.

Jessica removes a sharp.

Elizabeth turns over a card.

And so the game progresses around the circle. Adding or taking *Staff Sharps* off the *Staff Board* one at a time, or turning over an *Alphabet Card* if the key signature is completed. It's an excellent cooperative game.

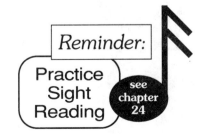

Reminder:
Practice Sight Reading
see chapter 24

GAME 19-8: CAN YOU TELL ME - SHARPS?

OBJECTIVE:
To identify the number of sharps for each key signature

IN BRIEF:
The caller says a letter (the key signature) and a student responds with a number (the number of sharps). Or a number is called out and a letter is the answer.

AGES:
Upper elementary and older

MATERIALS:
None

REPETITIONS:
Play for several minutes.

PROCEDURE:
You can be the caller at first to show them how the game works. Then it's much more fun if the students take turns being the caller.

"I'm going to call out a letter, for example . . . E. If it's your turn, you should answer . . . FOUR since the key of E has four sharps. Want to try it? Howard, you're first. B."

"I think it's . . . five," answers Howard.

"Right. E."

"Easy. Four," says Mary.

"Right. C."

"Gosh, that's a hard one. Zero," answers Ed.

"Right. G."

"Nineteen. Just kidding! One," giggles JoAnne.

"Very good. Mary, would you like to be the caller? This time, call out numbers and everyone will respond with the matching letter."

334

GAME 19-9: SHARP SCALE FINE

OBJECTIVE:
To help students think of adding sharps in sequential order as if they were playing the scale

IN BRIEF:
Students write the scale with *Alphabet Cards*, then place the *Pink Sharp Cards* on in order from left to right.

AGES:
Upper elementary and older

MATERIALS:
1) *Alphabet Cards*
2) *Blank Cards*
3) *Pink Sharp/Flat Cards*

REPETITIONS:
Through each scale at least once

PROCEDURE:
Give each student a set of *Alphabet Cards*, a *Blank Card* to match and six *Pink Sharp Cards*.

Call out a scale, "B major".

Students write out the scale using just the *Alphabet Cards*.

Then they add the *Pink Sharp Cards* in order, from left to right, rather than in the F C G D A order.

Repeat with other scales.

Children have never been very good at listening to their elders, but they have never failed to imitate them.

James Baldwin

335

OBJECTIVE:
To have fun writing scales in sequential order

IN BRIEF:
Alphabet Card snakes become scales.

AGES:
Upper elementary and older

MATERIALS:
1) *Alphabet Cards*
2) *Pink Sharp/Flat Cards*
3) One *Blank Card* per snake

REPETITIONS:
Several snakes in a session

PROCEDURE:
If your group of students is small, they can make one snake together. Otherwise divide the students into teams — three teams is best.

Mix up the *Alphabet Cards* and place them with the *Pink Sharp Cards* on the rug. Agree on a scale and say "GO!" They must put the *Pink Sharp Cards* in the snake above the *Alphabet Cards* as they go. "FINE!" cries Megan and her friends as they finish.

Note: Is this team's scale snake correct? The answer is at the end of the chapter.

The proper time to influence the character of a child is about a hundred years before he is born.

W. R. Inge

GAME 19-11: SHARPS SHOW ME

OBJECTIVE:
To practice identifying key signatures

IN BRIEF:
Students identify key signatures using *Alphabet Cards*.

AGES:
Upper elementary and older

MATERIALS:
1) *One* or *Grand Staff Board*
2) *Clefs Puzzle*
3) *Alphabet Cards* - one per student
4) *Staff Sharps*

REPETITIONS:
All the keys in a session

PROCEDURE:
Let the students place the clef(s) correctly. Pass out one set of *Alphabet Cards* to each student.

Write a key signature on the staff. Ask the students to turn the appropriate *Alphabet Card* face down.

Call out SHOW ME. They will turn their cards over.

"Hey, we're looking really good!"

337

OBJECTIVE:
When playing scales on the piano, it's easy to see how sharps (black notes) are added. On a string instrument it's not quite so clear. *Alphabet Cards* create a fingerboard and it becomes easy to understand.

IN BRIEF:
Violinists lay out *Alphabet Cards* into a fingerboard pattern using the BC and EF natural half steps. Different color cards represent the different strings. *Orange Symbol Cards* finger numbers help relate the *Alphabet Cards* to finger patterns. When a sharp is added to a card, it is moved up a space on the fingerboard or up a half step.

AGES:
Upper elementary and older

MATERIALS:
1) *Alphabet Cards* - four sets different colors
2) *Orange Symbol Cards* - finger numbers
3) Each student's instrument
4) *Mini Sharps*
5) One *Dictation Slate*
6) *Magic Notes* and *Magic Wands*
7) *Alphabet Kids*

REPETITIONS:
Several scales in a session

PROCEDURE:
Review 10-8: NATURAL HALF STEPS BC AND EF.

Lay out the violin fingerboard using a different color of *Alphabet Cards* for each string. Place the *Orange Finger Number Cards* along one side.

C MAJOR:

All cards not found in the scale should be turned face down. Because the C scale has no sharps or flats, no cards need to be changed.

Return all the cards on the fingerboard back to face up.

338

G MAJOR:

1. Fingerboard: Turn high A on the fingerboard face down. Say the names of the cards. When you come to F sharp, place a mini sharp on the card and slide it up a half-step.

2. Let them try this on their violins.

Slide each card back into position as you remove the *Mini Sharps.*

Continue through the other scales, playing them on the *Alphabet Card* fingerboard as well as the violins. Here is an example of the A major scale.

GAME IDEA: Play **FINGERBOARD MIX-UP**. After a fingerboard scale is made, mix it up for the students to fix.

Answer to GAME 19-6: SHARP KEY SIGNATURE FINE. In the key signature for B Major the bass clef A sharp should be on the lower space.

Answer to GAME 19-10: SHARP SCALE SNAKES. The snake is almost correct. E major has four sharps. This team forgot one G sharp.

Ability does not just come by nature without training. We have to educate it in ourselves. Everyone has to train his own self. Stop lamenting lack of talent and develop talent instead. To think that you are born with an ability that develops by itself is a mistake.

Shinichi Suzuki

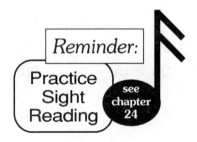

Reminder: Practice Sight Reading — see chapter 24

FLAT SCALES AND KEYS - EASY!

Now that you and your students have experienced learning sharp scales with sounds, cards and games you must agree that it is easier this way. Do you understand? Remember? Enjoy learning? Ready to begin learning flat scales?

Yes. Yes. Yes. Yes.

Okay. Let's go!

Since it worked well with sharps, let's do the same thing with flats. You can follow the same basic procedures for learning sharp scales. The difference: In sharps the new scale was found by moving up a fifth. With flats, the new scale is found by moving <u>down</u> a fifth. Simple.

Sharps go up.   **Flats go down.**

It's logical!

It's also simple for students to consistently use a fifth to think of the next scale and to move up for sharps and down for flats.

GAMES IN THIS CHAPTER

OBJECTIVE:
To introduce flat scales: F , B♭, E♭, A♭, D♭, G♭

IN BRIEF:
Students write each flat scale and discover that the new flat is found on the fourth degree of each scale.

AGES:
Upper elementary and older

REPETITIONS:
Once through each scale

MATERIALS:
1) Piano
2) *Alphabet Cards* - two sets, two colors
3) *Blank Cards*
4) Seven *Pink Sharp/Flat Cards*
5) One *Alphabet Kid*
6) Two *Dictation Slates*
7) *Magic Notes* and *Magic Wands*
8) *Cardboard Keyboards*
9) *Mini Flats*

PROCEDURE:
Flat scales can be learned with the students gathered around the piano or seated on the floor if the class is large.

STEP ONE: C MAJOR Write out a C scale.

"No sharps or flats, right?"

"Right."

"To find the scale with one sharp we moved . . . ," pause for them to tell you, ". . . right, up a fifth. Today we're learning the flat scales. Think about it. If we moved move up a fifth for sharp scales, how could we move for flat scales?"

"Is it down a fifth?"

"Absolutely! We move down a fifth from C to . . . right . . . F."

STEP TWO: F MAJOR Ask someone to write out the F scale with the *Alphabet Cards.*

Play the F scale without any flats.

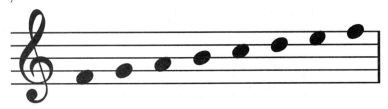

343

The students will quickly hear that B needs the flat. "What degree of the scale is B? . . . right, the fourth degree."

Play the corrected scale. Add the flat above B. Place the B card above the *Alphabet Card* scale. Let the students write out the key signature and scales.

"To find the scale with two flats? Down a fifth to . . ."

Looking at the cards, they will answer, "B." However, it needs to be B flat. This can be explained with two reasons.

1) Logic: "B is the scale with five sharps, remember? It can't have five sharps and three flats for the same scale, can it?"

2) The ear: Play the harmonic interval of F and C, a perfect fifth. "This is a perfect fifth. It's clear and easy to listen to, isn't it?"

"Listen to the sound of F to B. This is a tritone and it has a very different sound from the perfect fifth."

"If I play F to B flat, does that sound like a perfect fifth?"

They will be able to hear these differences. Put a *Pink Flat Card* on the B and the *Blank Card*. Remind them when they count flats not to count the B flats twice.

Go through all the remaining flat scales this same way.

B FLAT MAJOR

E FLAT MAJOR

A FLAT MAJOR

D FLAT MAJOR

G FLAT MAJOR

"Wow! We did it! Six flat scales just like that!"

NOTE: Students can memorize the order of flats without any extra game. Since the first four flats spell a word, it's easy to remember "bead". We just add "ga ca" and it's the whole list. "Bead ga ca" becomes the memory word for "B E A D G A".

*Rita Hauck, my good friend and colleague who has been teaching my theory games since 1977 stopped in for a visit during a break while we were both teaching in Hawaii. She's between me and Kaipo.

THE FOLLOWING GAMES ARE DESCRIBED IN THE PREVIOUS CHAPTER. THE ONLY CHANGE YOU NEED TO MAKE IS TO SUBSTITUTE THE FLAT SCALES OR KEY SIGNATURES.

GAME 20-2: WRITE A SCALE - FLATS

OBJECTIVE:
To give each student practice writing flat scales

IN BRIEF:
Individually, students write out flat scales using cards, *Cardboard Keyboards* and *Dictation Slates*.

MATERIALS:
1) *Alphabet Cards* - one per student
2) *Blank Cards* - one per student
3) Seven *Pink Sharp/Flat Cards* per student
4) *Dictation Slates*
5) *Magic Notes* and *Magic Wands*
6) *Cardboard Keyboards*
7) *Alphabet Kids*

PROCEDURE:

GAME 20-3: FIX THE FLATS

IN BRIEF:
As a group, students match the correct number of *Pink Flat Cards* to *Alphabet Cards* representing key signatures.

MATERIALS:
1) *Alphabet Cards* - one set
2) *Blank Card* - one pink
3) *Pink Sharp/Flat Cards*

PROCEDURE:

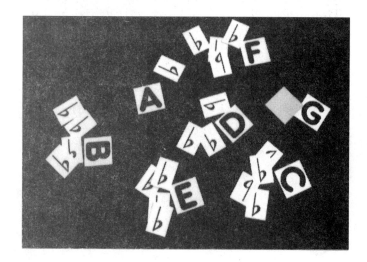

Can you spot any mistakes in this photo? The answer is at the end of the chapter.

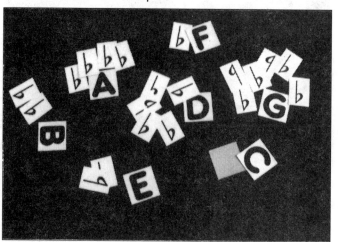

GAME 20-4: FIX THE FLAT KEY SIGNATURES

IN BRIEF:
Using the *One* or *Grand Staff Board*, students fix mixed-up key signatures.

MATERIALS:
1) *One* or *Grand Staff Board*
2) *Clefs Puzzle*
3) *Staff Flats*
4) *Alphabet Cards* - one set

PROCEDURE:

GAME 20-5: FLAT KEY SIGNATURE FINE

IN BRIEF:
Using *Alphabet Cards*, students repeatedly identify seven key signatures written on seven *Dictation Slates*.

MATERIALS:
1) Seven *Dictation Slates*
2) *Mini Flats*
3) *Alphabet Cards* - one set per student

PROCEDURE:

GAME 20-6: FLAT KEY SIGNATURE TURNS

IN BRIEF:
Using a *Staff Board* and *Alphabet Cards*, students take turns writing key signatures.

MATERIALS:
1) *One* or *Grand Staff Board*
2) *Clefs Puzzle*
3) *Staff Flats*
4) *Alphabet Cards* - one set

PROCEDURE:

GAME 20-7: CAN YOU TELL ME - FLATS?

IN BRIEF:
The caller says a letter (key signature) and the student responds with a number (the number of flats). Or the caller says a number and the student responds with a letter.

MATERIALS:
None

PROCEDURE:

GAME 20-8: FLAT SCALE FINE

IN BRIEF:
Students write scales with *Alphabet Cards* adding the *Pink Flat Cards* in order as they write.

MATERIALS:
1) *Alphabet Cards*
2) *Blank Cards*
3) *Pink Sharp/Flat Cards*

PROCEDURE:

GAME 20-9: FLAT SCALE SNAKES

IN BRIEF:
Students make snakes the way they did when they were younger, this time adding *Pink Flat Cards.*

MATERIALS:
1) *Alphabet Cards*
2) *Pink Sharp/Flat Cards*
3) One *Blank Card* per snake

REPETITIONS:
Several snakes in a session

PROCEDURE:

GAME 20-10: FLATS SHOW ME

IN BRIEF:
Students identify key signatures using *Alphabet Cards.*

MATERIALS:
1) *One* or *Grand Staff Board*
2) *Clefs Puzzle*
3) *Alphabet Cards* - one per student
4) *Staff Flats*

AGES:
Open

REPETITIONS:
All the keys in a session

PROCEDURE:

GAME 20-11: FLAT SCALES AND THE VIOLIN

IN BRIEF:
Using the violin as the example, students lay out *Alphabet Cards* into a fingerboard pattern. When a flat is added, the card is moved down a half step.

MATERIALS:
1) *Alphabet Cards*

2) *Orange Symbol Cards* - finger numbers
3) Each student's instrument
4) *Mini Flats*
5) *Dictation Slates*
6) *Magic Notes*
6) *Pink Sharp/Flat Cards*
7) One *Alphabet Kid*

PROCEDURE:

Answer to GAME 20-3: FIX THE FLATS. E flat should have three flats.

MASTERING TRIADS

Since your students are now comfortable identifying intervals by sight and sound, the study of triads will come easily. By this time, they have encountered a vast array of triads and chords in their repertoire. Perhaps they didn't always associate a label with the notes. Now is a perfect time to learn.

"We've talked about triads before, haven't we? All of you can recognize the distinctive sounds of the major and minor triads." If you are teaching piano students, ask: "Can anyone think of a triad in a piece you play?"

If anyone can recall using triads, let the students analyze the triad used. This will open up lots of discussion. If they need help, suggest a section of a piece and let a student or two discover the triads. Bring out the music book so they can see triads and their spellings.

The games in this chapter teach students to relate various kinds of triads to the tones in the major and minor scales. They will learn about inversions. The games begin with a simple C triad and advance to complex triads like B flat diminished or G sharp augmented. The sky's the limit!

You and your students use familiar materials to learn exciting new ideas.

Throughout the chapter specific colors are used to identify particular tonalities. These are reflected in the *Alphabet Cards* and the *Magic Notes*. This gives students a visual memory of triads as they occur in the scales.

Major	=	Purple	Minor	=	Blue
Diminished	=	Green	Augmented	=	Pink

GAMES IN THIS CHAPTER

OBJECTIVE:
To play triads and identify them by ear

IN BRIEF:
Students learn the four kinds of triads: major, minor, diminished and augmented and play them on the piano. Using *Number Slates* and/or four colors of *Magic Notes*, they identify them by ear.

AGES:
Upper elementary and older

MATERIALS:
1) Piano
2) *Cardboard Keyboards*
3) *Number Slates*
4) *Blank Cards*
5) *Magic Notes* and *Magic Wands*
6) *Seventh Chord Cards* - backside

REPETITIONS:
Repeat until students can play and identify the four kinds of triads.

PROCEDURE:
Students can learn to hear and play the major, minor, diminished and augmented triads. This is best practiced over several classes for short periods of time.

If your class is small enough, gather the students around the piano to watch how triads are formed. If the class is too large, have some of the students follow along with *Cardboard Keyboards* on the floor and switch after several examples.

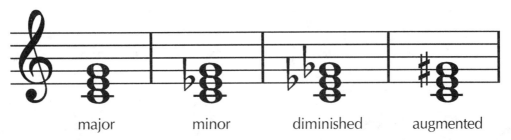

major   minor   diminished   augmented

Play several examples of these triads using the same root. Let each student play an example of each triad so s/he can feel as well as hear the differences. Talk about how the word diminished, like the word diminuendo, means to get smaller. Augmented means to get larger.

Ask them to practice playing triads at home.

VERSION 1: This game is similar to GAME 16-3: MAJOR OR MINOR? except diminished and augmented triads are included. Pass out a *Number Slate* to the students and ask them to prepare it as shown:

M	m	d	A

They can write the correct letter as you play the triads.

M	m	d	A
1	3	2	4

VERSION 2: Give each student four *Magic Notes*, one each of purple, blue, green and pink. If you want, give them each a white *Seventh Chord Card* on which to put their *Magic Notes*. To make it easier to remember which color represents which triad, prepare four *Number Slates* and four *Blank Cards* (purple, blue, green and pink) for them to see.

 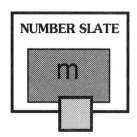 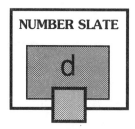 

Play four different triads using the same root. The students are to put their *Magic Notes* in order to match what they hear.

This game is very intriguing and challenging. Many times students request more triads to be played even though it is time to finish the lesson.

The greatest gift you can give to children is not to share
your riches with them but to reveal their riches to themselves.

Unknown

354

OBJECTIVE:
To learn the tonality of the triads on each note of the C major scale

IN BRIEF:
Students identify the triads by sound, guess the tonality using a *Magic Note* and together write it on a *Cardboard Keyboard* or *Dictation Slate*.

AGES:
Upper elementary and older

MATERIALS:
1) Five sets of *Alphabet Cards*:
     2 sets purple   1 set green
     1 set pink   2 sets blue
2) *Scale Triad Cards*
3) Piano
4) *Dictation Slates*
5) *Magic Notes* and *Magic Wands*
6) *Cardboard Keyboards*

REPETITIONS:
Spell all seven triads in one session

PROCEDURE:
Let each student take four *Magic Notes* - purple, blue, green and pink. These will be used to "guess" the triad tonality after it's played. The *Notes* should be held in one hand.

"Please listen then tell me the tonality of each triad built on the notes of the C major scale. We'll study them one at a time. Remember that even though I'm going to play only white notes for you, the triads won't all sound alike. After I play the first triad, hide the matching color *Magic Note* in your hand."

Play:

The students will think, then hide a note in their hands. After everyone's ready, say, SHOW ME, the signal to show the color *Magic Note* they chose.

Let's hope everyone heard it as a major triad and is holding a purple *Magic Note*.

"This is the first degree of the scale, and it's a major triad, so we use a large Roman numeral to identify it." Ask them to write out the C triad on their *Dictation Slates, Cardboard Keyboards* and *Alphabet Cards.* Everything should be purple since it's major.

Repeat this for each triad in the C scale, using the appropriate color *Magic Notes* and *Alphabet Cards.*

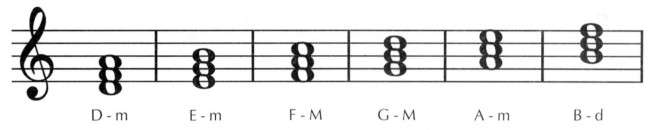

D - m   E - m   F - M   G - M   A - m   B - d

After all the triads are played the students may notice that they didn't use any pink *Alphabet Cards* or *Magic Notes.* They weren't needed but were available so as to not give the answer away.

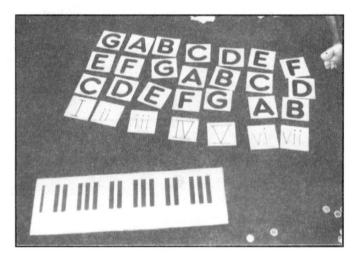

If the students have pianos at home, ask them to play these C scale triads as practice from today's class.

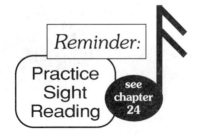

Reminder:

Practice
Sight
Reading

see
chapter
24

OBJECTIVE:
To help students remember the tonality of the triads in a major scale

IN BRIEF:
Using seven *Magic Notes*, students quickly arrange them in order to represent the tonalities of the scale triads.

AGES:
Upper elementary and older

MATERIALS:
1) *Magic Notes* - seven per student (3 purple, 3 blue and 1 green)
2) Backside of *Song Puzzle Cards*
3) *Scale Triad Cards* for reference
4) *Alphabet Cards*

REPETITIONS:
4-5 per session

PROCEDURE:
Pass out the *Magic Notes* to each student.

After you say "GO" they arrange their *Magic Notes* in the order of the triads. When finished they call out "Fine".

purple   blue   blue   purple   purple   blue   green

This is a fun, easy game and very helpful for remembering the triad patterns of the major scales.

This game can also be played as a group using the backside of three colors of *Alphabet Cards*.

357

GAME 21-4: SCALE TRIADS - I CAN WRITE IT

OBJECTIVE:
For each student to study the seven triads found in the C major scale

IN BRIEF:
Students use *Magic Notes* and *Alphabet Cards* in three colors to write out the C major scale triads.

AGES:
Upper elementary and older

MATERIALS:
1) Five sets of *Alphabet Cards*:
   2 purple, 2 blue and 1 set of green
2) *Magic Notes* and *Magic Wands*
3) *Dictation Slates*
4) *Scale Triad Cards*
5) Piano

REPETITIONS:
One C scale in a class session. May be repeated.

PROCEDURE:

"Everyone remember the colors for the triads? Great." Place the scale triad and *Alphabet Cards* nearby. Everyone needs a *Dictation Slate* and 21 (9 purple, 9 blue, 3 green) *Magic Notes*.

"Anyone remember what tonality the triad built on the first degree of the C scale is?" you can ask.

"I remember. It's major," says Eric. Everyone agrees after he plays it on the piano. Let someone write the triad with the *Alphabet Cards*, and ask all the students to write it on their *Dictation Slates*. Use purple for major.

Continue through the other triads in the same manner. Be sure each triad is played on the piano. →

By using the colors, they are developing a valuable visual memory of the tonality of the triads.

"Notice that the major triads are on I, IV and V, and the minor triads are on ii, iii and vi. The diminished triad is on vii."

Question them on this to help their memories. "Major triads are on which degrees of the scale? Minor triads? . . ."

Why not play mix-up with the cards? →

GAME 21-5: TRIADS AND OTHER SCALES

OBJECTIVE:
To discover if the triad tonalities of the C major scale are the same in other keys

IN BRIEF:
Students hear and identify each triad of a scale other than C using the same procedure.

AGES:
Upper elementary and older

MATERIALS:
1) Five sets of *Alphabet Cards*:
   2 purple, 2 blue and 1 green
2) *Magic Notes* and *Magic Wands*
3) *Dictation Slates*
4) *Scale Triad Cards*
5) *Mini Sharps and Flats*
6) *Pink Sharp/Flat Cards*
7) Piano

REPETITIONS:
One scale per class session

PROCEDURE:
"I am wondering. Do you think all the scales have this same arrangement of triads or is it just C?" you can ask.

"Oh, no . . . I bet we have to write out other scales." They will pretend to be dreading the thought of this effort.

"Hey, that's a great idea, Alexis."

"Oh no!" Alexis falls over on the rug, pretending to be exhausted.

Pass out *Dictation Slates*, *Magic Notes*, and *Mini Sharps* to each student. Place the *Alphabet Cards* and *Scale Triad Cards* in the middle of the group. Let them choose their scales.

Some students can figure out and write individual triads. They may come up with some correct answers and or at least some interesting ones. Encourage them to use the piano.

"Okay . . . four triads are correct and three aren't."

"Is mine right?"

"Did all of you remember to use the F sharp?"

In other sessions do different scales. This is excellent practice for writing triads and figuring tonalities.

GAME 21-6: FINE WITH SCALE TRIADS

OBJECTIVE:
Students practice writing scale triads quickly so they can quickly remember which degree of the scale is which tonality.

IN BRIEF:
Using *Dictation Slates* and *Magic Notes*, students write out the seven scale triads as quickly as possible using the appropriate colors.

AGES:
Upper elementary and older

MATERIALS:
1) *Dictation Slates*
2) *Magic Notes*:
   Each student needs 9 purple, 9 blue, 3 green
3) *Scale Triad Cards*
4) *Mini Sharps and Flats*

REPETITIONS:
4-5 times in a session

PROCEDURE:
Pass out one *Dictation Slate* and 21 *Magic Notes* to each student. If they need the review, show them the *Scale Triad Cards*. Then put them away.

"Please mix up your *Magic Notes* in the lower part of your *Dictation Slates*. When I say 'GO' you may write out the seven triads of the C major scale, using the right colors. When you finish, call out FINE!. Questions? Okay . . . ready . . . GO!"

They will enjoy this and quickly write their triads using the correct color *Magic Notes*.

Lay out the *Scale Triad Cards* so they can check themselves.

VARIATION: The game may be played as described above except lay out the *Scale Triad Cards* out of order. Students write their triads in that order.

VARIATION: Use different keys.

OBJECTIVE:
To relate scale triads to different key signatures

IN BRIEF:
One student arranges six triads from a scale of his choice using appropriate color *Magic Notes* on the *Dictation Slate*. Another student studies the triads to figure out the secret scale. Great game!

AGES:
Upper elementary and older

MATERIALS:
1) *Dictation Slates*
2) 18 *Magic Notes* per student: 9 purple, 9 blue
3) *Mini Sharps and Flats*
4) *Scale Triad Cards*
5) Piano

REPETITIONS:
Several rounds for each team of students

PROCEDURE:
This game may be played as a group but everyone gets more practice when the students are in pairs. Give each pair of students a *Dictation Slate* and the *Magic Notes*. Place the *Mini Sharps and Flats* nearby. Ask someone to arrange the *Scale Triad Cards* in order where everyone can see them if needed for reference.

"One person from each team decides on a secret scale. Using the correct color of *Magic Notes*, please write six of the triads from your scale <u>without</u> using sharps or flats on your *Dictation Slate*. Please write the triads out of order. Does anyone know which triad we're not using and why?" you can ask.

Michael raises his hand, "I think I know. Is it because we know that the diminished triad is always on the 7th degree in a major scale? If the diminished triad were there, it would be too easy just to go up a half-step from that triad and guess the scale. This way there's more for us to figure out. Is that right?"

"Exactly right. Good thinking, Michael. Okay, everyone go to it. Each of you may work on your own. When you figure out the secret scale your partner wrote, put the correct key signature on the staff. Please feel free to play the triads on the piano."

Here's one for you to guess. The answer is at the end of this chapter. Since this photo is black and white, the color arrangement is: B P B P P B

SECRET SCALE WITH LESS

This game is just like SECRET SCALE except fewer triads are written out, making it more interesting to figure out what the secret scale is.

Here are two examples using just two triads. Again, the answers are at the end of the chapter.

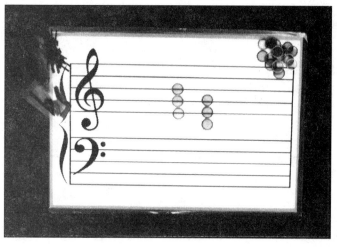

P   B

B   P

GAME 21-8: CHANCE MATCH

OBJECTIVE:
To play a sensational game of chance for remembering scale triads

IN BRIEF:
The *Scale Triad Cards* are placed face down out of order. Students place colored *Alphabet Cards* below the *Scale Triad Cards*. Each one that matches by chance is worth one *Magic Note*.

AGES:
Upper elementary and older

MATERIALS:
1) *Scale Triad Cards*
2) *Alphabet Cards* - purple, blue and green
3) *Magic Notes* and *Magic Wands*
4) *Mini Sharps and Flats* - for scales other the C major

REPETITIONS:
Each student will want several turns.

PROCEDURE:
C major is the example for this game, but do play it with other scales.

Lay out the *Scale Triad Cards* face down out of order.

Use these *Alphabet Cards*: Purple = C F G, Blue = D E A, Green = B. Mix them up and give them face down to the students.

"This is a game of chance. Place these *Alphabet Cards* below the *Scale Triad Cards* in hopes of making matches. Since you know purple is major, blue is minor and green is diminished you can at least put the right color card with the right *Scale Triad Card.*"

Turn them over to see how many are correct. Keep the correct *Alphabet Cards* by the *Scale Triad Cards* but move the incorrect ones down.

"Hey, I got three matches! B, E and G. Great! I get three *Magic Notes,*" exclaims Ann.

After several rounds of play Ann notices something. "Since B is the only diminished triad and we know it occurs on the 7th degree of the scale, that one is always an automatic winner."

"Very smart, Ann. This helps you remember that the 7th degree is diminished. Maybe you'll do composing when you're older and you can use lots of diminished chords in your compositions."

"I just might do that!" smiles Ann.

GAME 21-9: CHANGING TONALITIES

OBJECTIVE:
To practice changing the tonalities of triads

IN BRIEF:
Students choose *Alphabet Cards* and colored *Magic Notes* to indicate which tonality to use for writing many triads in a row.

AGES:
Upper elementary and older

MATERIALS:
1) *One Staff Board*
2) *Clefs Puzzle*
3) *Ledger Line Sheets*
4) *Notes With Letters*
5) *Staff Sharps and Flats*
6) *Magic Notes* and *Magic Wands*
7) *Cardboard Keyboards*
8) *Alphabet Cards* - purple, blue, green and pink
9) Piano

REPETITIONS:
Each student can do several triads in a session

PROCEDURE:
Set the *One Staff Board* between you and the students. Let them arrange the *Clefs*. Place the *Ledger Line Sheets*, *Notes With Letters* turned face down and *Staff Sharps and Flats* on the edge of the board. Ask them to take one *Cardboard Keyboard* and three *Magic Notes* of each of the four colors.

Select an assortment of *Alphabet Cards* (two or three times the number of students playing) and place the pile face down near the *Staff Board*.

Turn over the top card. It's an F. "Are you first, Rebecca?"

"Yes. I bet I can figure this out. It's pink. That means I'm to write an F augmented triad. Right?"

"Excellent! Would you like to play it on the piano? Everyone please write an F augmented triad on your *Cardboard Keyboard*. Next?"

Continue through the stack of *Alphabet Cards*.

Youth is not a time of life; it is a state of mind.

Samuel Ullman

OBJECTIVE:
To learn about inversions

IN BRIEF:
Students play inverted triads on the piano, write them on *Cardboard Keyboards* and *Dictation Slates*, then find them in printed music as 6 (first inversion) or $\frac{6}{4}$ chords (second inversion).

AGES:
Upper elementary and older

MATERIALS:
1) Piano
2) *Cardboard Keyboards*
3) *Dictation Slates*
4) *Magic Notes* and *Magic Wands*
5) *Mini Sharps and Flats*
6) One set of *Alphabet Cards*
7) *Number Slates*
8) Music books

REPETITIONS:
One or more sessions

PROCEDURE:
Gather the students around the piano. Discuss how the word invert means to reverse the order.

Play a C major triad. Place the *Alphabet Cards* C E and G on the music stand.

Explain that if we take the root C and play it at the end of the triad rather than at the beginning it becomes a first inversion triad. Place the C *Alphabet Card* after the G.

"Then if we take the E and put it on the end it's called a . "

" . . . a second inversion triad?" volunteers Francis.

"Exactly right, Francis." Move the E *Alphabet Card* after C.

Let the students play inversions of different triads, using *Alphabet Cards* for visual reference. Ask them to play inversions at home.

WRITING INVERSIONS

"Let's try writing out inversions of triads. Please take a *Cardboard Keyboard*, a *Dictation Slate*, three *Mini Sharps and Flats* and some *Magic Notes*. Sit so you can see the piano.

"Let's review C major first, okay?"

Give different students a chance to play the inversions and let everyone write out the root position, first inversion and second inversion on *Dictation Slates* and *Cardboard Keyboards*. Arrange the *Alphabet Cards* yourself.

After practicing several triads, ask them to name the interval between the lowest note and the highest note in a first inversion triad.

"It's a sixth," says Bita.

"What's the interval in a second inversion triad?"

"It's a sixth, too," says Josh. Write a six on each *Number Slate*.

"How can we tell the difference? Let's add the other interval from each one. It's not necessary to write ⁶₃ for first inversion triads. A 6 is all that's needed. But ⁶₄ is how second inversion triads are identified."

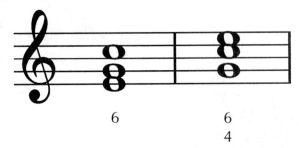

6   6
           4

Let them practice more triads, noticing the 6 and ⁶₄ intervals.

Then bring out music books and let them find inverted triads. They will become quick at this, and it's fun since they learned the concept in steps and understand it. It will help them with their music reading, too.

OBJECTIVE:
To practice spelling and identifying triad inversions

IN BRIEF:
Students arrange *Alphabet Card* triad inversions for each other to write and identify.

AGES:
Upper elementary and older

MATERIALS:
1) *Alphabet Cards*
2) *Mini Sharps and Flats*
3) *Dictation Slates*
4) *Magic Notes* and *Magic Wands*
5) Piano

REPETITIONS:
Several rounds

PROCEDURE:
Let each student take a *Dictation Slate*, a set of *Alphabet Cards* and three *Magic Notes*.

Ask everyone to think of a triad and write it as an inversion with the *Alphabet Cards*.

They are to look at the triad of the person to their right.

Then they write that triad on their own *Dictation Slate* and tell the person what the root is and which inversion it is.

Repeat for several rounds.

They may write triads with accidentals also.

GAME 21-12: INVERSION TURNS

OBJECTIVE:
To practice identifying inversions

IN BRIEF:
On the staff, students create triads from colored *Alphabet Cards* then change them into the correct tonality using accidentals.

AGES:
Upper elementary and older

MATERIALS:
1) *Alphabet Cards* - purple, blue, green, pink
2) *One Staff Board*
3) *Notes With Letters*
4) *Clefs Puzzle*
5) *Ledger Line Sheets*
6) *Staff Sharps and Flats*
7) Piano

REPETITIONS:
Several rounds

PROCEDURE:
Let the students place the clef on the *One Staff Board*. Set all the materials nearby.

Select three cards from each set of *Alphabet Cards* which spell a triad. The triads do not have to be from the same scale. For example:

purple	A C E	blue	G B D
green	D F A	pink	F A C

Place the cards <u>face down</u> in four piles (by color) in front of the students. Each part of a turn is taken by one student. This way everyone works together and turns are short. Ask the student sitting next to you to pick one *Alphabet Card* from the purple pile and place the matching *Note* on the *Staff*. That card, C, is the lowest note of the chord.

Next Rebecca picks up the other two purple *Alphabet Cards* and arranges them in order above the C and identifies the triad as a first inversion A chord. She also arranges the *Notes* on the *Staff*. →

Alexis decides if it's a major triad (since the cards are purple) and if it isn't, adds the necessary accidentals.

He makes the change. "We need a C sharp so it can be an A major triad," says Alexis.

Jessica goes to the piano to play the first inversion triad.

So the game continues with the other *Alphabet Cards* being drawn and triads spelled correctly. Enjoy!

GAME 21-13: INVERSION DROP

OBJECTIVE:
To practice writing inverted triads

IN BRIEF:
Students drop three *Magic Notes* on either a *Dictation Slate* or *Cardboard Keyboard*. They figure out what triad inversion the notes could become, moving the smallest possible interval(s). Students earn *Magic Notes* equal to intervals they move.

AGES:
Upper elementary and older

MATERIALS:
1) *Cardboard Keyboards*
2) *Dictation Slates*
3) *Magic Notes* and *Magic Wands*
4) *Mini Sharps and Flats*
5) Piano

REPETITIONS:
5-10 inversions

PROCEDURE:
Play this game using either the *Dictation Slate*, three *Magic Notes* and *Mini Sharps and Flats* or the *Cardboard Keyboard* and three *Magic Notes*. To use both at once will slow the momentum of the game. This game will be described using the *Cardboard Keyboards*. Pass out one *Cardboard Keyboard* plus three *Magic Notes* to each pair of students. Place a pile of *Magic Notes* nearby where everyone can reach them.

Demonstrate as you speak. "Alyssa, I'm going to drop these three *Magic Notes* one at a time on your *Cardboard Keyboard*. Then I'm going to move as few notes as possible to make a triad or its inversion." Here's what dropped and here's what it was changed to.

"I moved the note on B up a half step to C to make a C major triad, first inversion. My score is one *Magic Note*." Then Alyssa or another student plays the chord on the piano.

Student pairs can take turns dropping *Magic Notes* for each other. They are not in competition so the *Magic Notes* they take indicates their score together. Remind them to play each triad on the piano.

369

OBJECTIVE:
To practice spelling many chords. To help the mind become flexible thinking of all the possibilities of chords related to just one note

IN BRIEF:
Starting with one note, accidentals and notes are added and subtracted to spell many chords. May also be played with *Alphabet Cards* and *Cardboard Keyboards*.

AGES:
Upper elementary and older

MATERIALS:
1) *One Staff Board*
2) *Notes With Letters*
3) *Clefs Puzzle*
4) *Ledger Line Sheets*
5) *Staff Sharps and Flats*
6) Piano

REPETITIONS:
Several chords in one session

PROCEDURE:
This game can be played with *Alphabet Cards*, or the *One Staff Board* and *Notes With Letters*, or *Cardboard Keyboards*, or on the piano or everything all at once! It will be demonstrated using the *Staff* and *Notes*.

Set out the *Staff Board*, *Notes*, *Clefs*, *Ledger Line Sheets* and *Staff Sharps and Flats*. This game is like a previous one, GAME 20-12: INVERSION TURNS in that turns are taken around the circle, each student doing just one thing to the notes. Ask one student to stay at the piano, playing each triad.

Alyssa chooses the *Note* D and places it on the staff.

Bita adds two *Notes*, F and A to make a minor triad.

Each student makes one change, adding or taking away an accidental, identifying the triads.

Look at the possibilities! Can you think of others?

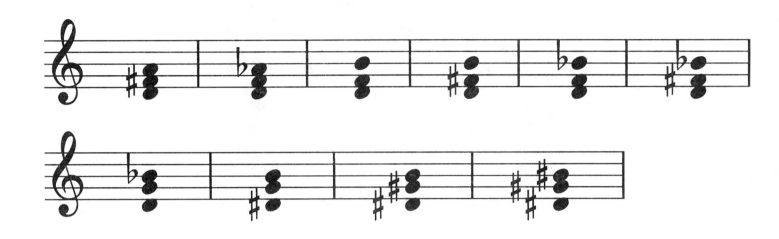

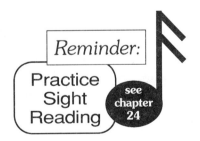

Answer to 21-7: SECRET SCALE

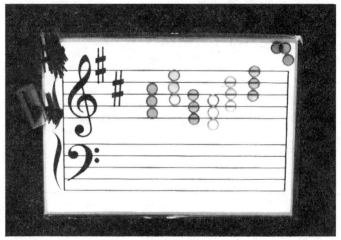

(Photo error: The first sharp should be on F, not G.)

Answer to 21-7: SECRET SCALE WITH LESS

Did you figure them out?

There is no result without cause. Wrong education and upbringing produces ugly personalities, whereas a fine upbringing and good education will bring forth superior sense and feeling, as well as nobility and purity of mind.

Shinichi Suzuki

SCALES AND CHORDS
PLUS SEVENTH CHORDS

S *cales and Chords*, is a unique, challenging and stimulating board game. It is designed to support students as they internalize the knowledge of scales, key signatures and chord spellings. During the game, students "play" scales and chords on the game board as well as on their instruments. They identify key signatures and triads and answer *Pink Question Cards* (some of which are really funny). They win *Magic Notes* and *Gold Coins* depending on how many sharps or flats are in the chord, scale or key signature. The more sharps or flats - the more money. Ah ha! Everyone suddenly wants to land on the hard scales! Clever, huh?

Students can begin playing *Scales and Chords* after playing most of the games in Chapter 19: SHARP SCALES AND KEYS - EASY!, Chapter 20: FLAT SCALES AND KEYS - EASY! and Chapter 21: MASTERING TRIADS. If the game is played before students understand the concepts, it's difficult and overwhelming. When they're ready, the game is intriguing and fun.

There is time in a one hour class to play the game. The students help you set it up, then let the *Dice* roll! Explain the game as they play. When they understand the game, step away and let them enjoy themselves.

Playing without too much teacher or parental participation once the rules are understood enables students to relax. They relate better to each other, respond to each other's answers and have more fun. As with all **Music Mind Games**, this game is for learning, but should be enjoyed in a playful atmosphere. Then it will be played often.

This versatile game can be played using any tonality of triads, chords, or scales. It's possible to practice chords as advanced as you want to study. What fun! Want to know a secret wish of mine? — seeing my theory professor from graduate school watching us enjoying augmented sixth chords in this way.

Seventh Chords

After GAME 22-1: *SCALES AND CHORDS*, seventh chords are introduced. Because they are simply extensions of triads, they can be smoothly absorbed by students who have developed a logical sense of memory from all the games they've played. Look for some neat new games, too.

Although these games do not expand to other chords such as ninths, elevenths, augmented sixth chords, neapolitan or harmonic chord progressions, the foundation is laid for them and you may proceed as desired.

GAMES IN THIS CHAPTER

GAME 22-1: SCALES AND CHORDS

OBJECTIVE:
To have fun identifying key signatures, playing scales, naming triads and being able to talk about and explain scales, chords and key signatures

IN BRIEF:
Students roll *Large Dice* and move *Alphabet Kids* around a large keyboard style game board using a chromatic scale. They draw cards that ask them to identify triads and key signatures, play scales (on their instruments or the game board) and answer questions. Humorous requests in the *Pink Question Cards* keep the game lighthearted. The number of *Magic Notes* or *Gold Coins* won is determined by the number of sharps or flats in each turn. Thus everyone hopes to get the hard scales like G flat and F sharp rather than the easy ones like C, F and G.

MATERIALS:
1) *Scales and Chords* game board
2) *Alphabet Kids*
3) *Scale and Chord Cards*
   Purple Play Scale Cards   *Pink Question Cards*
       Yellow Triad Cards   *Orange Key Signature Cards*
4) *Large Dice*
5) *Magic Notes* and *Magic Wands*
6) *Gold Coins*

AGES:
Upper elementary and older

REPETITIONS:
An hour of play will fly by! Play often.

PREPARATION:
Chapters 19, 20, 21 and study of the *Scale and Chord Cards*

DECISIONS:
The blue and green colors on the game board can be designated as different tonalities depending on what scales and chords want to be practiced. The most basic way to play *Scales and Chords* is for the blue to be major scales and the green to be major triads. At the end of these directions are suggestions for advanced play. Each time the game is played it must be decided what scales and triads will be used.

CARDS:
It is not necessary to use all the cards when first playing *Scales and Chords*. Use just those the students are good at, saving others as more knowledge is gained.

PIANO:
Students are encouraged to use the piano with each turn. This is a game <u>with</u> musical sound.

PLAYERS:
Although the game board is large, the flow of the game is best if not more than six players use one board. If there are more players than that, it's better to use more than one game board and have several independent games going at the same time. If that isn't possible, divide the students into small teams. Each team will move its *Alphabet Kid* and answer the questions together. They will enjoy helping each other, and the game maintains a quick pace.

PROCEDURE: **TO SET UP THE BOARD:**

Purple Play Scale Cards, Orange Key Signature Cards, Pink Question Cards and *Yellow Triad Cards* are placed <u>face up</u> on their corresponding color squares in the middle of the game board. Players can see which cards are next and be ready with the answers in case they draw one of them.

375

Containers of *Magic Notes* and *Gold Coins* are placed in the center of the game board.

Each player or team selects an *Alphabet Kid* and places it on any corner.

GENERAL RULES:

WHO ROLLS FIRST: After shuffling the deck, each player draws one *Orange Key Signature Card*.

Whoever drew the most number of sharps or flats will take the first turn. Whoever has the second most number of sharps or flats will go second and so on. In the case of a tie, the two players redraw cards without affecting the order of other players. All key signatures should be identified. Players rearrange themselves around the board in the order of play and return the *Orange Key Signature Cards* to the pile.

TURNS: To be fair, all players must have the same number of turns. When it's time to finish, the teacher should announce "This is the last round." The player who was last on the first round will be last to play.

Players move in the direction of the arrow.

Each player has one roll of the *Large Dice* on each turn unless doubles are rolled or s/he lands on a space with a star.

DOUBLES: If doubles are rolled, another turn may be taken. A second double in one turn is also worth an extra turn. However, if the third roll is also a double, the player moves backwards, does what the space asks and . . . the turn's over.

CARDS: Once cards are drawn, they should be kept face up in front of the players throughout the game. If put back under the bottom of the pile, cards cannot be learned. If kept in view, they may be easier to remember the next time.

STARS: If a turn is answered correctly on a space with a star, the student may take one extra turn.

MAGIC NOTES: A *Magic Note* is won for every sharp or flat in the turn. For example:

1. Jessica plays an A major scale on the blue *S & C Keyboard*. 3 sharps = 3 *Magic Notes*.

2. Student plays a B major triad on the green *S & C Keyboard*. 2 sharps = 2 *Magic Notes*.

3. Student plays a C major scale on the blue *S & C Keyboard*. 0 sharps or flats = 1 *Magic Note*.

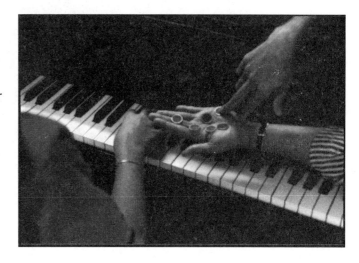

4. Rebecca draws a purple play card to play a G flat major scale on her instrument. 6 flats = 6 *Magic Notes*.

5. Elizabeth draws an *Orange Key Signature Card* of D flat major. 5 flats = 5 *Magic Notes*.

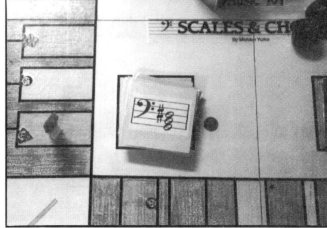

6. Student draws a *Yellow Triad Card* of G augmented. 1 sharp = 1 *Magic Note*.

7. Rebecca draws a *Pink Question Card*. A *Magic Note* is won for answering the card correctly. Another *Magic Note* is won if the card asks for something silly and she does it.

If a card is not answered correctly or something is not done correctly, no money is given up.

Teachers may choose to let students collect *Magic Notes* for answering a card or whatever the turn requires, even if it requires some assistance. Gaining confidence is an important step to learning.

GOLD COINS: Ten *Magic Notes* may be traded in for a *Gold Coin*.

The description given is the simplest way to play:

SAMPLE ROLLS: The player rolls both *Large Dice* and moves counter-clockwise around the board, moving a chromatic scale. All turns should include the piano or other instrument. If s/he lands on:

BLUE = SCALE Play a major scale on the *S & C Keyboard*.
1. Name the note
2. Name the number of sharps or flats in the scale
3. Name the sharps or flats
4. Play a one octave ascending scale on the *S & C Keyboard*. Say the notes out loud and move the *Alphabet Kid*.
5. Stay on the new note and the turn is complete.

GREEN = TRIAD Play a major triad on the *S & C Keyboard*.
1. Name the note
2. Play an ascending triad on the *S & C Keyboard* saying the notes out loud while moving the *Alphabet Kid*.
3. Stay on the new note (the fifth) and the turn is complete.

PINK Take top *Pink Question Card*. Answer the question or do what the card asks. Enjoy the fun stuff! One card says: "Move up a minor seventh then stand on your head," so Jessica and I did!

YELLOW Take top yellow card. Identify the triad.

PURPLE Take top *Purple Play Scale Card*. Play the scale on the piano or other instrument.

ORANGE Take top *Orange Key Signature Card*. Identify the key signature.

ROLL FOR DOUBLES Student has three chances to roll doubles. If they are rolled, student may move that amount, win one *Magic Note* and answer the new space. If doubles aren't rolled, nothing happens.

ROLL AGAIN Student gets another turn.

GOLD COIN Win a *Gold Coin*!

CORNER SHARP Elizabeth names all the sharp scales in order. She says the scale, number of sharps and what the sharps are.

CORNER FLAT Name all the flat scales in order. Say the scale, number of flats and what the flats are.

ADVANCED PLAY IDEAS: Since the game board is coded only by color, it may be changed as students acquire more knowledge about scales and chords.

1. **BLUE** When players understand minor scales: (Example) Player lands on blue space F. S/he is to move the *Alphabet Kid* down a minor third to D and play the <u>relative</u> minor scale. S/he may choose either the natural, melodic or harmonic.

<u>OR</u> Player lands on the blue space F. S/he is to play the <u>parallel</u> minor scale, f minor, relative to A flat major. S/he may choose either the natural, melodic or harmonic.

2. **GREEN** Play all the triads: major, minor, diminished and augmented.

<u>OR</u> Play a seventh chord

3. New *Yellow Cards* could also be made to spell seventh chords. Or the student could spell a seventh chord based on what triad s/he drew.

<u>OR</u> Any sort of scale or chord structure could be applied to this game. How about studying the Greek modes? or the Church Modes? or whole tone scales? or pentatonic scales? or Neapolitan sixth or augmented sixth chords?

<u>OR</u> Just practice intervals. Roll the *Large Dice*. (four) Move. (to A flat) Student to your left calls out an interval

("minor sixth") and student on your right calls out up or down ("down"). You move your *Alphabet Kid* down a minor sixth to C. Good turn!

OR   Make up some of your own fun.

CLEANUP: All players pitch in to sort the cards and put everything away so *Scales and Chords* is ready for the next exciting class.

ADAPTATIONS: It's all right for *Scales and Chords* to be changed to fit the needs of the players.

FOR THE FOLLOWING GAMES, REFER TO SIMILAR GAMES IN CHAPTER 21. FEEL FREE TO ADD INNOVATIVE IDEAS OF YOUR OWN.

GAME 22-2: SIX KINDS OF SEVENTH CHORDS

OBJECTIVE:
To play seventh chords and identify them by ear

IN BRIEF:
Students learn the six kinds of seventh chords

SIMILAR TO:
GAME 21-1: FOUR KINDS OF TRIADS

AGES:
Junior high and older

MATERIALS:
1) Piano
2) *Seventh Chord Cards*
3) Five sets of *Alphabet Cards*:
   2 sets purple, 1 set blue, 1 set green, 1 set pink
4) *Cardboard Keyboards*
5) *Magic Notes* and *Magic Wands*

REPETITIONS:
Repeat over several sessions until students can play and identify the six kinds of seventh chords.

PROCEDURE:

Gather students around the piano to hear and learn how to play seventh chords.

M = major   m = minor
d = diminished   A = augmented

380

1. MM7   2. Mm7   3. mm7   4. dm7   5. dd7   6. AM7

dm7 = half diminished dd7 = fully diminished

As you learn about each chord, use the backside of the *Alphabet Cards* to illustrate this. Let the students figure out how to arrange the *Alphabet Cards* in colors appropriate to the tonality of the triad and the seventh. A game of FIX THE CARDS is helpful.

M = purple   m = blue   d = green   A = pink

Also have the students try writing these chords using *Cardboard Keyboards* and *Magic Notes*.

Ask them to practice these chords at home.

Those who love the young best stay young longest.

Edgar I. Friedenberg

OBJECTIVE:
To practice remembering which triads and sevenths form the six seventh chords

IN BRIEF:
The backside of colored *Alphabet Cards* are used to spell seventh chords.

AGES:
Junior high and older

MATERIALS:
1) Five sets of *Alphabet Cards*:
   2 sets purple, 1 set blue, 1 set green, 1 set pink
2) *Seventh Chord Cards*
3) Piano

REPETITIONS:
Several times in a session

PROCEDURE:
Review the six seventh chords at the piano giving students practice playing and identifying them.

Sit back on the rug and review seventh chords with the cards. Give everyone a chance to study them for a moment. Mix up all the cards and put them in a pile. Place the *Seventh Chord Cards* on top. The *Alphabet Cards* must be face down since we're not using the letter side.

Take turns around the circle, one by one placing cards back in the right places. The first students will turn over the *Seventh Chord Cards*. They should identify the chord and how it's formed.

"This is a fully diminished seventh chord, and it has a diminished triad and a diminished seventh," says Elizabeth.

After the *Seventh Chord Cards* are laid out, the *Alphabet Cards* will be placed in the proper places, one at a time. Since they are mixed up, students will need to decide where to place them, based on their color and the order of the *Seventh Chord Cards*.

OBJECTIVE:
To learn the tonality of seventh chords on each note of the C major scale

IN BRIEF:
Students identify seventh chords built on each tone of a major scale by sound, guessing their tonality using *Magic Notes*. They are written with *Alphabet Cards*, and on a *Cardboard Keyboard* and/or *Dictation Slates*.

SIMILAR TO:
GAME 21-2: MAJOR SCALE TRIADS

AGES:
Junior high and older

MATERIALS:
1) Piano
2) Five sets of *Alphabet Cards*:
   2 sets purple, 2 sets blue, 1 set green
3) *Seventh Chord Cards*
4) *Dictation Slates*
5) *Magic Notes* and *Magic Wands*
6) *Cardboard Keyboards*

REPETITIONS:
Once through the C major scale, plus a bit of time spent with the sound of the augmented/major seventh chord

---

PROCEDURE:
"Since you know the scale triads so well, you need to listen most for the tonality of the seventh interval."

Let each student take six *Magic Notes*, two each of purple, blue and green. Play each chord, giving them time to guess the tonality by placing two colors of *Magic Notes* in their hands.

"Here's the first seventh chord built on the tones of the C major scale."   Play:

Students who hear it correctly will hide two purple *Magic Notes* in their hands.

Continue through each seventh chord in the C major scale, letting the students guess the tonalities they hear.

Write out the C major scale seventh chords with *Alphabet Cards* and with *Magic Notes* on a *Dictation Slate*.

Use these and other earlier game ideas to help the students remember this order.

GAME: MIX-UP Both of the above can be mixed up for the students to fix. This doesn't have to be done quickly and can be done in a group. Continue having students play the chords on the piano.

GAME: FINE Students have their own set of materials which are mixed up. After you say go, they are to arrange the *Alphabet Cards* and/or *Magic Notes* as quickly as possible, calling out FINE when finished.

In a later session, the students can practice writing seventh chords with different scales.

GAME: SECRET SCALE One student arranges six seventh chords from a scale of his choice using appropriate color *Magic Notes* on the *Dictation Slate*. Another student studies the chords to figure out the secret scale. The answer to this secret scale is at the end of this chapter.

color clue: PP PB BB PP

384

OBJECTIVE:
Each student writes the six varieties of seventh chords using accidentals.

IN BRIEF:
Using the *Alphabet Cards, Dictation Slates, Cardboard Keyboards* and the piano, students write six seventh chords with the same root.

AGES:
Junior high and older

MATERIALS:
1) *Alphabet Cards* - purple, blue, green, pink
2) *Seventh Chord Cards*
3) *Dictation Slates*
4) *Cardboard Keyboards*
5) *Magic Notes* and *Magic Wands*
6) *Mini Sharps and Flats*

REPETITIONS:
Write all six seventh chords in a session

PROCEDURE:
Each student needs a *Dictation Slate, Cardboard Keyboard, Mini Sharps and Flats* and a generous handful of *Magic Notes*. Place the *Alphabet Cards, Seventh Chord Cards,* and *Mini Sharps and Flats* in the center of the group.

Ask someone to lay out one of each *Seventh Chord Cards* in a row.

| MM7 | Mm7 | mm7 | dm7 | dd7 | AM7 |

Working together and using the piano as reference, students write seventh chords with the *Alphabet Cards*, using the appropriate colors and adding *Mini Sharps and Flats*.

Individually, they can use their *Dictation Slates, Magic Notes* and *Mini Sharps and Flats* to spell each seventh chord, using colors to reflect the tonalities. When using *Cardboard Keyboards*, use only <u>RED</u> *Magic Notes*. It's easier than trying to use the colors.

GAME 22-6: CHANGING TONALITIES - SEVENTH CHORDS

OBJECTIVE:
To practice changing the tonalities of seventh chords

IN BRIEF:
A seventh chord is written on the staff. Students draw two *Magic Notes*, indicating how to change the chord. Game may also be played in pairs with *Dictation Slates* and *Magic Notes*.

AGES:
Junior high and older

MATERIALS:
1) *One* or *Grand Staff Board*
2) *Clefs Puzzle*
3) *Ledger Line Sheets*
4) *Notes With Letters*
5) *Magic Notes* and *Magic Wands*
6) *Cardboard Keyboards*
7) *Staff Sharps and Flats*
8) Piano

REPETITIONS:
Each student should do several chords. This game can be played over and over in later sessions.

PROCEDURE:

Using the blank side of the *Notes With Letters*, a seventh chord is written on the staff.

Rebecca draws two *Magic Notes*. First she drew purple, indicating the triad should be major. Then she drew blue indicating the seventh should be minor. Rebecca changes the chord to a major / minor seventh chord.

Then Jessica draws purple and pink *Magic Notes*. She adjusts the chord so it is augmented.

Play for several rounds. Encourage them to use the piano.

OBJECTIVE:
To practice writing seventh chord inversions

IN BRIEF:
Students are shown an *Alphabet Card* and told it's either the root, third, fifth, or seventh of a chord. They are to write it on their *Cardboard Keyboards* and *Dictation Slates.*

AGES:
Junior high and older

MATERIALS:
1) Piano
2) *Cardboard Keyboards*
3) *Dictation Slates*
4) *Magic Notes* and *Magic Wands*
5) *Mini Sharps and Flats*
6) *Pink Sharp/Flat Cards*
7) *Alphabet Cards*
8) *Seventh Chord Cards*
9) *Number Slates*

REPETITIONS:
Several inversions per session

PROCEDURE:
Everyone needs a *Cardboard Keyboard,* a *Dictation Slate,* four each of the *Mini Sharps and Flats* and eight *Magic Notes.* Keep the *Alphabet Cards* and *Seventh Chord Cards* for yourself.

"Today we're studying inversions of seventh chords. I know you're terrific at triad inversions, and this is the same with one more note."

Place an E *Alphabet Card* with a *Pink Flat Card* in front of it saying, "This is the third of the seventh chord." Then randomly select a *Seventh Chord Card.* Let's say a minor/ minor card was picked.

With that information they write a c minor/minor seventh chord first inversion on their *Cardboard Keyboards* and on their *Dictation Slates.* Write the full chord yourself with the *Alphabet Cards* and *Pink Flat Cards* so they can check their work. Let someone play it on the piano.

Repeat with many inverted seventh chords. This is the perfect time to help them discover how the inversions are labeled. Use the *Number Slates* to write the symbols.

387

GAME 22-8: INVERSION DROP - SEVENTH CHORDS

OBJECTIVE:
To practice writing inverted seventh chords

IN BRIEF:
Students drop four *Magic Notes* on either a *Dictation Slate* or *Cardboard Keyboard.* They figure out what inversion the notes could become by moving the least steps. Students take *Magic Notes* to match the intervals they moved.

SIMILAR TO:
GAME 21-13: INVERSION DROP

AGES:
Junior high and older

MATERIALS:
1) *Cardboard Keyboards* or *Dictation Slates*
2) *Magic Notes* - red
3) Piano
4) *Mini Sharps and Flats*

REPETITIONS:
5-10 inversions

PROCEDURE:
Use either the *Dictation Slate* or the *Cardboard Keyboard.*

Drop four red *Magic Notes* on each student's *Dictation Slate.* Red is used since it's neutral. This color does not indicate any tonality.

Students move the *Magic Notes* to correctly spell a seventh chord, keeping track of intervals they moved. *Magic Notes* are collected to match the intervals. This chord change earned five notes.

The G was moved down a second to F = 2 *Magic Notes*
The A was moved up a third to C = 3 *Magic Notes*

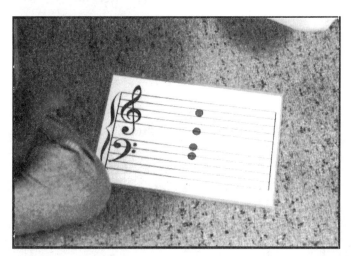

It's fun to play this game in pairs with students taking turns dropping *Magic Notes,* figuring out how to move them and checking the chord spelling. The students are not in competition so the *Magic Notes* are collected as a team score.

OBJECTIVE:
To practice inversions of seventh chords

IN BRIEF:
To write many seventh chords in a scrabble formation. Alphabet cards, mini sharps and flats are used.

SIMILAR TO:
GAME 2-6: ALPHABET SCRABBLE

AGES:
Junior high and older

MATERIALS:
1) *Alphabet Cards* — <u>many</u> sets
2) *Mini Sharps and Flats*

REPETITIONS:
One scrabble in a session

PROCEDURE:
Mix up the *Alphabet Cards* on the rug. If the students have played *Alphabet Card* scrabble games before, you can let them play on their own.

Get them started by arranging several chords. Make certain your letters read <u>up and not down like the regular scrabble game.</u> Add *Mini Sharps and Flats* as needed.

Answer to SECRET SCALE from GAME 22-4: MAJOR SCALE SEVENTH CHORDS

Reminder:
Practice Sight Reading
see chapter 24

On children: You may house their bodies but not their souls, for their souls dwell in the house of tomorrow, which you cannot visit, not even in your dreams.

Kahlil Gibran

There exists a passion for comprehension, just as there exists a passion for music. That passion is rather common in children, but gets lost in most people later on.

Albert Einstein

Ability does not just come by nature without training. We have to educate it in ourselves. Everyone has to train his own self. Stop lamenting lack of talent and develop talent instead. To think that you are born with an ability that develops by itself is a mistake.

Shinichi Suzuki

EXPANDING TO MINOR KEYS

The intricate beauty of the minor tonality is woven into the fabric of our rich musical life. When expressive feelings cannot be served by the brightness of the major sounds, it is the minor tones that bring forth emotions and passions.

In ancient Greek music as well as during the middle ages, musicians and composers had a variety of distinctive modes to choose from. Although many of the historical facts are still obscure, it was once thought that the modes of the middle ages were derived from the Greek modes. This is now considered an oversimplification.

The names dorian, phrygian, lydian, mixolydian, aeolian, and ionian were all used to identify different scale patterns of tones and semitones. It wasn't until the 16th century that the modes on **c** and **a**, which correspond to our major and minor, were recognized theoretically.

Although composers continue to push the boundaries of tonal thinking, music students will most commonly encounter pieces in major or minor tonalities. The major scales studied in Chapters 19 and 20 should be thoroughly understood by students before venturing into this chapter. A few games of review with major scales is advised and will surely be welcomed by the students.

PART
TWO

23

GAMES IN THIS CHAPTER

GAME 23-1: KEY SIGNATURES IN THE MUSIC

OBJECTIVE:
To identify key signatures in the music book

IN BRIEF:
Students look at a variety of music to determine key signatures. The concept of minor keys is introduced.

AGES:
Junior high and older

MATERIALS:
Music books - Advanced music will have the most varieties of key signatures.

REPETITIONS:
5-10 pieces

PROCEDURE:
Ask the students to gather around a music book you've placed on the floor. If you have a large group, try to get several copies of the same music.

Open the book and let the students identify the key signature of a piece by looking at the music. Have them notice that the key is found on the beginning of each line of music, not just at the beginning as the time signature is.

Also have them notice if there is a key change in the middle of a piece and if it changes back again.

Explain that minor keys use the same sharps or flats as their relative majors. So the key signature could look major, but really be minor. Besides listening to the piece, it's possible to look at the beginning and/or ending notes to determine if it's major or minor.

After analyzing the music, let them hear the piece.

393

GAME 23-2: MAKE IT MAJOR - MAKE IT MINOR

OBJECTIVE:
To prepare students to quickly identify minor and major third intervals

IN BRIEF:
Using *Cardboard Keyboards*, *Dictation Slates* and the piano, students practice spelling major and minor thirds.

AGES:
Upper elementary and older

MATERIALS:
1) Piano
2) *Cardboard Keyboards*
3) *Dictation Slates*
4) *Magic Notes* - four per student
5) *Alphabet Cards* - two sets same color
6) *Blank Cards*
7) *Pink Sharp/Flat Cards*
8) *Mini Sharps and Flats*

REPETITIONS:
Repeat until students can spell thirds easily. May be repeated in several sessions

PROCEDURE:
Pass out a *Cardboard Keyboard*, *Dictation Slate* and four *Magic Notes* to each student.

This game is mind expanding. It helps students get used to spelling major and minor thirds up and down the keyboard. In a class, one girl in particular was really enjoying herself as she tried her best to come up with the correct answers. "Oh, I get it now," Elizabeth would say with every new note. Then she would smile with pleasure at her ability to understand something she knew was tricky.

Elizabeth's mother, Patty, was thoroughly amazed at what they were learning. Several times she smiled and said, "I can't tell you how far beyond my ability this is!"

Step one: Ascending thirds Ask the students to put one *Magic Note* on C on their *Cardboard Keyboards*.

"Now, can you put your other note on the key a major third higher than C?" Encourage them to think of the spelling of major triads.

"That's exactly right. Now, can you make it a minor third?"

While they write the intervals on their *Dictation Slates* and *Cardboard Keyboards*, reinforce their work with *Alphabet Cards* and the *Pink Sharp/Flat Cards*.

Let students take turns playing the intervals, comparing the sounds and note placement.

Continue with all the white notes of the keyboard, D, E, F, G, A and B, letting the students figure out the major and minor thirds.

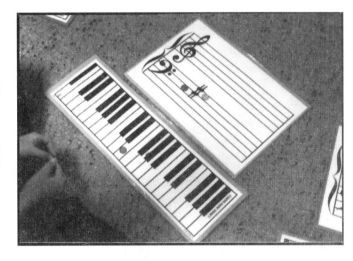

Step two: Descending intervals Either in the same session or in a later session, let the students spell successive minor thirds, moving down the keyboard.

OBJECTIVE:

To introduce the natural minor scale by learning the relative minor for each major scale. Harmonic and melodic scales will be taught in GAME 23-5.

IN BRIEF:

Using the piano, *Cardboard Keyboards* and *Alphabet Cards*, students write out minor scales based on their knowledge of major scales and minor thirds.

AGES:

Upper elementary and older

MATERIALS:

1) *Alphabet Cards*
2) *Blank Cards*
3) *Pink Sharp/Flat Cards*
4) *Cardboard Keyboards*
5) *Magic Notes* and *Magic Wands*

REPETITIONS:

Until all the minor scales have been introduced

PROCEDURE:

Set out the materials and let each student select a set of *Alphabet Cards*, a matching color *Blank Card*, several *Pink Sharp/Flat Cards*, a *Cardboard Keyboard* and eight *Magic Notes*.

"Let's talk for a moment about relatives. There are certain similarities that you and your relatives may share — such as the same last name, similar body build, the same hair type or skin color, or even a similar way of laughing. Can you think of ways you and your relatives are alike? There are also many differences between you and your relatives.

"Today we're going to learn about relative minor scales and what makes them the same and what makes them different from their relative major scales. You all know the sound of the minor scale from pieces you have played, sung or heard."

Now is a good time to either play a few examples of minor scales, songs or pieces or let the students do so. Play around with the scales or simple songs, changing the third degree of the scale from major to minor to review that the third gives the scales their particular sound.

"What makes a minor scale related to a particular major scale is that they have the same key signature. But what makes them different is that the scale begins on a different note." Discuss this around the circle until you are confident they understand.

"Let's write a C major scale with your *Alphabet Cards* and your *Cardboard Keyboards*."

"To find the relative minor scale to C major, we find the note a minor third below C."

"Is it a?"

"It is a. Please move your *Magic Notes* and cards so they are A B C D E F G A rather than C D E F G A B C. Will you add any sharps or flats?"

"No, the key signature for C major and a minor are the same," says Rebecca as the students rearrange their *Magic Notes* and *Alphabet Cards.*

After they are finished, let them take turns playing the a minor scale on the piano.

"It's just that simple. Remember that the minor scale is found a minor third below the major scale. Put another way, major scale "is on top" and the minor scale "is on the bottom". You always go **down** to find the minor scale." This distinction is very important for the students to lock into their understanding of relative minor scales.

Do several more scales in this session, continuing the others in later sessions.

Why do all children possess the marvelous ability to speak their mother tongue quite effortlessly? Therein lies the secret of how to educate all human ability.

Shinichi Suzuki

GAME 23-4: MINOR SCALE FINE

OBJECTIVE:
To practice matching major and minor keys using *Alphabet Cards*

IN BRIEF:
Three rows of cards are arranged in order. Top row is major (purple *Alphabet Cards*), middle row is the number of sharps in the key and bottom row is minor (blue *Alphabet Cards*).

AGES:
Upper elementary and older

MATERIALS:
1) *Alphabet Cards* - two sets purple and blue
2) *Pink Sharp/Flat Cards*
3) *Cardboard Keyboards*
4) *Magic Notes* and *Magic Wands*

REPETITIONS:
Several times in a session - may be repeated

PROCEDURE:

First students lay out the purple *Alphabet Cards* to represent the major key signatures. All of them aren't represented since their relative minor scales aren't very common.

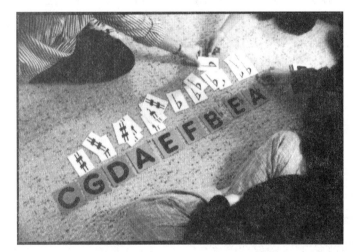

Next they lay out the *Pink Sharp/Flat Cards* to represent the key signatures.

Next they lay out the blue *Alphabet Cards* to represent the relative minor key signatures. Students can use *Cardboard Keyboards* and the piano for help.

Can you spot an error in this photo? The answer is at the end of this chapter.

398

Play FIX THE CARDS. These girls decided to rearrange the *Alphabet Cards* so that the minor scales are underneath the major scales since the relative minors are a third <u>below</u> the majors. Sharp music minds at work!

OBJECTIVE:
To teach students the three different minor scales

IN BRIEF:
After being shown the different minor scales, students write out natural, harmonic and melodic minor scales using *Cardboard Keyboards* and *Dictation Slates*.

AGES:
Upper elementary and older

MATERIALS:
1) Piano
2) *Cardboard Keyboards*
3) *Magic Notes* and *Magic Wands*
4) *Dictation Slates*
5) *Mini Sharps and Flats*

REPETITIONS:
Usually one session

PROCEDURE:
Seat yourself at the piano and ask the students to gather around you.

Explain that there are three kinds of minor scales.

"You have already learned one of them. Because it is the same as its relative major, we call it the <u>natural</u> or <u>pure</u> minor scale." Play several scales in different keys to refresh their memories.

"The other two scales are simply slight variations of the natural minor scale. One is called harmonic and one is called melodic. These three scales are all popular with composers. Let me play several harmonic minor scales so you can hear the distinctive sound. Then I want you to tell me how it is different from the natural minor scale."

Harmonic minor

With the students gathered around the piano with you, play several natural and harmonic minor scales until they understand how the harmonic minor scale is formed.

"I know," says Art. "The harmonic scale has a raised seventh!"

Ask the students to sit on the floor and with the *Dictation Slates* and *Cardboard Keyboards* practice writing out various natural and harmonic minor scales. →

Melodic minor

Ask the students to gather around the piano again while you demonstrate several melodic minor scales. They will be able to describe how the melodic scale is formed.

"The melodic minor scales raises the 6th and 7th tones on the way up, but lowers them back to the natural minor scale on the way down," explains Elizabeth.

"Exactly right, Elizabeth."

Give the students a chance to play different minor scales on the piano. Assign home practice.

Ask them to return to their *Dictation Slates* and *Cardboard Keyboards* and as a group, write out several melodic minor scales. →

In this photo, the ascending scale is in the lower octave on the *Cardboard Keyboard*. The upper octave is the descending scale. Can you find the error in this photo? The answer is at the end of the chapter.

"You know I don't usually give you tricks for remembering," you can say. "But I can't help but share this one with you."

"What is it?" They are curious.

"Which minor scale raises the 7th tone one note?" you can ask.

"Uh . . . the harmonic minor."

"Right. Harmonic starts with the letter "h" and an "h" has one hump. Now in the melodic minor scale, two notes, the sixth and seventh tones are raised going up and lowered going down, right? The word melodic starts with the letter "m" and an "m" has two humps. Get it? — harmonic - "h" - one hump - one raised note . . . melodic - "m" - two humps - two notes raised or lowered. Will that help your musical minds remember?"

If there's time, proceed to the next game, GAME 23-6: MINOR SCALE DICTATION.

GAME 23-6: MINOR SCALE DICTATION

OBJECTIVE:
To practice identifying the three minor scales by ear

IN BRIEF:
Students write out the correct minor scales using *Dictation Slates* and *Magic Notes* while the scales are played on the piano.

AGES:
Upper elementary and older

MATERIALS:
1) Piano
2) *Dictation Slates*
3) *Cardboard Keyboards*
4) *Magic Notes* and *Magic Wands*

REPETITIONS:
Until students can hear the difference between the three minor scales

PROCEDURE:
Pass out a *Dictation Slate*, *Cardboard Keyboards* and *Magic Notes* to each student. Choose a natural minor scale and help them write it on their slates.

Just as you've done throughout the other games in **Music Mind Games**, allow the students to learn through self-discovery. This is a highly superior teaching technique than just telling them.

"Let's compare the difference between the melodic and the harmonic minor scales. I will play the natural minor and then either the harmonic or the melodic. You simply rewrite your scale to match what I played."

"I understand. This will be a cinch!"

Truthfully, it should be fairly easy.

Practice using different scales, each time discussing how the minor scale was formed from the relative major.

OBJECTIVE:
To learn the whole step, half step sequence for major and minor scales

IN BRIEF:
Students write and play scales, comparing whole step, half step patterns. The blank orange *Alphabet Cards* represent whole steps and blank yellow *Alphabet Cards* represent half steps.

AGES:
Upper elementary and older

MATERIALS:
1) *Alphabet Cards - one set each orange and yellow*
2) *Cardboard Keyboards*
3) *Dictation Slates*
4) *Magic Notes* and *Magic Wands*
5) *Mini Sharps and Flats*

PROCEDURE:
Pass out everything but the *Alphabet Cards* to the students. Ask them to write out a C major scale on the *Cardboard Keyboard* and the *Dictation Slate*.

"Let's learn the half step/whole step pattern for major scales. Remember, a whole step is a major second and a half step is a minor second." Review this to make certain everyone knows it.

Using the backside of the *Alphabet Cards* explain that:

orange cards = whole steps
yellow cards = half steps.

MAJOR: "Can you tell me the sequence for the C major scale?"

"Whole . . . whole . . . half . . . whole . . . whole . . . whole . . . half." Using the appropriate colors, let them lay out the *Alphabet Cards* in this order. Repeat with several other major scales.

MINOR - NATURAL: "whole . . . half . . . whole . . . whole . . . half . . . whole . . . whole."

402

HARMONIC: "whole . . . half . . . whole . . whole . . . half . . . one and a half . . . half." You can use both an orange and yellow card for the step and a half.

MELODIC: Ascending -- "whole . . . half . . . whole . . . whole . . . whole . . . whole . . . half.

Descending: whole . . . whole . . . half . . . whole . . . whole . . . half . . . whole.

Child, give me your hand
That I may walk in the light of your faith in me.

Hannah Kahn

Reminder:

Practice Sight Reading

see chapter 24

GAME 23-8: FOUR SCALE GAME

OBJECTIVE:
To practice writing major, pure minor, harmonic minor and melodic minor scales

IN BRIEF:
The materials create a game for students to write out scales and play on the piano.

AGES:
Junior high and older

MATERIALS:
1) *Cardboard Keyboards* - four
2) *Alphabet Kids*
3) *Large Dice*
4) *Magic Notes* and *Magic Wands*
5) *Number Slate* - one
6) *Blank Cards* - one each of purple, blue, pink, green
7) Piano

REPETITIONS:
Each student should get several turns

PROCEDURE:
Set up the game as shown in the photo. To help students remember the scale tonalities, on the *Number Slate* write:

M	=	major
m	=	minor/natural
mm	=	minor/melodic
mh	=	minor/harmonic

Place an appropriate color *Magic Note* next to each letter.

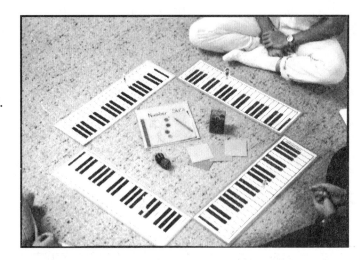

In brief: student rolls *Large Dice*
          student moves a chromatic scale on the *Cardboard Keyboard*
          student draws a *Blank Card* to determine scale tonality
              major   = purple
              minor/natural   = blue
              minor/melodic   = green
              minor/harmonic = pink
          student lays out *Magic Notes* on the *Cardboard Keyboard* to form the scale
          student checks answer by playing the scale on the piano
          student takes *Magic Notes* for number of sharps and flats in the scale

"Anyone want to be first?" you can ask.

"I do!" exclaims Rebecca. "Come on, lucky *Dice*! . . . Four! One . . . two . . . three . . . four. I'm on E. What do I do now?

Jessica holds out the four *Blank Cards*. "Close your eyes, Rebecca," she asks.

"Oh, I got pink. Let me check the *Number Slate*. Pink is the harmonic minor scale. Right?"

"Right, Rebecca. You catch on quickly," teases Elizabeth.

"I don't remember the key signature for e minor, but I bet I can figure it out. Okay, let me think out loud. The relative major scale is a minor third up from E. That would be . . . G?" asks Rebecca.

"G is right, Rebecca," Jessica assures her.

Rebecca continues, "I know what I'm doing here. G has one sharp - F sharp, so e minor must have F sharp, too. Okay, give me those notes and I'm set to write out this baby. e, f sharp, g, a, b, c, d, e. Right?"

"Almost."

Rebecca snaps to attention. "Oh, right. I'm writing a harmonic minor scale so I have to raise the, let's see . . . I have to raise the 7th degree. That means D has to be sharp. D sharp is it!"

"Now, I have to play it on the piano? Piece of cake." Rebecca walks confidently over to the piano and plays the e harmonic minor scale without hesitation.

"Hey, can you tell I've been practicing?" Rebecca giggles.

"You're great. We can just barely stand it," tease her friends. "Okay, scale expert. Take your earnings."

"Okay. F sharp is in the key and I added D sharp, so I win two *Magic Notes*. Right? . . . wait . . . All that for just two *Magic Notes*?" Rebecca falls over in mock shock.

The game is simple to play and is most enjoyable. At this age, students like having a few more rules to keep track of and will learn right along with each turn.

GAME 23-9: PARALLEL MAJOR AND MINOR

OBJECTIVE:
To practice writing parallel major and minor scales

IN BRIEF:
Using two *Cardboard Keyboards*, students write a major scale on one and the parallel minor scale on the other. Students discover the interesting fact that when sharps and flats are added or subtracted between the major and the natural minor scales, the answer is always three.

AGES:
Junior high and older

MATERIALS:
1) *Cardboard Keyboards*
2) *Magic Notes* and *Magic Wands*
3) *Alphabet Cards* - purple and blue
4) Two *Pink Sharp/Flat Cards*

REPETITIONS:
Enough for all scales

PROCEDURE:
Ask the students to take two *Cardboard Keyboards* and a handful of *Magic Notes*.

Choose a scale for them to write and place those *Alphabet Cards* so everyone can see them. Ask students to write the major scale on the top *Cardboard Keyboard* and the minor scale on the bottom *Cardboard Keyboard*.

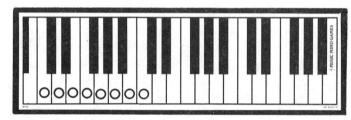

Repeat for several scales.

After writing several scales, see if the students can figure out that if the number of flats or sharps are added or subtracted between the major and the natural minor scales, the answer is always three. Try it!

For example:
1. e♭ minor = 6 flats   subtract and answer = 3
   E♭ major = 3 flats

2. C major = 0 flats   add and answer = 3
   c minor = 3 flats

3. b♭ minor = 5 flats   subtract and answer = 3
   B♭ major = 2 flats

4. g minor = 2 flats   add and answer = 3
   G major = 1 sharp

5. D major = 2 sharps   add and answer = 3
   d minor = 1 flat

6. F# major = 6 sharps   subtract and answer = 3
   f# minor = 3 sharps

406

OBJECTIVE:
To practice minor scales

IN BRIEF:
Ideas from past games are borrowed

AGES:
Junior high and older

MATERIALS:
Whatever!

REPETITIONS:
Whenever!

PROCEDURE:
Use ideas from the previous chapters to practice remembering minor scales. Enjoy!

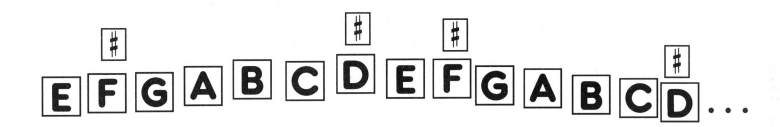

Answer to GAME 23-4: MINOR SCALE FINE.

The relative minor scale of B flat major is g minor, not g flat minor.

Answer to GAME 23-5: NATURAL, HARMONIC AND MELODIC MINOR SCALES:

The error in the third photo is the missing C natural from the descending scale. The *Cardboard Keyboard* is correct.

LET'S READ MUSIC

Although this chapter is at the end of *Music Mind Games*, this doesn't mean students should wait to complete all the games before opening a music book and beginning to read. Rather, as basic theory concepts are acquired through the games, students will find it exciting to begin reading.

Since my students study piano using the Suzuki method, we don't begin actual reading at the keyboard until they have developed the ability to sound out music by ear, play with a secure, natural hand and body position, demonstrate fine tone and rhythmic accuracy and play with an even tempo. At the beginning of the second of seven repertiore books, my students are usually ready to begin reading from supplementary materials.

It's a happy, exciting time when students take a reading book home for the first time. The games take on new significance and credibility. Reading skills improve as more *Music Mind Games* are played. They are mutually beneficial.

WHEN CAN READING BEGIN?

Although your criteria may be different from mine, I've listed the chapters or portions of chapters that my students usually complete before they begin reading. In round figures, they have completed a little more than one-third of *Music Mind Games*.

Chapter 1	JUST THE ABCS	all
Chapter 2	SNAKES!	all
Chapter 3	LINES AND SPACES	all
Chapter 4	BLUE JELLO - INTRODUCING RHYTHM	all
Chapter 5	I CAN HEAR IT - DICTATION PART 1	all
Chapter 6	GRAND STAFF C'S	all
Chapter 7	NOTES AND RESTS - PART 1	half
Chapter 8	THIRDS ARE ONE MORE THAN SECONDS	one-third
Chapter 9	NOTES ON THE STAFF - DICTATION PART 2	half
Chapter 10	GRAND STAFF NEIGHBORS	half
Chapter 11	SIGNS AND SYMBOLS	one-fourth
Chapter 12	TEMPOS	one-fourth
Chapter 13	REAL RHYTHMS	one-third

To summarize, at the onset of reading at the piano, my students feel comfortable with the musical alphabet and understand the concept of intervals. They know lines from spaces, the significance of the clefs, and the names of some notes and their location on the keyboard.

Having taken melodic dictation successfully, they grasp the concept of sound moving up, down or being repeated. They are secure at manipulating notes on a staff to match the sounds they hear. As stated before, I feel dictation is the single most beneficial factor in developing an understanding of reading music. Students who have had the chance to write simple melodic patterns before they are asked to read music are better equipped to handle the whole reading process. This is because they learned the relationship of sound to the written symbol by playing simple games.

In the category of rhythm, the students learn to maintain a steady pulse and read rhythms that fall on and around the beat. Usually the concepts we do in our rhythm games are much more difficult than the simple rhythms they encounter in their early reading experiences. The students also have learned a few of the common musical signs and symbols.

PART
TWO

24

GAMES IN THIS CHAPTER

READING FROM A MUSIC BOOK

Your choice of reading books will vary with your musical goals for your students, depending on if they play an instrument or sing. There are many choices of music books and perhaps you already have some favorites ones.

My experience is with piano music, however nonpianists will find suggestions here to guide their selections.

1. **QUALITY PRINTING**   The music must be of fine quality printing, distinctive and clear. The ink color must be dark and even.

2. **GOOD SIZED NOTES** The notes should be large, but not too large. The spacing of the notes must be far enough to be easily read, but not too far apart, for the eye must develop a smooth flow as it moves from note to note.

3. **FEW DRAWINGS** The pages should not contain lots of drawings to distract the student. I enjoy cute drawings very much, but in a reading book, the music must be the most prominent feature.

4. **FINGER NUMBERS** There should be finger numbers. Reading music is accomplished through playing the right note with the right finger. The numbers must be edited carefully and be there only when needed. If numbers are used for all notes within a five finger position, students may take the easy way out and look at just the numbers, not a helpful habit to acquire. However, numbers are essential when hand positions change. They shouldn't be too large or too small.

5. **WELL WRITTEN MUSIC** The music must have a pleasant sound and be artistically written. Who wants to learn to play a piece that sounds dull or unmusical?

6. **PROGRESS IN SMALL STEPS**   The books should not progress too quickly. Students need lots of practice at slowly increasing levels of difficulty in order to master the mechanics of reading. It's also very helpful for students who have been reading for years to practice reading very simple pieces. This checks their basic understanding of reading.

7. **BOOK STAYS OPEN**   The book should stay open on its own. There's nothing more frustrating than a book that fights to close up while you're trying to play! If needed, though, check your music store for a simple, one piece, metal, four-pronged creation that really works to hold books open.

8. **WELL EDITED** There must not be any mistakes in the music. Students must be able to trust what they see since they are taught to study everything on the page.

Here are a few games which are reading related.

GAME 24-1: LOTS OF INTERVALS

OBJECTIVE:
To help students instantly recognize intervals on the staff and locate them on the keyboard. Students who develop this ability will be better readers.

IN BRIEF:
Using *Dictation Slates* and *Cardboard Keyboards*, the students quickly identify an interval. Then they race to write the interval on their staff, *Cardboard Keyboard* and the piano.

AGES:
Any student who is reading music

MATERIALS:
1) *Dictation Slates*
2) *Cardboard Keyboards*
3) *Magic Notes*
4) Piano or students' instruments

REPETITIONS:
6 - 10 intervals in a session. Repeat game often.

PROCEDURE:
Let each student take a *Cardboard Keyboard*, a *Dictation Slate* and four *Magic Notes*. Keep a *Dictation Slate* and two *Magic Notes* for yourself.

The game is simple to play.

Snap your fingers so the students will close their eyes. Arrange two *Magic Notes* into an interval on your *Dictation Slate*.

Clap your hands.

The students are to call out the interval as soon as they know it.

"Third. Down."

Then as quickly as possible, they are to write it on their *Dictation Slates* and then on their *Cardboard Keyboards*. They can race to the piano and play it in the correct octave.

Remember to do simple intervals like seconds and thirds or even the same note.

Children have more need of models than of critics.

Joseph Joubert

GAME 24-2: *MELODIC AND RHYTHMIC BINGO MEMORY*

OBJECTIVE:
To develop memory of small patterns

IN BRIEF:
A roll of the *Large Dice* decides which pattern the student is to look at very quickly, then play on his or her instrument.

AGES:
Anyone who's reading

MATERIALS:
1) *Melodic* or *Rhythm Bingo Cards*
2) One or two *Large Dice*
3) Piano or students' instruments

REPETITIONS:
Several turns for each student

PROCEDURE:
Place the stack of *Bingo Cards* in front of the students and set the *Large Dice* on the cards. Select someone to take the first roll using the *Large Dice*.

Explain that each space has a number, counting across each row. A roll of the *Large Dice* will tell them which space they are to play. They may choose to roll one or two *Large Dice*.

After rolling the dice, the student will count left to right, by row to find the appropriate space. S/he may look at it for just a moment before you slap your hand over it! Everyone will laugh!

As the student plays it from memory, let the other students watch the pattern.

Melodic Bingo Cards - students play the pattern
Rhythmic Bingo Cards - students play a melody to fit the rhythm

Both at once — Wow!

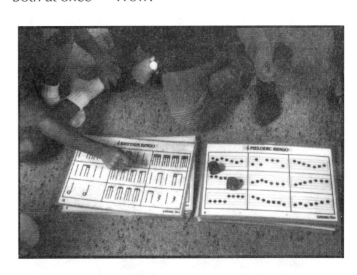

GAME 24-3: SONG PUZZLE DRAW

OBJECTIVE:
To practice remembering one measure of music. This game helps students see groups of notes similar to how in regular reading, they way we read words rather than individual letters.

IN BRIEF:
Students draw one *Song Puzzle Card*, look at it for a few seconds, then try to play it from memory.

AGES:
Elementary and older

MATERIALS:
1) *Song Puzzle Cards*
2) Piano or students' instruments

REPETITIONS:
A couple of turns each

PROCEDURE:
Hold up an example such as a cover of a book or anything showing a small group of words that can be easily read. Ask them to notice how they see the entire word rather than looking at each letter individually. "It's much quicker and easier to read words rather than letters."

"This game encourages you to do the same thing with music notes. Each of you will draw one *Song Puzzle Card*. Rather than reading one note at a time, try to see the group of notes all together.

"In a few seconds, notice the starting note, the rhythm pattern and the melodic pattern on the card. The rhythmic pattern may be notes of all the same value, or there might be a *Jello* on the second beat or the third beat. Or there might be a half note followed by two quarter notes. The melodic pattern might be stepwise ascending only. Or stepwise except for a third at the end. With practice, you can see these in a flash."

Fan out the cards, face down, like you would playing cards, asking someone to draw one card.

"Please <u>do not</u> look at the card you draw, Josh. I am going to hold up your card for you. Then you may go and play it for us. The trick is . . . I am going to hold it up for only a few seconds."

Everyone will groan in mock disbelief. Several will fall to the floor as if they have just died. I casually ignore this reaction, fond as I am of it.

"In a flash, you can train your eye to see and remember the measure you are going to play. It's just like reading words."

Without letting anyone see it, pick up Josh's card. Look at it yourself, turning it right side up (face on the bottom). "Ready, Josh?"

"Sure, anytime," smiles Josh.

Hold the card at eye level for Josh for a few seconds. →

"Oh, eeeaaasy," says a confident Josh. He stands up and heads for the piano.

Turn the card so the rest of the students can read it while Josh plays it. Let them tell you if he did it correctly or not.

If he didn't, show it to him a second time . . . briefly.

Depending on circumstances, it's up to you if he gets a third peek at the card. If he doesn't get it on the third peek, hand him the card to put on the music stand and let him read and play it.

Progress around the circle, letting each student have a turn.

The only rational way of educating a child is to be an example—of what to avoid, if one can't be the other sort.

Albert Einstein

LENDING LIBRARY

Sometimes my students purchase their reading materials, but mostly they borrow them from our studio library. Over the years, the parents in my program have contributed small amounts of money to buy duplicate copies of reading books that may be used by all the students. It definitely saves money for the parents and allows the students to have a larger selection of reading materials. This also gives them a wonderful sense of belonging and of having others share their goal of learning how to read.

READING - DAILY

The most influential point to developing a student into a good reader is to ask him or her to spend time reading every day.

Dr. Suzuki tells his students that they don't have to practice everyday, just on the days that they eat. I've always loved that expression simply because it is so true. If we were to stop nourishing our bodies we would not be able to move forward with life. If students skip too many days of practicing, they will not progress.

So, ask your students to make reading a part of each day's practice session. It's an excellent idea to do the reading first. This insures it will be done.

I don't always make specific reading assignments such as, "Prepare this page for next week," or "Read one page a day," or "Read as much as you can." Instead, I give them guidelines on how to read and let their own appetites set the pace.

What I do is hear what they have prepared for each lesson. Just as in practice, we do reading first, before we get involved in repertoire.

STEPS TO READING

There are two aspects of reading development.

1. The first is acquiring the basic ability to read—to play what's on the page, to understand the symbols and produce the musical sounds represented on the printed page.

2. The second is developing the ability to read at sight. That is to create the sound of the written music with just a try or two.

Obviously, the first skill must be thoroughly developed if the second one is to have any hope of blossoming.

IMPORTANT POINTS

I give my students a few guidelines as they begin to read, then they continue to fine tune their reading as the months go by.

Discuss important information found at the beginning of the music.

We notice the clefs, the key and time signatures and the beginning notes.

Take a quick trip through the music with our eyes.

I simplify the piece by looking for patterns, repeats and similarities. We notice repeat signs and other information so they aren't faced with too many surprises as they learn to read.

Eyes on the music

I ask them to look only at the music while they are reading. If they glance back and forth from music to hands to music to hands, they might lose their place and stumble.

I tell them that their fingers already know how to play. Learning how to read is mostly training for their eyes, mind and ears. We want to train the eyes to move from one note to the next without interruption.

For this reason, I look for beginning reading books that stay within a five finger position. This way the student doesn't have to look down at the piano, and the sense of where the keys are found becomes dependable.

For students who may have unconsciously developed the habit of looking down to check keys, simply hold a large piece of paper over their hands. Use a blank sheet since a busy print would be distracting. Show the parent how to hold the paper so this habit can be corrected quickly.

Choose the correct tempo

If a student is missing notes, the tempo must be changed. And once tempo games have been played it will be more meaningful to say, "Let's take the tempo down a notch to andantino, okay? Then your eyes will have more time to see the notes more accurately. After it's easy to play, you can speed it up again." Students generally don't like to be told to play something more slowly.

Pointing

While a student's eyes are getting accustomed to following a row of notes, it helps if I point along the top of the notes while s/he reading. Since I'm encouraging the eye to move a little ahead of where the student is actually playing, I keep my finger just ahead of the notes. It's necessary to tell the student why I'm ahead, or s/he may try to catch up to my finger and race through the piece.

Of course, teach a parent to point at home.

No stopping

Of all my suggestions, this is the strongest. A good reader has an eye that stays on track and moves only forward through the music. If the student gets into the habit of stopping and fixing missed notes, the eye loses its momentum.

I tell my students the following scenario so they realize how silly it is to stop and correct missed notes as they read.

"Pretend that you and your mom or dad are driving down the road in your car. The car hits a hole in the road. Does your mom keep going or does she turn the car around, drive back down the road and then go forward again, trying to miss the pothole? And if she hits it again, does she back up and try again and again to miss it?" Everyone is smiling at the thought of seeing this car going back and forth trying to miss a pothole in the road.

I suggest the sensible alternative. "Or does she notice the bump and then the next time she drives down that road, try to miss it?"

"That's what she does," smiles the student.

"Good choice," I say. "Now, when you are reading music and you miss a note, should you stop to fix it, or just keep on going?"

"I will try to keep going."

As you are practicing this technique, remember two things:

1. If there are lots of misses, just slow down the tempo.

2. If the student stops, the teacher or parent pointing should keep on pointing in the same tempo, to help the student keep his/her eyes flowing and soon come back in.

With practice the student will then be able to keep his/her eye moving. The mind and eye work together to quickly send the correct message to the fingers.

Even after much discussion, playing without going back to correct mistakes seems to go against some students' natural tendencies.

"But, I want to go back and fix the note I missed even though I know I'm not supposed to!"

"I know, most of us feel that way. But when you keep going, your eye is more careful and you will make fewer mistakes. Just try not to go back too much, and it will gradually become easier."

ROAD REPAIR   If there are some bumps that aren't fixed after the first few playings then it's time to call in the road repair crew and give special attention to the "hole in the road". As with working on a repertoire piece, the student should practice the few tricky notes hands alone then hands together until they are mastered.

Then it helps immensely to back up a few measures from the old "bump" to see if it holds together when approached again.

One very important point: A wise teacher or parent should never refer to tricky parts as "problems." One teacher I had would point to a spot that I couldn't play well and say, "You have a problem here." It seemed to put a lasting label there. Even after I'd perfected it, I still felt a tiny sense of panic as I approached the "problem spot". It could instantly be transformed into its former monster self and grab me as I went by. Naturally, this sense of panic was always heightened during a performance.

These spots are not problems, they are often just concentrated collections of newer material that the brain and fingers haven't encountered in just that combination before. It may be the rhythm, fingerings, note sequences or tempos that startles the reader. I like to think of them as new tricks rather than "problems" or even temporary traps.

REPEAT SIGNS? WHERE? Sometimes a student will play the same few notes over and over, not being able to move forward. "Hold it. Show me where it says to repeat those notes four times. That's a symbol I can't see," I will joke.

(Pianists) Read hands together

The human mind has amazing capacity for learning and if approached correctly it can develop amazing skills.

One of these is the ability to read two lines of music at the same time, one for each hand. This is best trained if the student practices this way.

For a few pages we study reading each hand by itself until the students are secure with the concepts. Then I ask them to read their reading pieces with both hands. They should do this for the first half dozen playings. In this way, they learn to read wide — two staves at once — and get used to it.

In addition they can study the piece hands alone and work on the tricky parts. When it's back together, two staves together, it will be more solid.

Counting

It's fine for the teacher and parent to count ("one two three one two three') if it's helpful for the student. Sometimes just a gentle tapping can help the student feel the beat. This is kinder than a metronome which can cause panic.

Some teachers like their students to count aloud when they play. Personally, I've found this to be too confusing to talk and play at the same time.

Quality reading

How difficult should the reading pieces be? Although this will not hold true for every case, the piece should not take more than 10 - 15 playings to be read accurately and sound like a good piece. At this point it should sound musical, with few misses and with good rhythm.

If pieces take much more than this, then perhaps they are better categorized as repertoire pieces. Although they must be musically strong, reading pieces are primarily meant to improve the skill of reading.

OTHER READING TIPS FOR THE STUDENT

Reading by interval rather than note name

Years ago I had a young student named Eva who's nonmusically trained mother was very dedicated to helping her. They made quick progress. One day in lesson she told me that she had been distressed that week when she asked Eva to stop in the middle of her reading piece and Eva couldn't immediately name any of the notes she was playing.

I smiled and thanked her for asking me a good question. To me, I'd never thought about naming the notes as I played, and obviously Eva didn't either. But her mother, relying on note names to figure out music, thought that her daughter should be doing just that.

Although names of notes may pop into one's mind from time to time, it is the relationship of one note to the other that enables the player to play the music.

Therefore it is logical to use music with seconds and thirds until the student is secure and proficient at this level.

Often it is helpful to ask the student to point to the music and identify the interval one note at a time. "Second up, second up, third up, second down . . ."

Look for triad and chord positions

One of my students was reading a short piece, and struggling through it. "Rebecca," I said, "what are the chords used in the left hand?" She looked at the music for a moment then realized there were just two chords and one other pattern. When playing it again, she played more smoothly and with just a few minor stumbles.

Please don't compose. Play what's written.

Sometimes this simple statement reminds the students to read accurately.

Bring a piece to theory class.

We often take a few minutes of class time to gather around the piano, so students can take turns reading a song of their choice. The other students watch carefully to see if the music has been read correctly, thus becoming actively involved in strengthening their own reading skills rather than being passive listeners.

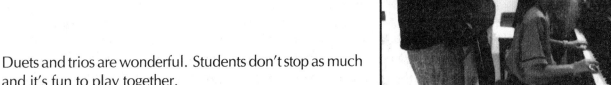

Duets and trios are wonderful. Students don't stop as much and it's fun to play together.

To help with key signatures.

Remembering to use the sharps or flats indicated by the key signature may be difficult for some students. They continue to read the note as "plain F" even though the key signature indicates "F sharp". It will help to take a few moments before playing the piece, for the student to find and point to all the F sharps. Let him quickly glide a finger over the music, stopping whenever an F sharp appears.

" . . . Here! . . . here . . . Another here . . ."

READING CONTEST

When my daughter was in third grade at school, her teacher, Mr. Mark Danzler, had many innovative ways to make learning enjoyable. When they read <u>Strega Nona</u> by Tomi de Paulo, I went into class and helped them make pasta.

To learn fractions they covered their desks with shaving cream and drew in it. Great way to clean the desks, too.

In November he had a reading contest. It was very non-stressful. He encouraged me to keep it fun and let my daughter set her own goals. There was no requirement on what was to be read; each student was to turn in papers listing book title, author, illustrator and number of pages as books were completed. The five top readers were announced each day in the classroom. Although there were times she read a lot, there were other times she didn't. I did notice though that I was signing a lot of papers and that her retention and speed were impressive.

Happily, she won as the top reader, and he gave her some nice books as a present. Her top count—a staggering 4,519 pages in one month!

For weeks I wondered how I could do this in my studio to encourage my students to read more. From past experiences I had found that contests are encouraging for the motivated students but terribly discouraging for the others. Taking that into account, I thought carefully about making it a positive experience for each of my students.

Here are the details and the outcome.

1. I gave students several pages of the contest sheet to keep track of their reading. It was simple to use with a minimum amount of items to write down.
2. Students could read anything.
3. Each page counted as one, no matter the difficulty.
4. I preferred they read both hands at once, but if the music was too advanced they could read one hand then the other and count the page twice.
5. Each time the music was read, they could count it again.
6. They understood that the goal was to become better readers.

1. The contest ran for seven weeks.
2. Each week I recorded each student's cumulative score on a chart I kept in the studio.
3. The last two weeks I kept the scores secret so they wouldn't know their standing. A little suspense kept the reading on their minds!

Each week I listened to something the student had read or gave him or her something to sight read. It was easy to spot improvement, so I always offered encouragement for specific points of progress. "Wow! You read the whole duet with me without looking down at your hands. I can't believe it!" or "What good reading! You and I both know that you couldn't read like that before the reading contest." Smiles! "Hey, you're actually reading, aren't you!"

On the next page is a copy of the reading contest form.

Better to be driven out from among men than to be disliked of children.

R. H. Dana

READING CONTEST

My name _____ Sheet no. _____

DATE	BOOK	COMPOSER	PAGES	TOTAL
_____	_____	_____	_____	_____
_____	_____	_____	_____	_____
_____	_____	_____	_____	_____
_____	_____	_____	_____	_____
_____	_____	_____	_____	_____
_____	_____	_____	_____	_____
_____	_____	_____	_____	_____
_____	_____	_____	_____	_____
_____	_____	_____	_____	_____
_____	_____	_____	_____	_____
_____	_____	_____	_____	_____
_____	_____	_____	_____	_____
_____	_____	_____	_____	_____
_____	_____	_____	_____	_____
_____	_____	_____	_____	_____
_____	_____	_____	_____	_____

TOTAL _____

Parent's signature _____

Here are the results of the contest. It was astonishing to see the pages of reading these students did!

name	grade in school	week: 1	2	3	4	5	6	7
Alexis	10	183	293	423	504	566	594	647
Aya	6	84	163	229	229	229	337	403
Bita	2	32	110	238	289	345	425	475
Christina	3	65	129	145	200	251	410	513
Elizabeth	4	95	126	164	326	391	442	549
Francis	7	58	121	251	286	424	522	641
Jessica	10	118	197	272	310	394	472	518
Josh	6	37	86	118	136	187	229	285
Maria	3	31	82	222	226	233	308	456
Meredith	3	43	134	201	321	390	500	531
Rebecca	7	90	126	155	170	181	231	291
Sarah	1	21	50	167	180	190	270	310

Some personal tales:

Much of Alexis' reading was Bach Preludes and Fugues, Bartok or Prokofiev.

Although she could play Beethoven's "Fur Elise" and a Haydn Sonata, Rebecca had resisted reading, relying mostly on her ears. Reading was not her favorite thing. As a result of the contest it was apparent that she was actually reading, relating notes by interval, and making the rhythms she understood so well, work for her.

Bita, Sarah and Maria had been reading for about nine months and made great leaps in their reading skills. Even now reading is one of Bita's favorite activities.

Meredith was preparing duets for a workshop in San Diego during the contest. She was certainly prepared!

PRIZES: Everyone received a prize. Students "competed" only with the two or three friends in their theory class. Prizes were small — music pens, a music folder, a music notebook. Alexis, the grand prize winner won an extra prize, a deck of music cards.

Each student was applauded for his or her incredible score. Because of their great efforts during our contest, all of them were definitely much better at reading music—an ability they will have forever. As with the **Music Mind Games** they had played, they developed a positive attitude, enjoyed learning and gained knowledge as well as self-confidence.

APPENDIX

Directions for Making Materials

Number Slates

The backing board for *Number Slates* is sold with the other **Music Mind Game** materials. To help keep your costs low, they are not sold with the "magic" slate and pencil.

Please buy 12 magic slates from a toy store.

Since the drawings may be distracting and not appropriate you can easily make yours match your other **Music Mind Game** materials. They will also be more compact for traveling.

Remove the pencils and set aside.

Carefully remove the magic slate from the backing cardboard. Discard the backing.

Glue the magic slate in place.

Number Cards

To make a set of *Number Cards*, use colored posterboard in the same colors as the *Music Mind Games Materials*. Cut cards measuring 2 1/2" x 3 1/2". Using a broad, black magic marker pen, write one number on each card. You'll need about 5 each of numbers 1 2 3 4 and 5. It's fine to mix the colors.

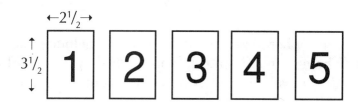

List of *MUSIC MIND GAMES* MATERIALS

Alphabet Kids
Alphabet Cards
Bingo Dots
Bingo Cards
Blank Cards
Blue Jello Cards
Blue Jello Rhythm Puzzle
Cardboard Keyboards
Clefs Puzzle
Dictation Slates
Gold Coins
Grand Staff Cards
Grand Staff Board or One Staff Board
Large Dice
Ledger Line Sheets
Magic Notes
Magic Wands
Melodic Bingo Cards
Mini Sharps
Mini Notes
Mini Flats
Musopoly Game Board
    Fermata Cards
Notes and Rests Cards

Notes and Rests Game Board
Notes With Letters
Number Cards
Number Slates
Orange Symbol Cards
Pink Sharp/Flat Cards
    or Pink Sharp Cards or Pink Flat Cards
Real Rhythm Cards
Rhythm Playing Cards or Rhythm Money
Rhythm Bingo Cards
Scale & Chords Cards:
    Pink Question Cards
    Orange Key Signature Cards
    Yellow Triad Cards
    Purple Play Scale Cards
Scale Triad Cards
Scales and Chords Game Board
Seventh Chord Cards
Song Puzzle Cards
Staff Flats
Staff Sharps
Toss Note
Yellow Tempo Cards

IMPORTANT HINTS

PUZZLES

Put foam core under the platforms in the *Blue Jello Rhythm Puzzle* and the *Clefs Puzzle* so when they are pushed upon by small, eager and enthusiastic hands, the platforms won't collapse. You won't have to keep telling everyone to "be careful".

Store both Lauri puzzles with the lids on to keep the crepe plastic supple. Lots of light can make some puzzles less flexible after years of exposure.

ORANGE SYMBOL CARDS

There are a few blank orange symbol cards in case you have some extra ones you want to include.

LAMINATION

After speaking with many teachers, we made the decision not to laminate the **Music Mind Games** materials. Many teachers have access to laminating machines which would be a savings to having to buy them laminated.

It is recommended that you laminate your materials or cover them in a clear plastic adhesive to protect them and extend their lifespans.

REFERENCES

Apel, Willi <u>Harvard Dictionary of Music</u>, Belnap Press of Harvard University Press (1969) 935 pp.

Doman, Glenn <u>How to Teach Your Baby to Read</u> Random House (1964) 166 pp.

Feldstein, Sandy <u>Pocket Dictionary of Music</u> Alfred Publishing Company (1985) 240 pp.

Read, Gardner <u>Music Notation: a Manual of Modern Practice</u> Crescendo Publishing Company (1979) 482 pp.

Shinichi Suzuki, <u>Nurtured by Love</u> (Exposition Press), c. 1969 121 pp.

<u>The Fairy Tale Book</u> Golden Press, Inc. (1958) 156 pp.

INDEX OF GAMES BY TITLE

INDEX OF GAMES BY SUBJECT

MUSICAL ALPHABET AND INTERVALS - 27 games

THE GRAND STAFF - 35 games

INDEX OF GAMES BY SUBJECT AND TEACHING SEQUENCE

ABOUT THE AUTHOR

Michiko is a native of Arizona, spending early years in Sedona and school years in Mesa. She has played piano since she was a toddler, violin since she was in fourth grade, and sang in church and school choirs. In 1969 she won the Phoenix Symphony Young Musicians Concerto Competition. She received her undergraduate music degree from Ohio University in Piano Performance where she studied with George Katz (Juilliard). She did graduate work in music theory at Ohio University where she began work on her original theory ideas.

Since 1973 she has enjoyed a successful, private piano studio and is a registered Teacher Trainer with the Suzuki Association of the Americas. She has traveled to Hawaii, Newfoundland, Canada, Puerto Rico, Alaska, Australia, New Zealand and points inbetween sharing her ideas at over 150 music workshops.

In 1979 her book, No H in Snake: Music Theory for Children (Alfred) was published. She formed Music 19 about that time to distribute her game products.

In 1985-86 she was National Chairperson for the SAA Children to Children African Relief Project. Students raised over $85,000 during a two week Practice-a-Thon.

In 1990 Warner Bros. Publications Inc. acquired Music 19. Michiko is Creative Director of Music 19.

She makes her home in Maryland. She is on the faculty of the Levine School of Music (Washington D.C.) as co-ordinator of the Suzuki Piano Program.